The Institute of Chartered Accountants in England and Wales

PRINCIPLES OF TAXATION
FA 2012

Professional Stage Knowledge Level

For exams in 2013

Study Manual

ICAEW

www.icaew.com

Principles of Taxation
The Institute of Chartered Accountants in England and Wales Professional Stage

ISBN: 978-0-85760-458-3

Previous ISBN: 978-0-85760-228-2

First edition 2007
Seventh edition 2012

British Library Cataloguing-in-Publication Data
A catalogue record for this book has been applied for from the British Library

Printed in the United Kingdom by Polestar Wheatons

Polestar Wheatons
Hennock Road
Marsh Barton
Exeter
EX2 8RP

Your learning materials are printed on paper sourced from traceable,
sustainable forests.

Welcome to ICAEW

I am delighted that you have chosen to study for our chartered accountancy qualification, the ACA or the Certificate in Finance, Accounting and Business (CFAB).

If you are a CFAB student, you will be gaining essential knowledge of how businesses work. As your understanding develops you may be surprised by the variety of roles that chartered accountants take on. To gain further insight and develop your career, I hope that you choose to continue onto the ACA qualification.

The ACA will open doors to a highly rewarding career as a financial expert or business leader. Once you are an ICAEW member, you will join over 138,000 others around the world who work at the highest levels across all industry sectors, providing valuable financial and business advice. Some of our earlier members formed today's global Big Four firms, and you can find an ICAEW Chartered Accountant on the boards of 80% of the UK FTSE 100 companies.

As part of a worldwide network of over 19,000 students, you will have access to a range of resources including the online student community, where you can interact with fellow students. Our student support team is dedicated to helping you every step of the way. Take a look at the key resources available to you on page viii.

I wish you the very best of luck with your studies and look forward to supporting you throughout your career.

Michael Izza
Chief Executive
ICAEW

Contents

1 Introduction

1.1 What is the Principles of Taxation module and how does it fit within the ACA Professional Stage?

Structure

The ACA syllabus has been designed to develop core technical, commercial, and ethical skills and knowledge in a structured and rigorous manner.

The diagram below shows the twelve modules at the ACA Professional Stage, where the focus is on the acquisition and application of technical skills and knowledge, and the ACA Advanced Stage which comprises two technical integration modules and the Case Study.

If you are studying for CFAB, you will only complete the first six knowledge modules. However, you may decide to progress to the ACA after you have completed the CFAB qualification.

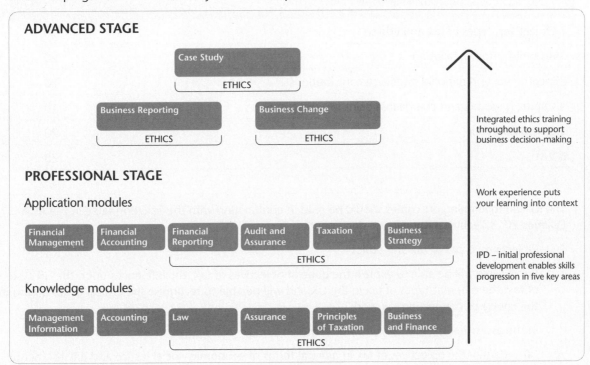

The knowledge level

The aim of the Principles of Taxation module is to enable students to understand the general objectives of tax and to calculate income tax, national insurance contributions, capital gains tax, corporation tax and VAT in straightforward scenarios.

Progression to ACA application level

The knowledge base that is put into place here will be taken further in the Application level Taxation module, where the aim will be to enable students to prepare tax computations and provide tax advice to individuals and companies, again in straightforward scenarios. The above taxes introduced at Knowledge level are taken to a higher level, and in addition inheritance tax is covered at Application level.

Progression to ACA Advanced Stage

The Advanced Stage papers – Business Reporting (BR) and Business Change (BC) – then take things further again, also introducing stamp duty and stamp duty land tax. The aims of BR are that students can apply analysis techniques, technical knowledge and professional skills to resolve real-life compliance issues faced by businesses – including circumstances where overseas taxes affect national taxes. In the BC paper taxation is particularly important. The aim is to ensure that students can provide technical advice in respect of issues arising in business transformations, eg mergers and acquisitions.

The above illustrates how the knowledge of taxation principles gives a platform from which a progression of skills and taxation expertise is developed.

2 Specification grid for Principles of Taxation

2.1 Module aim

To enable students to understand the general objectives of tax and to calculate income tax, national insurance contributions, capital gains tax, corporation tax and VAT in straightforward scenarios.

2.2 Specification grid

This grid shows the relative weightings of subjects within this module and should guide the relative study time spent on each. Over time the marks available in the assessment will equate to the weightings below, while slight variations may occur in individual assessments to enable suitably rigorous questions to be set.

Syllabus area	Weighting (%)
1 Objectives, types of tax and ethics	10
2 Administration of taxation	20
3 Income tax and national insurance contributions	20
4 Capital gains tax and chargeable gains for companies	10
5 Corporation tax	20
6 VAT	20
	100

The following learning outcomes should be read in conjunction with the Taxation table in the ACA Syllabus 2013 Technical Knowledge document.

1 Objectives, types of tax and ethics

Candidates will be able to explain the general objectives of tax, the influences upon the UK system of tax, the different types of tax in the UK, and will be able to recognise the ethical issues arising in the course of performing tax work.

In the assessment, candidates may be required to:

(a) identify the objectives of tax in general terms of economic, social justice and environmental issues, the range of tax opportunities open to the government and the relative advantages of different types of tax in meeting the government's objectives

(b) recognise the impact of external influences, including EU tax policies, on UK tax objectives and policies

(c) classify entities as individuals, partnerships, or companies for tax purposes and state how they are taxed

(d) identify who is liable for the following taxes, how the taxes apply to income, transactions and assets, identify the government bodies responsible for the taxes, and determine when an individual or entity comes within the scope of the taxes:

- capital gains tax
- corporation tax
- income tax
- national insurance
- VAT

(e) recognise the importance of the budget cycle, tax year and the following sources of UK tax law and practice:

- legislation

- case law

- HM Revenue & Customs manuals, statements of practice, extra-statutory concessions and press releases

(f) identify the five fundamental principles given in the IFAC Code of Ethics for Professional Accountants and ICAEW Code of Ethics, and the guidance in relation to a tax practice with regard to:

- the threats and safeguards framework
- ethical conflict resolution

(g) identify the following:

- conflicts of interest

- money laundering

- tax avoidance and tax evasion

2 Administration of taxation

Candidates will be able to identify the obligations the UK system of tax imposes on taxpayers and the implications for taxpayers of non-compliance.

In the assessment, candidates may be required to:

(a) identify the records which companies and individuals must retain for tax purposes and state the periods for which the records must be retained

(b) identify the key features of the PAYE and national insurance system and calculate PAYE tax codes for employees

(c) identify the key features of the self assessment system for both companies and individuals

(d) determine, in straightforward cases, due dates for:

- companies', sole traders', partnerships' and individuals' tax returns, tax payments and payments on account

- businesses' VAT returns and payments

- employers' PAYE and national insurance returns and payments

(e) identify and calculate the interest and penalties due for:

- late submissions of and/or incorrect returns, and

- late and/or incorrect payments of tax

(f) identify the periods within which HM Revenue & Customs can enquire into a taxpayer's returns or other information and tax liabilities and recognise the taxpayer's right of appeal and the process for dealing with disputes.

3 Income tax and national insurance contributions

Candidates will be able to calculate the amount of income tax owed by or owed to individuals and the amount of national insurance payable.

In the assessment, candidates may be required to:

(a) recognise the main sources of taxable and non-taxable income

(b) calculate the personal allowance available to an individual according to personal circumstances including personal age allowances and married couples allowance

(c) calculate assessable employment income for an employee or director, including taxable and exempt benefits

(d) recognise the badges of trade

(e) allocate given items of business expenditure as allowable or disallowable for tax purposes and calculate the adjusted trading profits after capital allowances on plant and machinery of a sole trader or partnership

(f) allocate the tax adjusted profits of a partnership to each partner and calculate the final assessable profits for each partner for any given tax year

(g) calculate the assessable trading profits for a new unincorporated business and identify the overlap profits on the commencement of trade

(h) calculate the final assessable trading profits for an unincorporated business ceasing to trade

(i) calculate total taxable income and the income tax payable or repayable for employed and self-employed individuals.

(j) calculate the total national insurance contributions payable by employees, employers and self-employed individuals.

4   Capital gains tax and chargeable gains for companies

Candidates will be able to calculate the amount of capital gains tax payable by individuals and the chargeable gains subject to corporation tax.

In the assessment, candidates may be required to:

(a) classify persons, assets and disposals as either chargeable or exempt for capital gains purposes

(b) calculate the chargeable gains and losses on the disposal of assets, including indexation where appropriate

(c) calculate total taxable gains for both individuals and companies and for individuals calculate the capital gains tax payable

5   Corporation tax

Candidates will be able to calculate the amount of corporation tax payable by companies.

In the assessment, candidates may be required to:

(a) identify chargeable accounting periods for a company

(b) recognise the effect of having one or more associated companies on corporation tax payable

(c) allocate given items of business expenditure as allowable or disallowable for tax purposes and calculate the adjusted trading profits after capital allowances on plant and machinery

(d) calculate the taxable total profits and the corporation tax payable for a company resident in the UK which has no associated companies and an accounting period of 12 months or less.

6   VAT

Candidates will be able to calculate the amount of VAT owed by or owed to businesses.

In the assessment, candidates may be required to:

(a) classify supplies in given straightforward situations as exempt, zero-rated, standard-rated, subject to a reduced rate of 5% or outside the scope of VAT

(b) recognise the implications of supplies being classified as standard-rated, zero-rated or exempt

(c) identify when a business could or should register or deregister for VAT and state the time limits

(d) determine the tax point for a supply of goods or services

(e) state the principles of VAT payable or repayable on the supply of goods or services by a taxable person and calculate the monthly, quarterly and annual VAT payable or repayable by a business

(f) state the alternative schemes for payment of VAT by businesses.

3 Key Resources

STUDENT SUPPORT TEAM

T +44 (0)1908 248 250
E studentsupport@icaew.com

STUDENT WEBSITE

icaew.com/students student homepage
icaew.com/exams exam applications, deadlines, regulations and more
icaew.com/cpl credit for prior learning/exemptions
icaew.com/examresources examiners comments, syllabus, past papers, study guides and more
icaew.com/examresults exam results

TUITION

If you are receiving structured tuition, make sure you know how and when you can contact your tutors for extra help.

If you aren't receiving structured tuition and are interested in classroom, online or distance learning tuition, take a look at our tuition providers in your area on icaew.com/exams

ONLINE STUDENT COMMUNITY

The online student community allows you to ask questions, gain study and exam advice from fellow ACA and CFAB students and access our free webinars. There are also regular Ask an Expert and Ask a Tutor sessions to help you with key technical topics and exam papers. Access the community at icaew.com/studentcommunity

THE LIBRARY & INFORMATION SERVICE (LIS)

The Library & Information service (LIS) is ICAEW's world-leading accountancy and business library. You have access to a range of resources free of charge via the library website, including the catalogue, LibCat. icaew.com/library

4 Syllabus and learning outcomes

Covered
in chapter

1 Objectives, types of tax and ethics

Candidates will be able to explain the general objectives of tax, the influences upon the UK system of tax, the different types of tax in the UK and will be able to recognise the ethical issues arising in the course of performing tax work.

In the assessment, candidates may be required to:

(a) Identify the objectives of tax in general terms of economic, social justice and environmental issues, the range of tax opportunities open to the government and the relative advantages of different types of tax in meeting the government's objectives.   1

(b) Recognise the impact of external influences, including EU tax policies, on UK tax objectives and policies.   1

(c) Classify entities as individuals, partnerships, or companies for tax purposes and state how they are taxed.   1

(d) Identify who is liable for the following taxes, how the taxes apply to income, transactions and assets, identify the government bodies responsible for the taxes, and determine when an individual or entity comes within the scope of the taxes: 1

- Capital gains tax
- Corporation tax
- Income tax
- National insurance
- VAT

(e) Recognise the importance of the budget cycle, tax year and the following sources of UK tax law and practice: 1

- Legislation
- Case law
- HM Revenue & Customs manuals, statements of practice, extra statutory concessions and press releases

(f) Identify the five fundamental principles given in the IFAC Code of Ethics for Professional Accountants and the ICAEW Code of Ethics, and the guidance in relation to a tax practice with regard to: 13

- The threats and safeguards framework
- Ethical conflict resolution

(g) Identify the following: 13

- Conflict of interest
- Money laundering
- Tax avoidance and tax evasion

2 Administration of taxation

Candidates will be able to identify the obligations the UK system of tax imposes on taxpayers and the implications for taxpayers of non-compliance.

In the assessment, candidates may be required to:

(a) Identify the records which companies and individuals must retain for tax purposes and state the periods for which the records must be retained.   11,12

(b) Identify the key features of the PAYE and national insurance system and calculate PAYE tax codes for employees. 3, 7

(c) Identify the key features of the self assessment system for both companies and individuals. 12

(d) Determine, in straightforward cases, due dates for:

- Companies', sole traders', partners' and individuals' tax returns, tax payments and payments on account 12

- Businesses' VAT returns and payments 11

- Employers' PAYE and national insurance returns and payments 3,12

(e) Identify and calculate the interest and penalties due for:

- Late submissions of and/or incorrect returns, and 12
- Late and/or incorrect payments of tax 12

(f) Identify the periods within which HM Revenue & Customs can enquire into a taxpayer's returns or other information and tax liabilities and recognise the taxpayer's right of appeal and the process for dealing with disputes. 12

3 Income tax and national insurance contributions

Candidates will be able to calculate the amounts of income tax owed by or owed to individuals and the amounts of national insurance payable.

In the assessment, candidates may be required to:

(a) Recognise the main sources of taxable and non-taxable income. 2

(b) Calculate the personal allowance available to an individual according to personal circumstances including personal age allowances and married couples allowance. 2

(c) Calculate assessable employment income for an employee or director, including taxable and exempt benefits. 3

(d) Recognise the badges of trade. 4

(e) Allocate given items of business expenditure as allowable or disallowable for tax purposes and calculate the adjusted trading profits after capital allowances on plant and machinery of a sole trader or partnership. 4, 5

(f) Allocate the tax adjusted profits of a partnership to each partner and calculate the final assessable profits for each partner for any given tax year. 6

(g) Calculate the assessable trading profits for a new unincorporated business and identify the overlap profits on the commencement of trade. 6

(h) Calculate the final assessable trading profits for an unincorporated business ceasing to trade. 6

(i) Calculate total taxable income and the income tax payable or repayable for employed and self-employed individuals. 2

(j) Calculate the total national insurance contributions payable by employees, employers and self-employed individuals. 7

4 Capital gains tax and chargeable gains for companies

Candidates will be able to calculate the amount of capital gains tax payable by individuals and the chargeable gains subject to corporation tax.

In the assessment, candidates may be required to:

(a) Classify persons, assets and disposals as either chargeable or exempt for capital gains purposes.   8

(b) Calculate the chargeable gains and losses on the disposal of assets, including indexation where appropriate.   8

(c) Calculate total taxable gains for both individuals and companies and for individuals calculate the capital gains tax payable.   8

5 Corporation tax

Candidates will be able to calculate the amount of corporation tax payable by companies.

In the assessment, candidates may be required to:

(a) Identify chargeable accounting periods for a company.   9

(b) Recognise the effect of having one or more associated companies on corporation tax payable.   9

(c) Allocate given items of business expenditure as allowable or disallowable for tax purposes and calculate the adjusted trading profits after capital allowances on plant and machinery.   9

(d) Calculate the taxable total profits and the corporation tax payable for a company resident in the UK which has no associated companies and an accounting period of 12 months or less.   9

6 VAT

Candidates will be able to calculate the amount of VAT owed by or owed to businesses.

In the assessment, candidates may be required to:

(a) Classify supplies in given straightforward situations as exempt, zero rated, standard rated, subject to a reduced rate of 5% or outside the scope of VAT.   10

(b) Recognise the implications of supplies being classified as standard rated, zero rated or exempt.   10

(c) Identify when a business could or should register or deregister for VAT and state the time limits.   10

(d) Determine the tax point for a supply of goods or services.   10

(e) State the principles of VAT payable or repayable on the supply of goods or services by a taxable person and calculate the monthly, quarterly and annual VAT payable or repayable by a business.   10, 11

(f) State the alternative schemes for payment of VAT by businesses.   11

4.1 Technical knowledge

The tables contained in this section show the technical knowledge in the disciplines of financial reporting, audit and assurance, ethics and taxation covered in the ACA syllabus by module.

For each individual standard the level of knowledge required in the relevant Professional Stage module and at the Advanced Stage is shown.

The knowledge levels are defined as follows:

Level D

An awareness of the scope of the standard.

Level C

A general knowledge with a basic understanding of the subject matter and training in its application sufficient to identify significant issues and evaluate their potential implications or impact.

Level B

A working knowledge with a broad understanding of the subject matter and a level of experience in the application thereof sufficient to apply the subject matter in straightforward circumstances.

Level A

A thorough knowledge with a solid understanding of the subject matter and experience in the application thereof sufficient to exercise reasonable professional judgement in the application of the subject matter in those circumstances generally encountered by Chartered Accountants.

Key to other symbols:

→   the knowledge level reached is assumed to be continued

TAXATION

Title	Principles of Taxation	Taxation	Advanced Stage
	Professional Stage		
Objectives of taxation	C	→	→
Ethics	A	→	→
HM Revenue & Customs	B	→	→
Tax evasion and avoidance	C	B	A
BUSINESS TAXATION			
Administration	B	→	→
Appeals	C	→	→
Payments	B	A	→
Penalties and interest	B	A	→
Self assessment	B	A	→
Chargeable gains			
Chargeable assets	C	B	→
Chargeable disposals	C	B	→
Chargeable persons	C	B	→
Chattels: wasting and non-wasting	B	→	→
Costs of acquisition and disposal	C	B	→
Indexation	B	A	→
Leases			A
Nil gain/nil loss transfers		A	→
Part disposals		B	→
Pre 31 March 1982 assets		A	→
Qualifying corporate bonds			A
Relief for capital losses		A	→
Reorganisations and reconstructions			A
Shares and securities (including bonus and rights issues)		A	→
Chargeable gains reliefs			
Entrepreneurs' relief		A	→
Gift relief		A	→
Incorporation relief		A	→
Rollover relief		A	→
Substantial shareholding exemption		A	→
Trading profits			
Adjustments to profits	B	A	→
Badges of trade	B	A	→
Capital allowances	B	A	→
Foreign currency transactions			A
Long periods of account	C	A	→
Pension contributions		B	A
Royalty payments		B	→
Royalty receipts		B	→
Unincorporated businesses			
Basis of assessment – current year basis	B	A	→
Change of accounting date		B	→
Commencement and cessation of trade	B	A	→
Overlap profits and treatment of opening year losses	B	A	→
Partnerships	B	A	→

Title	Principles of Taxation	Taxation	Advanced Stage
Trading losses		A	→
Companies – Taxable total profits			
Property income (including lease premiums)		A	→
Trading profits	B	A	→
Loan relationships	B	A	→
Loan relationships – worldwide debt cap			B
Intangible assets		B	A
Research and development expenditure		B	A
Research and development tax credits			A
Miscellaneous income	B	A	→
Chargeable gains	B	A	→
Indexation		A	→
Qualifying donations	B	A	→
Relief for capital losses		A	→
Trading losses		A	→
Use of deficit on non-trading loan relationships		A	→
Corporation tax computation			
Chargeable accounting periods	C	B	A
Close companies		A	→
Corporation tax liability	B	A	→
Distributions		B	→
Double tax relief (including underlying tax and withholding tax)			B
Liquidation			A
Provision of services through a company			A
Rates of tax	B	A	→
Residence	C	B	→
Groups			
Associated companies	C	B	A
Capital gains groups		A	→
Changes in group structure			A
Change in ownership		B	A
Consortium relief			A
Controlled foreign companies			A
Degrouping charges			A
Group loss relief		A	→
Group relationships		A	→
Non-coterminous accounting periods		A	→
Overseas companies and branches			A
Pre-acquisition gains and losses			A
Rollover relief		A	→
Transfer of assets		A	→
Transfer of pricing			A
Stamp Duty and Stamp Duty Land Tax			
Basic principles			B
Chargeable occasions			B
Exemptions			B

Title	Professional Stage		Advanced Stage
	Principles of Taxation	Taxation	
VAT			
Administration	B	→	→
Appeals	C	→	→
Capitals goods scheme			A
Group aspects		A	→
Input VAT	A	→	→
Output VAT	A	→	→
Overseas aspects		A	→
Partial exemption		B	→
Payments	A	→	→
Penalties and interest	A	→	→
Property transactions		A	→
Registration and deregistration	A	→	→
Small business reliefs	A	→	→
Taxable person	A	→	→
Taxable supplies	A	→	→
Transfer of a business as a going concern		B	→
VAT records and accounts	A	→	→
PERSONAL TAXATION			
Administration			
Administration	B	→	→
Appeals	C	→	→
PAYE	B	→	→
Payments	B	A	→
Penalties and interest	B	A	→
Self assessment	B	A	→
Employees			
Allowable deductions against employment income		A	→
Employment income	B	A	→
Share schemes			A
Statutory Mileage Rates Scheme		A	→
Taxable and exempt benefits	B	A	→
Termination payments		B	→
Other income			
Dividends from UK companies	B	A	→
Enterprise Investment Scheme			B
Investment income	B	A	→
ISAs	B	B	→
Property income	C	A	→
Lease premiums		A	→
Savings income	B	A	→
Venture Capital Trusts			B
Income tax computation			
Exempt income	B	A	→
Gift Aid	B	A	→
Income tax liable and payable	B	A	→
Income tax charge on child benefit		B	→
Independent taxation and jointly owned assets		B	A

Title	Principles of Taxation	Taxation	Advanced Stage
Married couples allowance	B	A	→
Pension contributions: provision for retirement		B	A
Pension contributions: tax reliefs		B	A
Personal age allowance	B	A	→
Personal allowance	B	A	→
Rates of tax	B	A	→
Taxable persons	C	A	→
Capital gains tax			
Annual exempt amount	B	A	→
Chargeable assets	C	B	→
Chargeable disposals	C	B	→
Chargeable persons	C	B	→
Chattels: wasting and non wasting	B	→	→
Connected persons		A	→
Converted trading losses		B	→
Costs of acquisition and disposal	C	B	→
Leases			A
Nil gain/nil loss transfers		A	→
Part disposals		B	→
Pre 31 March 1982 assets		A	→
Qualifying corporate bonds			A
Rate of tax	B	A	→
Relief for capital losses		A	→
Reorganisations and reconstructions			A
Shares and securities (including bonus and rights issues)		A	→
Capital gains tax reliefs			
Letting relief		A	→
Principal private residence relief		A	→
Reinvestment relief under EIS			B
National insurance contributions			
Administration	C	B	→
Classes of NIC	C	B	→
Directors		B	→
Maximum contributions		C	→
Taxable benefits		B	→
Basic principles of inheritance tax			
Chargeable persons		B	→
Chargeable property		B	→
Excluded property		B	→
Inter-spouse transfers		A	→
Rates of tax		A	→
Related property		B	→
Seven year accumulation period		A	→
Inheritance tax on lifetime transfers			
Discretionary trusts		A	→
Potentially exempt transfers		A	→

Title	Professional Stage		Advanced Stage
	Principles of Taxation	Taxation	
Inheritance tax on death			
Death estate		A	→
Deeds of variation		B	→
Lifetime transfers		A	→
Reliefs and exemptions from inheritance tax			
Agricultural property relief		B	→
Annual exemption		B	→
Business property relief		A	→
Gifts to charities and political parties		A	→
Gifts with reservation of benefit		B	→
Marriage exemption		A	→
Normal expenditure out of income		A	→
Quick succession relief		B	→
Small gifts exemption		A	→
Taper relief		A	→
Overseas aspects of personal taxation			
Arising basis			A
Deemed domicile for IHT			A
Domicile			A
Foreign assets income and gains			A
Double tax relief			A
Ordinary residence			A
Remittance basis			A
Residence			A
Temporary absence			A
UK taxation of non-domiciled individuals			A

Ethics Codes and Standards

Ethics Codes and Standards	Level	Professional Stage modules
IFAC Code of Ethics for Professional Accountants (parts A, B and C and Definitions)	A	Assurance Business and Finance Law Principles of Taxation
ICAEW Code of Ethics (icaew.com/regulations)	A	Audit and Assurance Business Strategy Financial Reporting Taxation
APB Ethical Standards 1-5 (revised) Provisions Available to Small Entities (revised)	A	Assurance Audit and Assurance

ICAEW

5 Faculties and Special Interest Groups

The faculties and special interest groups are specialist bodies within ICAEW which offer members networking opportunities, influence and recognition within clearly defined areas of technical expertise. As well as providing accurate and timely technical analysis, they lead the way in many professional and wider business issues through stimulating debate, shaping policy and encouraging good practice. Their value is endorsed by over 40,000 members of ICAEW who currently belong to one or more of the seven faculties:

- Audit and Assurance
- Corporate Finance
- Finance and Management
- Financial Reporting
- Financial Services
- Information Technology
- Tax

The special interest groups provide practical support, information and representation for chartered accountants working within a range of industry sectors, including:

- Charity and Voluntary sector
- Entertainment and Media
- Farming and Rural Business
- Forensic
- Healthcare
- Interim Management
- Non-Executive Directors
- Public Sector
- Solicitors
- Tourism and Hospitality
- Valuation

Students can register free of charge for provisional membership of one special interest group and receive a monthly complimentary e-newsletter from one faculty of your choice. To find out more and to access a range of free resources, visit icaew.com/facultiesandsigs

6 ICAEW publications for further reading

ICAEW produces publications and guidance for its students and members on a variety of technical and business topics. This list of publications has been prepared for students who wish to undertake further reading in a particular subject area and is by no means exhaustive. You are not required to study these publications for your exams. For a full list of publications, or to access any of the publications listed below, visit the Technical Resources section of the ICAEW website at icaew.com

ICAEW no longer prints a Members Handbook. ICAEW regulations, standards and guidance are available at icaew.com/regulations This area includes regulations and guidance relevant to the regulated areas of audit, investment business and insolvency as well as materials that was previously in the handbook.

The TECH and AUDIT series of technical releases are another source of guidance available to members and students. Visit icaew.com/technicalreleases for the most up-to-date releases.

Audit and Assurance Faculty – icaew.com/aaf

- **Right First Time with the Clarified ISAs**, ICAEW 2010, ISBN 978-0-85760-063-9

  Clarified ISAs provide many opportunities for practitioners in terms of potential efficiencies, better documentation, better reporting to clients, and enhanced audit quality overall.

  This modular guide has been developed by ICAEW's ISA implementation sub-group to help medium-sized and smaller firms implement the clarified ISAs and take advantage of these opportunities. This modular guide is designed to give users the choice of either downloading the publication in its entirety, or downloading specific modules on which they want to focus.

  An international edition is also available.

- **Quality Control in the Audit Environment**, ICAEW 2010, ISBN 0-497-80857-605-5

  The publication identifies seven key areas for firms to consider. Illustrative policies and procedures are provided for selected aspects of each key area, including some examples for sole practitioners. The guide also includes an appendix with answers to a number of frequently asked questions on the standard.

  An international edition is also available.

- **The Audit of Related Parties in Practice** ICAEW 2010, ISBN 978-1-84125-565-6

  This practical guide to the audit of related party relationships and transactions is set in the context of the significant change in approach that is required under the revised ISA and highlights the importance of planning, the need to involve the entire audit team in this, to assign staff with the appropriate level of experience to audit this area and upfront discussions with the client to identify related parties.

  An international edition is also available.

- **Alternatives to Audit** ICAEW, 2009, ISBN 978-1-84152-819-9

  In August 2006, the ICAEW Audit and Assurance Faculty began a two-year consultation on a new assurance services (the ICAEW Assurance Service), an alternative to audit based on the idea of limited assurance introduced by the International Auditing and Assurance Standards Board (IAASB). This report presents findings from the practical experience of providing the ICAEW Assurance Service over the subsequent two years and views of users of financial information that help in assessing the relevance of the service to their needs.

- **Companies Act 2006 – Auditor related requirements and regulations third edition – March 2012** ICAEW, 2012, ISBN 978-0-85760-442-2

  This third edition of the guide provides a brief summary of the key sections in the Companies Act 2006 (the Act) which relate directly to the rights and duties of auditors. It covers the various types of reports issued by auditors in accordance with the Act. It is designed to be a signposting tool for practitioners and identifies the other pieces of guidance issued by ICAEW, APB, FRC, POB and others to support implementation of the Act.

- **Auditing in a group context: practical considerations for auditors** ICAEW, 2008, ISBN 978-1-84152-628-7

  The guide describes special considerations for auditors at each stage of the group audit's cycle. While no decisions have been taken on UK adoption of the IAASB's clarity ISAs, the publication also covers matters in the IAASB's revised and redrafted 'ISA 600 Special Considerations - Audits of Group Financial Statements (Including the Work of Component Auditors)'. The revised publication contains suggestions for both group auditors and component auditors.

Corporate Finance Faculty – icaew.com/corpfinfac

- **Private equity demystified – an explanatory guide** Second Edition, Financing Change Initiative, ICAEW, March 2010, John Gilligan and Mike Wright

  This guide summarises the findings of academic work on private equity transactions from around the world. Hard copies of the abstract and full report are free and are also available by download from icaew.com/thoughtleadership

- **Best Practice Guidelines**

  The Corporate Finance Faculty publishes a series of guidelines on best-practice, regulatory trends and technical issues. Authored by leading practitioners in corporate finance, they are succinct and clear overviews of emerging issues in UK corporate finance. icaew.com/corpfinfac

- **Corporate Financier magazine**, ISSN 1367-4544

  The award-winning *Corporate Financier* magazine is published ten times a year for members, stakeholders and key associates of ICAEW's Corporate Finance Faculty.

  Aimed at professionals, investors and company directors involved in corporate finance, it covers a wide range of emerging regulatory, commercial and professional development issues.

  The magazine includes features, news, analysis and research, written by experts, experienced editors and professional journalists.

  In 2011, three major themes were introduced: Innovation & Corporate Finance; Financing Entrepreneurship; and Deal Leadership.

Corporate governance – icaew.com/corporategovernance

- **The UK Corporate Governance Code 2010**

  The UK Corporate Governance Code (formerly the Combined Code) sets out standards of good practice in relation to board leadership and effectiveness, remuneration, accountability and relations with shareholders. All companies with a Premium Listing of equity shares in the UK are required under the Listing Rules to report on how they have applied the UK Corporate Governance Code in their annual report and accounts.

  The first version of the UK Corporate Governance Code was produced in 1992 by the Cadbury Committee. In May 2010 the Financial Reporting Council issued a new edition of the Code which applies to financial years beginning on or after 29 June 2010.

  The UK Corporate Governance Code contains broad principles and more specific provisions. Listed companies are required to report on how they have applied the main principles of the Code, and either to confirm that they have complied with the Code's provisions or – where they have not – to provide an explanation.

- **Internal Control: Revised Guidance on Internal Control for Directors on the Combined Code (Now the UK Corporate Governance Code)**

  Originally published in 1999, the Turnbull guidance was revised and updated in October 2005, following a review by the Financial Reporting Council. The updated guidance applies to listed companies for financial years beginning on or after 1 January 2006.

- **The FRC Guidance on Audit Committees** (formerly known as the Smith Guidance)

  First published by the Financial Reporting Council in January 2003, and most recently updated in 2010. It is intended to assist company boards when implementing the sections of the UK Corporate Governance Code dealing with audit committees and to assist directors serving on audit committees in carrying out their role. Companies are encouraged to use the 2010 edition of the guidance with effect from 30 April 2011

- **The UK Stewardship Code**

  The UK Stewardship Code was published in July 2010. It aims to enhance the quality of engagement between institutional investors and companies to help improve long-term returns to shareholders and the efficient exercise of governance responsibilities by setting out good practice on engagement with investee companies to which the Financial Reporting Council believes institutional investors should aspire.

  A report summarising the actions being taken by the Financial Reporting Council and explaining how the UK Stewardship Code is intended to operate was also published in July 2010.

Corporate responsibility – icaew.com/corporateresponsibility

- **Sustainable Business** January 2009

  The new thought leadership prospectus acts as a framework for the work that ICAEW do in sustainability/corporate responsibility. It argues that any system that is sustainable needs accurate and reliable information to help it learn and adapt, which is where the accounting profession plays an important role. A downloadable pdf is available at icaew.com/sustainablebusiness

- **Environmental issues in annual financial statements** ICAEW, May 2009, ISBN 978-1-84152-610-2

  This report is a joint initiative with the Environment Agency. It is aimed at business accountants who prepare, use or audit the financial statements in statutory annual reports and accounts, or who advise or sit on the boards of the UK companies and public sector organisations. It offers practical advice on measuring and disclosing environmental performance. A downloadable pdf is available at icaew.com/sustainablebusiness

- **ESRC seminar series – When worlds collide: contested paradigms of corporate responsibility**

  ICAEW, in conjunction with the British Academy of Management, won an Economic and Social Research Council grant to run a seminar series which aims to bring academics and the business community together to tackle some of the big challenges in corporate responsibility. icaew.com/corporateresponsibility

- **The Business Sustainability Programme (BSP)**

  The Business Sustainability Programme is an e-learning package for accountants and business professionals who want to learn about the business case for sustainability. The course is spread across five modules taking users from definitions of sustainability and corporate responsibility, through case studies and finally towards developing an individually tailored sustainability strategy for their business. The first two modules are free to everyone. For more information and to download a brochure visit icaew.com/bsp

Ethics – icaew.com/ethics

- **Code of Ethics** (part of icaew.com/regulations)

  The Code of Ethics helps ICAEW members meet these obligations by providing them with ethical guidance. The Code applies to all members, students, affiliates, employees of member firms and, where applicable, member firms, in all of their professional and business activities, whether remunerated or voluntary.

- **Instilling integrity in organisations** ICAEW June 2009

  Practical guidance aimed at directors and management to assist them in instilling integrity in their organisations. This document may also be helpful to audit firms discussing this topic with clients and individuals seeking to address issues in this area with their employers.

- **Reporting with Integrity** ICAEW May 2007, ISBN 978-1-84152-455-9

  This publication brings ideas from a variety of disciplines, in order to obtain a more comprehensive understanding of what is meant by integrity, both as a concept and in practice. Moreover, because this report sees reporting with integrity as a joint endeavour of individuals, organisations and professions, including the accounting profession, the concept of integrity is considered in all these contexts.

Finance and Management Faculty – icaew.com/fmfac

- **Finance's role in the organisation** November 2009, ISBN 978-1-84152-855-7

  This considers the challenges of designing successful organisations, written by Rick Payne, who leads the faculty's finance direction programme.

- **Investment appraisal** SR27: December 2009, ISBN 978-1-84152-854-4

  This special report looks at the key issues and advises managers on how they can contribute effectively to decision making and control during the process of investment appraisal.

- **Starting a business** SR28: March 2010, ISBN 978-1-84152-984-2

  This report provides accountants with a realistic and motivational overview of what to consider when starting a business.

- **Developing a vision for your business** SR30: September 2010, ISBN 978-0-85760-054-7

  This special report looks at what makes a good vision, the benefits of having one, the role of the FD in the process, leadership, storytelling and the use of visions in medium-sized businesses.

- **Finance transformation – the outsourcing perspective** SR31: December 2010, ISBN 978-0-85760-079-0

  The authors of this outsourcing special report share their expertise on topics including service level agreements, people management, and innovation and technology.

- **The Finance Function: A Framework for Analysis September 2011**, ISBN 978-0-85760-285-5

  This report is a source of reference for those analyzing or researching the role of the finance function and provides a foundation for considering the key challenges involved, written by Rick Payne, who leads the faculty's finance direction programme.

Financial Reporting Faculty – icaew.com/frfac

- **EU Implementation of IFRS and the Fair Value Directive** ICAEW, October 2007, ISBN 978-1-84152-519-8

  The most comprehensive assessment to date of compliance with the requirements of IFRS and the overall quality if IFRS financial reporting.

  The Financial Reporting Faculty makes available to students copies of its highly-regarded factsheets on UK GAAP and IFRS issues, as well as its journal, *By All Accounts*, at icaew.com/frfac

Financial Services Faculty – icaew.com/fsf

- **Audit of banks: lessons from the crisis,** (Inspiring Confidence in Financial Services initiative) ICAEW, June 2010 ISBN 978-0-85760-051-6

  This research has looked into the role played by bank auditors and examined improvements that can be made in light of lessons learned from the financial crisis. The project has included the publication of stakeholder feedback and development of a final report

- **Measurement in financial services,** (Inspiring Confidence in Financial Services initiative) ICAEW, March 2008, ISBN 978-1-84152-546-4

  This report suggests that more work is required on matching measurement practices in the financial services industry to the needs of different users of financial information, despite the fact that the financial services industry has the greatest concentration of measurement and modelling skills of any industry. A downloadable pdf is available at icaew.com/thoughtleadership

- **Skilled Persons' Guidance – Reporting Under s166 Financial Services and Markets Act 2000 (Interim Technical Release FSF 01/08)**

  This interim guidance was issued by ICAEW in April 2008 as a revision to TECH 20/30 to assist chartered accountants and other professionals who are requested to report under s166 Financial Services and Markets Act 2000. A downloadable pdf is available at icaew.com/technicalreleases

Information Technology Faculty – icaew.com/itfac

The IT Faculty provides ongoing advice and guidance that will help students in their studies and their work. The online community (ion.icaew.com/itcountshome) provides regular free updates as well as a link to the faculty's Twitter feed which provides helpful updates and links to relevant articles. The following publications should also be of interest to students:

- **Make the move to cloud computing** ICAEW, 2012, ISBN 978-0-85760-617-4

  Cloud computing in its purest form is pay-as-you-go IT, online and on demand. The IT capabilities provided as a service to businesses include: single software applications or software suites; online software development platforms; and virtual computing infrastructure, ranging from data storage to computer grids.

- **Bringing employee personal devices into the business – a guide to IT consumerisation** ICAEW, 2012, ISBN 978-0-85760-443-9

  The gap between business and consumer technology has been growing over the last few years, with the consumer market now leading in terms of ease of use and portability.

- **Making the most of social media – a practical guide for your business** ICAEW, 2011, ISBN 978-0-85760-286-2

  This guide will enable the business manager to develop a philosophy that allies social media's potential with the business's objectives and capabilities, to set objectives and protect against pitfalls, and then to take the first practical steps in a mass communications medium very different from any that British business has encountered before.

Tax Faculty – icaew.com/taxfac

The Tax Faculty runs a Younger Members Tax Club which provides informal presentations, discussions and socialising. All young professionals interested in tax are welcome to attend. See the website for more details icaew.com/taxfac

- **Tax news service**

  You can keep up with the tax news as it develops on the Tax Faculty's news site icaew.com/taxnews. And you can subscribe to the free newswire which gives you a weekly round up. For more details visit icaew.com/taxfac

- **Demystifying XBRL**

  This booklet, produced jointly by KPMG, the Tax Faculty and the Information Technology Faculty, explains exactly what iXBRL is all about and what must be done in order to e-file corporation tax returns using the new standard.

- **Implementing XBRL**

  This booklet, produced jointly by Thompson Reuters, the Tax Faculty and the Information Technology Faculty, is a practical guide for accountants in business and practice, and follows on from Demystifying XBRL.

- **TAXline Tax Practice series of detailed briefings on current topics:**

  TAXline Tax Practice 27
  Let property - a brief guide by Rebecca Cave (published November 2011)

TAXline Tax Practice 26
The new pension rules by Anne Redston (published July 2011)

TAXline Tax Practice 25
Tax Credits by Robin Williamson (published April 2011)

TAXline Tax Practice No 23
HMRC Powers - an overview of the new powers and penalties regime by Paula Clemett (published October 2010)

CHAPTER 1

Introduction to taxation

Introduction

Examination context

Topic List

Summary and Self-test

Answers to Self-test

Learning outcomes

- Identify the objectives of tax in general terms of economic, social justice and environmental issues, the range of tax opportunities open to the government and the relative advantages of different types of tax in meeting the government's objectives ☐

- Recognise the impact of external influences, including EU tax policies, on UK tax objectives and policies ☐

- Classify entities as individuals, partnerships, or companies for tax purposes and state how they are taxed ☐

- Identify who is liable for the following taxes, how taxes apply to income, transactions and assets, identify the government bodies responsible for the taxes, and determine when an individual or entity comes within the scope of the taxes: ☐

    - capital gains tax
    - corporation tax
    - income tax
    - national insurance
    - VAT

- Recognise the importance of the budget cycle, tax years and the following sources of UK tax law and practice: ☐

    - legislation
    - case law
    - HM Revenue & Customs manuals, statements of practice and press releases

Specific syllabus references for this chapter are: 1a, b, c, d, e.

Syllabus links

The topics covered in this chapter are essential background knowledge which will underpin the whole of your taxation studies.

Examination context

In the examination candidates may be required to:

- Identify the social justice principles being applied for taxation purposes
- Recognise external influences on the UK taxation system
- Understand which taxes apply to different taxpayers eg partnerships, companies
- Identify the responsibilities of HM Revenue & Customs

For extra question practice on these topics go to the section of the Question Bank covering this chapter.

1 Objectives of taxation

Section overview

- The UK tax system has developed piecemeal and has been changed by successive governments in accordance with their political objectives.

- Governments use taxation to encourage or discourage certain types of economic activity.

- Taxation may be used to promote social justice but there is no political consensus on what is meant by this term.

- Environmental concerns have led to changes in taxation policy.

- External influences are increasingly important, in particular the European Union.

1.1 Introduction

The purpose of this chapter is to provide background information which will assist your understanding of the framework of the UK taxation system, why governments impose tax and the principles of taxation.

The UK taxation system has developed over centuries on a piecemeal basis. Successive governments have changed the taxation system in accordance with their political objectives. There has never been an all-party political consensus about how the UK taxation system should be changed and there probably never will be.

1.2 Management of the economy

The government has an effect on the level of economic activity in the UK by its withdrawal of money from the economy through taxation and the injection of money into the economy through public sector spending.

In the past, governments tended to make changes to taxation in the light of short-term changes in the economy such as inflation, unemployment and the balance of trade between imports and exports.

More recently, governments have believed that the impact of taxation takes a long time to have an effect. Government policies have therefore moved to longer-term planning. The government has also delegated the setting of interest rates to the Bank of England within specific targets for inflation, instead of trying to manage inflation by short-term interest rate changes.

Within the longer-term planning, the government aims to encourage or discourage certain types of economic activity.

The government encourages:

- Savings, for example by offering tax incentives such as Individual Savings Accounts (ISAs) and tax relief on pension contributions

- Donations to charity, for example through the Gift Aid Scheme

- Investment into business, for example through Venture Capital Trust relief and the Enterprise Investment Scheme

- Entrepreneurs who build their own businesses, through reliefs from capital taxes

The government discourages:

- Office buildings, for which there are no tax allowances
- Smoking and alcoholic drinks, through substantial taxes on each type of product
- Motoring, through vehicle excise duty and fuel duties

Governments argue that these latter two taxes to some extent mirror the extra costs to the country of such behaviour, such as the burden placed on the National Health Service and maintenance of the road network.

However, the government also needs to raise money for other areas of public expenditure such as defence, law and order, overseas aid and the running of the government and parliament. There is no real link between taxation and this type of expenditure.

1.3 Social justice

Social justice lies at the heart of politics. What some think of as just is regarded by others as completely unjust. Attitudes to the redistribution of wealth are a clear example.

Some people believe in a free-market approach where individuals are allowed to generate income and capital and spend it as they choose, with relatively low levels of taxation. It is argued that since the economy overall increases in the free market, every individual will benefit in the long term.

The free-market approach could be criticised for resulting in the rich becoming richer and the poor poorer since economic power may become concentrated in relatively few hands.

Some people argue that taxation should be used to redistribute income and wealth away from the rich towards the poor. This is a key argument in favour of taxes on capital which, relative to the tax raised, cost a great deal to collect. The introduction of tax credits which benefit those on lower incomes, especially those with children, can also be seen as an attempt at wealth redistribution through taxation.

There are a number of principles which either side might invoke in the debate over social justice:

- The direct/indirect principle
    - direct taxes (eg income tax, capital gains tax, corporation tax, national insurance contributions) are only paid by those who generate the funds to pay the tax
    - indirect taxes (eg value added tax, excise duty) relate to consumption and it is up to individuals whether they spend money on such goods
- The progressive/regressive principle
    - progressive taxes rise as a proportion of income as that income rises. For example, the lowest rate of income tax is 10% which is payable on the first few thousand pounds of certain taxable income, whereas the rate of income tax on taxable income of over £42,475 is 40% and that on taxable income of over £150,000 is 50%
    - regressive taxes rise as a proportion of income as income falls. The amount of duty paid on a packet of cigarettes is the same, regardless of the income of the purchaser. That amount will be a greater proportion of the income of a person with a low income than a person with a higher income. The argument that a regressive tax is just hinges on the benefit principle (below)
- The unit/value principle
    - a unit tax is calculated as a flat rate per item, regardless of value. Again, this hinges on the benefit principle (below)
    - a value tax is based on a percentage of the value of the item, such as value added tax. This argument partly hinges on the ability to pay principle (below)
- The income/capital/expenditure principle
    - income tax is paid only by those who generate income
    - capital taxes are just because people should not be able to live off the sale of capital assets without generating income
    - taxes on expenditure are paid only by those who incur the expenditure
- The ability to pay/benefit principle
    - taxes should be based on the ability of the taxpayer to pay them eg income tax, capital gains tax
    - taxes should be based, at least partly, on the benefit that the taxpayer receives. For example, everyone should pay towards defence or law and order
- The neutrality principle
    - tax should be neutral so as not to distort choice (but the examples given in 1.2 show that governments do not always want taxes to be neutral)

- The equity principle

    - tax should be equitable or just. However, there are many different views as to what is equitable

- The efficiency principle

    - the cost of collecting the tax should be low in relation to the tax raised. Governments are generally only concerned with the cost to them of administration, not with costs incurred by the taxpayer, for example under the Pay As You Earn scheme or value added tax

1.4 Environmental concerns

The taxation system is slowly moving to accommodate environmental concerns such as sources of energy and global warming.

Many would agree that it is for the government to make sure that such concerns are dealt with through government policy, including taxation, instead of leaving it to individuals to modify their behaviour.

Examples of such taxes are:

- Climate change levy on businesses in proportion to their energy consumption

- Landfill tax to discourage the use of landfill sites for waste disposal and to encourage recycling

- Taxes on motor vehicles based on carbon emissions, such as cars provided to employees and vehicle excise duty, to encourage use of more environmentally friendly vehicles

1.5 External influences

In the past, the UK government tended to set its taxation policies based on domestic concerns with little external influence. However, over the last forty years, with the entry of the UK into the European Union (EU) and increased globalisation, the UK government has had to take much more account of external influences in setting its taxation policies.

We have already seen that the impact of environmental concerns has led to changes in UK taxation. This has been partly brought about by the influence of the international community and agreements entered into by the UK government such as the Kyoto Treaty on reduction of greenhouse gases, principally carbon dioxide.

However, the main external influence on UK taxation policy is the EU.

The overall aim of the EU is the creation of a single European market with no internal trade barriers and common policies relating to trade outside the EU.

There is no general requirement for member states to move to a common system of taxation. However, states may provide for a common code of taxation within particular areas of their taxation system.

The most important example is value added tax (VAT) where the UK is obliged to pass its laws to conform to rules laid down by European law. There is a certain amount of flexibility between the member states, for example on rates of taxation.

There have been limited examples of specific European laws in relation to direct taxes.

However, under the EU treaties, member states are also obliged to permit freedom of movement of workers and capital and freedom to establish business operations within the EU. These treaty provisions can be invoked by taxpayers. An example was a UK company which wished to make use of losses in a subsidiary based in another EU country. This was prohibited by UK tax law. The success of the UK company's case in the European Court has led to a change to UK tax law in this area.

A further example of how external influences affect UK taxation policy is the ongoing impact of the recent banking crisis. In January 2011, the government introduced a systemic risk tax on financial institutions called the bank levy. It is hoped that this tax will help reduce the risks and impact of future such crises and would be best coordinated globally. The levy has been introduced by the UK, France and Germany.

The tax proceeds will go into general taxation of the government and are not an insurance policy for financial institutions.

2 Liability to tax and tax administration

Section overview

- Individuals, partnerships and companies are liable to tax.
- Taxes in the UK are administered by HM Revenue & Customs (HMRC).

2.1 Individuals

An individual may be liable to the following taxes:

- Income tax (IT), for example on income from investments, income from employment and income from a business which he operates as a sole trader or as a member of a partnership

- Capital gains tax (CGT) on the disposal of capital assets owned by him as investments or used in his sole trade or partnership

- National insurance contributions (NICs) as an employee, as a sole trader or partner, and as an employer

- Value added tax (VAT) as the supplier of goods and services or as the final consumer of goods or services

An individual is taxed annually on his income and gains arising in a tax year.

Definition

Tax year: 6 April in one calendar year to 5 April in the next calendar year. The tax year running from 6 April 2012 to 5 April 2013 is called the 2012/13 tax year.

2.2 Partnerships

A partnership is a group of persons carrying on a business together with a view to making a profit.

Each partner is liable to tax on his share of income and gains of the partnership in a tax year, but not for tax on the shares of income and gains of the other partners.

The partners are jointly and severally liable for the following taxes:

- Income tax of employees deducted under the Pay As You Earn (PAYE) system

- National insurance contributions (NICs) as an employer (employer contributions and employee contributions are collected under the PAYE system)

- Value added tax (VAT) as the supplier of goods and services or as the final consumer of goods or services

'Joint and several' liability means that these taxes can be recovered from all or any of the partners.

2.3 Companies

A company is a legal person formed by incorporation under the Companies Acts. It is legally separate from its owners (shareholders) and its managers (directors).

A company is liable for the following taxes:

- Corporation tax (CT) on its income and gains

- Income tax of employees deducted under the Pay As You Earn (PAYE) system

- National insurance contributions (NICs) as an employer (employer contributions and employee contributions collected under the PAYE system)

- Value added tax (VAT) as the supplier of goods and services or as the final consumer of goods or services

The rate of corporation tax is determined by reference to the financial year.

Definition

Financial year: 1 April in one calendar year to 31 March in the next calendar year. The financial year running from 1 April 2012 to 31 March 2013 is called Financial Year (FY) 2012.

2.4 HM Revenue & Customs

All taxes in the UK are administered by HMRC.

The Commissioners of HMRC are a body of civil servants appointed by the Queen who exercise their duties on behalf of the Crown. They have a duty to implement the law relating to taxation and oversee the administration of taxation.

The Commissioners appoint 'Officers of Revenue & Customs' (known as Officers) to carry out the day-to-day work of HMRC. These officers mainly work in one of several hundred local district offices which are the front line point of contact between HMRC and the taxpayer.

The responsibilities of HMRC are:

- To collect and administer IT, CGT, NIC, CT and VAT
- To pay and administer working tax credit, child tax credit and child benefit
- To collect repayments of student loans
- To ensure all employers meet the minimum wage rules
- To protect UK society from tax fraud, alcohol and tobacco smuggling and illegal importation of drugs

3 Sources of tax law and practice

Section overview

- Tax law is set out in statute, supplemented by statutory instruments.

- A Finance Act is passed each year, following Budget proposals.

- Case law interpreting statute law must usually be followed in later cases.

- HMRC publishes its interpretation of tax law in various ways.

3.1 Legislation

3.1.1 Statutes

The basic rules of the UK taxation system are in a number of tax statutes (Acts of Parliament).

The tax law is amended each year by the **Finance Act**. This is based on proposals in the Budget put forward by the Chancellor of the Exchequer in March or April each year. The Finance Act generally relates to the tax year and financial year starting in April of that year. Therefore, the Finance Act 2012 relates mainly to the tax year 2012/13 and the Financial Year 2012.

Most of the statutory tax law is found in consolidated statutes which contain the law enacted by Finance Acts over the years. For example, value added tax is dealt with in the Value Added Tax Act 1994 (*VATA 1994*).

The main direct tax law has also recently been rewritten in plainer English. An example is the Corporation Tax Act 2010 *(CTA 2010)*.

3.1.2 Statutory instruments

Some tax statutes set out a general principal but provide for the detail to be changed, as required, in secondary or 'delegated' legislation. This is usually in the form of a statutory instrument (SI), introduced either by a parliamentary minister or a local authority.

The reason for this is that the procedure for making changes to a SI is less complicated than for a statute. A SI is simply laid before Parliament and usually automatically becomes law within a stated period, unless any objections are raised to it.

SIs most commonly take the form of regulations, which deal with these detailed provisions. They are the biggest single source of tax law each year.

3.2 Case law

Over the years, many thousands of tax cases have been brought before the courts where the interpretation of statute law is unclear.

Decisions made by judges to resolve these cases form case law. Many judgements are precedent for future cases which means that they must be followed unless superseded by legislation or the decision of a higher court.

Knowledge of specific case names is not examinable.

3.3 HMRC publications

HMRC must act according to tax law, but it has some discretion over how it applies the law. HMRC therefore publishes details of how the law is to be implemented in practice, for example on its website – www.hmrc.gov.uk.

These publications have no legal backing but do provide information on HMRC's interpretation of the law which will be adhered to unless successfully challenged by a taxpayer in the courts.

HMRC publications include:

- Manuals, primarily for the guidance of its own staff but also mostly available to taxpayers and tax professionals on the HMRC website

- Statements of practice (SP) setting out HMRC's interpretation of tax legislation

- Extra-statutory concessions (ESC) which provide for a relaxation of the strict legal position to resolve anomalies and relieve hardship. An ESC may be given statutory effect by means of a Treasury Order. ESCs are gradually being codified or withdrawn as their legality was successfully challenged in 2005

- Press releases and explanatory notes dealing with changes in tax law, for example Budget proposals

- Leaflets which are mainly aimed at ordinary taxpayers and explain the tax system in non-technical language

Summary and Self-test

Summary

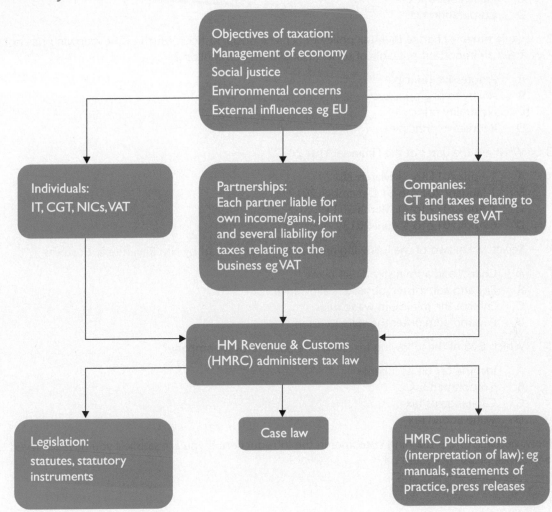

Self-test

Answer the following questions.

1   Which **two** of the following are direct taxes?

   A   Excise duty
   B   Capital gains tax
   C   Value added tax
   D   Corporation tax

2   Governments change their tax policy to achieve 'social justice'. Which of the following has **not** been an important principle of social justice in modern politics?

   A   Progressive principle
   B   Ability to pay principle
   C   Neutrality principle
   D   Regressive principle

3   What are the dates of the Financial Year 2012?

   A   1 April 2011 to 31 March 2012
   B   1 January 2012 to 31 December 2012
   C   1 April 2012 to 31 March 2013
   D   6 April 2012 to 5 April 2013

4   Select which **two** of the following are functions carried out by HM Revenue & Customs

   A   Collect and administer direct taxes
   B   Pay and administer jobseekers allowance
   C   Enforce the minimum wage rules
   D   Pay and administer the state pension

5   Which **two** of the following taxes may be payable by a company?

   A   Income tax on its income
   B   Corporation tax
   C   Capital gains tax
   D   Value added tax

Now, go back to the Learning outcomes in the Introduction. If you are satisfied you have achieved these objectives, please tick them off.

Answers to Self-test

1   B and D – capital gains tax and corporation tax

    The others are indirect taxes.

2   C – the neutrality principle (taxes should not distort choice).

    The encourage/discourage examples show that governments do not generally want taxes to be neutral.

3   C – Financial Year 2012 runs from 1 April 2012 to 31 March 2013.

4   A and C – collect and administer direct taxes and enforce the minimum wage rules.

5   B and D – corporation tax (payable by a company on its income and gains) and value added tax (as a supplier and a final consumer of goods and services).

Principles of Taxation

CHAPTER 2

Introduction to income tax

Introduction

Examination context

Topic List

    1   Chargeable and exempt income

    2   Computation of taxable income

    3   Computing tax payable

    4   Allowances for taxpayers aged 65 and over

Summary and Self-test

Technical reference

Answers to Interactive questions

Answers to Self-test

Introduction

Learning outcomes

- Recognise the main sources of taxable and non-taxable income
- Calculate the personal allowance available to an individual according to personal circumstances including personal age allowances and married couples allowance
- Calculate total taxable income and the income tax payable or repayable for employed and self-employed individuals

The specific syllabus references for this chapter are: 3a, b, i.

Syllabus links

The topics covered in this chapter are fundamental to your understanding of income tax.

You will be using this knowledge again when you tackle the Taxation paper later on in the Professional Stage and it will also underpin the technical aspects at the Advanced Stage.

Examination context

In the examination, candidates may be required to:

- Differentiate between items which are taxable and exempt for income tax purposes
- Calculate taxable income where income has been received net of income tax or without deduction of tax at source
- Categorise taxable income as non savings, savings or dividend income and calculate the tax liability
- Identify how tax relief is given for Gift Aid
- Compute the allowances available for taxpayers aged 65 and over

For extra question practice on these topics go to the section of the Question Bank covering this chapter.

Candidates have historically prepared well for this area of the syllabus. Better prepared candidates are able to perform well in the more difficult areas of Gift Aid and allowances for taxpayers aged 65 and over.

1 Chargeable and exempt income

Section overview

- Income may be chargeable to income tax or exempt from income tax.

- Chargeable income is employment income, trading income, property income, savings income, dividend income and miscellaneous income.

- Exempt income includes income from Individual Savings Accounts and premium bond prizes.

1.1 Sources of income

Income can be broadly divided into two main types:

- Income which is chargeable to income tax – this may be called taxable income or chargeable income

- Income which is exempt from income tax – this may be called non-taxable income or exempt income

The first stage of an income tax computation is to prepare a computation of taxable income. To do this you will need to identify whether the income received by the taxpayer is chargeable or exempt.

1.2 Chargeable income

The main types of chargeable income are:

- Income from employment
- Income from trading
- Income from renting out property
- Income from investments such as interest on loans, bank and building society accounts
- Income from investments such as dividends
- Income from other sources (pensions income, some social security benefits, income from casual work)

1.3 Exempt income

Some income is specifically exempt from income tax including the following:

- Interest on National Savings Certificates
- Income from Individual Savings Accounts (ISAs) including Junior ISAs
- Betting, competition, lottery and premium bond winnings
- Some social security benefits such as housing benefit and child benefit
- Scholarships
- Income tax repayment interest

2 Computation of taxable income

Section overview

- Some income is received with tax already deducted at source, such as most interest and employment income, and must be included gross in the income tax computation.

- Other income is received without tax being deducted at source, such as trading income and property income.

- Dividend income has a tax credit attached to it which must be included in the tax computation.

- There are three types of income in a total chargeable income computation: non-savings income; savings income; and dividend income.

- The total of all chargeable income is called 'net income'.

- Taxable income is net income less the personal allowance.

2.1 Income taxed at source

Some income is received by the taxpayer net of tax, which means that tax is already deducted at the source of the income. This simplifies the collection of tax for HMRC. You may be told in a question that the amount received is **net of income tax**. However, when working out the chargeable income you must include any tax deducted at source, and use the **gross** amount.

Most forms of interest are received net of 20% tax deducted at source. This includes most bank and building society interest and interest on loan stock issued by UK companies. Net interest must be **grossed up** by multiplying the net amount by 100/(100 – 20) (ie 100/80) to obtain the gross equivalent. For example, if you are given a figure for bank interest received of £160 in a question, you must multiply this figure by 100/80 to obtain the gross figure of £200 on which tax of £200 × 20% = £40 has been suffered. Alternatively, the question may give you the gross bank interest figure of £200.

Employment income is received net of income tax deducted under the Pay As You Earn (PAYE) system. The amounts of tax deducted under PAYE will vary according to the income and personal circumstances of the individual. The PAYE system is dealt with later in this text. For examination purposes, questions will normally quote employment income as the amount of income **before** any tax deducted, that is in **gross** terms. If required for the answer, the amount of income tax deducted at source via PAYE will be given separately.

Dividends from UK companies are received with a deemed tax credit. They are treated differently from other sources of income.

2.2 Income received without deduction of tax at source

The other sources of income are generally received without deduction of tax at source. This is called income received gross. You simply need to include the gross figure as given in the question as the chargeable income. The main types of income received gross are trading income and property income.

Some interest is received gross:

- Interest on National Savings and Investments (NS&I) Direct Saver and Investment Accounts

- Interest on government securities (gilt-edged securities or gilts) such as Exchequer Stock and Treasury Stock

- Interest received gross by an individual who has signed a declaration of non-taxpayer status and supplied a certificate to the bank or building society. This is called self-certification and is used mainly by children and pensioners

- Interest on non-commercial investments, such as a loan between friends

2.3 Dividend income

Dividends received from UK companies are dividend income. Dividend income is received with a deemed tax credit of 10% of the grossed up dividend. The dividend must be grossed up by 100/90 to obtain the gross equivalent. For example, if you are given a figure for a dividend received of £450 in a question, you must multiply the dividend by 100/90 to obtain the gross figure of £500 on which there is a tax credit of £500 × 10% = £50. Alternatively the question may give you the gross dividend income figure of £500.

2.4 Types of income

When you set out a taxable income computation, you need to use a standard format which divides the income into three types. This is because there are different rates of tax for each type of income.

The three types of income are:

- Non-savings income: Employment income, Trading profits, Property income, Miscellaneous income. Income that is not categorised as from a specific source is taxed as miscellaneous income.

- Savings income: Interest from investments

- Dividend income: Dividends from UK companies

Note that income received from a pension (pension income) and taxable social security benefits such as jobseeker's allowance (social security income) are taxed in the same way as employment income.

Income that is not categorised as from a specific source is taxed as miscellaneous income.

Definition

Net income: The total chargeable income before deducting the personal allowance (see later in this chapter).

Worked example: Net income

Andrew received the following income in 2012/13:

- Salary from his employment £10,000
- Building society interest £240
- Premium bond winnings £250
- Property income £2,000
- Dividends from UK companies £720

Requirement

What is Andrew's net income for 2012/13?

Solution

Net income

	Non-savings income £	Savings income £	Dividend income £	Total £
Employment income	10,000			
Property income	2,000			
Building society interest				
£240 × 100/80		300		
Dividends				
£720 × 100/90			800	
Net income	12,000	300	800	13,100

Premium bond winnings are exempt income and, therefore, not included in the above computation.

Interactive question 1: What type of income?   [Difficulty level: Easy]

Classify the following types of income as non-savings income, savings income or dividend income and show the taxable amount of each type of income that you would enter in the computation of taxable income.

Question	Fill in your answer
(a) Bank interest received from HSBC of £600	
(b) Property income of £1,000	
(c) Dividend received from UK company of £495	
(d) Interest received on Treasury Stock of £525	
(e) Trading profits of £5,000	
(f) Interest received on NS&I investment account of £600	

See **Answer** at the end of this chapter.

2.5 Personal allowance

Definition

Taxable income: Net income after deduction of the personal allowance.

There is one further step that you need to undertake in order to arrive at the amount of taxable income. This is to deduct the personal allowance. Every individual taxpayer who is resident in the UK is entitled to a personal allowance from birth.

The basic personal allowance for 2012/13 is £8,105. There are enhanced personal allowances for taxpayers aged 65 and over which are covered later in this chapter.

The personal allowance is deducted from the different types of income in the following order:

- Non-savings income
- Savings income
- Dividend income

The full personal allowance of £8,105 is not available for individuals with an adjusted net income of more than £100,000. The personal allowance is reduced by £1 for every £2 that the individual's adjusted net income exceeds £100,000.

The personal allowance will be withdrawn completely where adjusted net income exceeds £116,210. Therefore any taxpayer subject to the additional rate of tax (see later in this chapter) will not be entitled to a personal allowance.

Worked example: Taxable income

Charlotte receives the following income in 2012/13:

- Trading profits £6,600
- Bank interest £500
- Dividends from UK companies £1,350

Requirement

What is Charlotte's taxable income for 2012/13?

Solution

Charlotte

Taxable income

	Non-savings income £	Savings income £	Dividend income £	Total £
Trading profits	6,600			
Bank interest				
£500 × 100/80		625		
Dividends				
£1,350 × 100/90			1,500	
Net income	6,600	625	1,500	8,725
Less personal allowance	(6,600)	(625)	(880)	(8,105)
Taxable income	Nil	Nil	620	620

Interactive question 2: Computing taxable income   [Difficulty level: Exam standard]

Max received the following income in 2012/13:

- Employment income £20,000
- Interest on Individual Savings Account £600
- Interest on Barclays Bank account £280
- Dividends from UK companies £990

Requirement

Using the standard format below, compute Max's taxable income for 2012/13.

Max

Taxable income

	Non-savings income £	Savings income £	Dividend income £	Total £
Employment income				
Interest				
Dividends				
Net income				
Less personal allowance				
Taxable income				

See **Answer** at the end of this chapter.

3 Computing tax payable

Section overview

- Income tax is calculated first on non-savings income, then on savings income and lastly on dividend income.

- There are different rates of tax for each of the three types of income.

- Income tax may be payable by (or repayable to) a taxpayer after taking into account tax credits and tax deducted at source.

- Cash gifts to charity are given tax relief under Gift Aid, and affect the taxpayer's basic rate and higher rate band.

3.1 Computing tax liability

Definition

Tax liability: The total amount of income tax due from a taxpayer.

Once taxable income has been computed, you can calculate the income tax liability. Tax on the three types of income is calculated in the following order:

- Non-savings income
- Savings income
- Dividend income

For 2012/13, the rates of income tax for non-savings income are as follows:

First £34,370 of taxable income	basic rate band	20%
Taxable income between £34,370 and £150,000	higher rate band	40%
Remainder over £150,000	additional rate band	50%

Worked example: Income tax liability on non-savings income

Krishan has trading profits of £45,000 in 2012/13. This is his only source of income in this tax year.

Requirement

What is Krishan's income tax liability for 2012/13?

Solution

Krishan

Income tax liability

	Non-savings income
	£
Trading profits/Net income	45,000
Less personal allowance	(8,105)
Taxable income	36,895

Tax

	£
£34,370 × 20%	6,874
£2,525 × 40%	1,010
£36,895	
Income tax liability	7,884

Worked example: Income tax liability on non-savings income

Lois has employment income of £169,000 in 2012/13. This is her only source of income in this tax year.

Requirement

What is Lois's income tax liability for 2012/13?

Solution

Lois

	Non-savings income £
Employment income/Net income	169,000
Less personal allowance (note)	–
Taxable income	169,000
Tax	
£34,370 × 20%	6,874
£115,630 × 40%	46,252
£150,000	
£19,000 × 50%	9,500
£169,000	
Income tax liability	62,626

Note

As Lois' net income exceeds £116,210 her personal allowance is restricted to nil.

Interactive question 3: Computing tax on non-savings income

[Difficulty level: Exam standard]

Henry is an employee of Tilbury Ltd. His gross salary for 2012/13 is £45,465.

Requirement

Using the standard format below, compute Henry's income tax liability for 2012/13.

Henry

Income tax liability

	Non-savings income £
Employment income/Net income	
Less personal allowance	_____
Taxable income	_____
Tax	
	£
× 20%	
× 40%	
_____	
£ _____	
Income tax liability	_____

See **Answer** at the end of this chapter.

A taxpayer is entitled to only one set of rate bands. The rate bands are used firstly by **non-savings income**. To the extent that any of the rate bands remain, they are used by savings income and then by dividend income. You will see how this works in the example below.

For 2012/13, the rates of income tax for savings income are as follows:

• First £2,710 of savings income	starting rate band 10%
• Next £31,660 of taxable income	basic rate band 20%
• Taxable income between £34,370 and £150,000	higher rate band 40%
• Remainder over £150,000	additional rate band 50%

The starting rate band of 10% for savings income applies **only** to taxpayers who have taxable non-savings income not exceeding £2,710. Where non-savings income, after deduction of the personal allowance (or personal age allowance) exceeds £2,710, the starting rate does not apply to savings income.

Worked example: Income tax liability on non-savings and savings income

Evie received the following income in 2012/13:

- Property income £8,194
- Building society interest £38,648

Requirement

What is Evie's income tax liability for 2012/13?

Solution

Evie
Income tax liability

	Non-savings income £	Savings income £	Total £
Property income	8,194		
Building society interest			
£38,648 × 100/80		48,310	
Net income	8,194	48,310	56,504
Less personal allowance	(8,105)		(8,105)
Taxable income	89	48,310	48,399

	£		£
Tax on non-savings income	89	× 20%	18
Tax on savings income:			
– in starting rate band	2,621	× 10%	262
	2,710		
– in basic rate band	31,660	× 20%	6,332
	34,370		
– in higher rate band	14,029	× 40%	5,612
	48,399		
Income tax liability			12,224

The £89 of non-savings taxable income is taxed first at 20%, the basic rate of tax for non-savings income.

Savings income is taxed next on a cumulative basis. Since the taxable non-savings income was less than £2,710 there is £2,621 of savings income in the starting rate band to tax at 10%.

On a cumulative basis a total of £2,710 of taxable income has been taxed so far. This leaves £31,660 (£34,370 – £2,710) of the basic rate band to tax the savings income at the basic rate of 20%.

Finally £14,029 of savings income falls in the higher rate band which is taxed at 40%.

For 2012/13, the rates of income tax for dividend income are as follows:

- First £34,370 of taxable income   basic rate band   10%
- Between £34,370 and £150,000   higher rate band   32.5%
- Remainder over £150,000   additional rate band   42.5%

Worked example: Income tax liability on all types of income

George receives the following income in 2012/13:

- Employment income £32,325
- Bank interest £4,040
- Dividends from UK companies £8,428

Requirement

What is George's income tax liability for 2012/13?

Solution

George

Income tax liability

	Non- savings income £	Savings income £	Dividend income £	Total £
Employment income	32,325			
Bank interest				
£4,040 × 100/80		5,050		
Dividends				
£8,428 × 100/90			9,364	
Net income	32,325	5,050	9,364	46,739
Less personal allowance	(8,105)			(8,105)
Taxable income	24,220	5,050	9,364	38,634

	£			£
Tax on non-savings income	24,220	× 20%		4,844
Tax on savings income:				
– in basic rate band	5,050	× 20%		1,010
	29,270			
Tax on dividend income:				
– in basic rate band	5,100	× 10%		510
	34,370			
– in higher rate band	4,264	× 32.5%		1,386
	38,634			
Income tax liability				7,750

Since the taxable non-savings income was more than £2,710 there is no starting rate band remaining to tax any savings income at 10%. All of the savings income therefore falls in the basic rate band and is taxed at 20%.

On a cumulative basis a total of £29,270 of taxable income has been taxed so far. This leaves £5,100 (£34,370 – £29,270) of the basic rate band to tax the dividend income at the basic rate of 10%.

Finally £4,264 of dividend income falls in the higher rate band which is taxed at 32.5%.

Worked example: Income tax liability on all types of income

Elise receives the following income in 2012/13:

- Employment income £95,875
- Property income £31,700
- Bank interest £21,140
- Dividends from UK companies £15,300

Requirement

What is Elise's income tax liability for 2012/13?

Solution

Elise

	Non-savings income £	Savings income £	Dividend income £	Total £
Employment income	95,875			
Property income	31,700			
Bank interest				
£21,140 × 100/80		26,425		
Dividends				
£15,300 × 100/90			17,000	
Net income	127,575	26,425	17,000	171,000
Personal allowance	–			
Taxable income	127,575	26,425	17,000	171,000

	£			£
Tax on non-savings income	34,370	× 20%		6,874
	93,205	× 40%		37,282
	127,575			
Tax on savings income				
– in higher rate band	22,425	× 40%		8,970
	150,000			
– in additional rate band	4,000	× 50%		2,000
Tax on dividend income				
– in additional rate band	17,000	× 42.5%		7,225
	171,000			
Income tax liability				62,351

3.2 Computing tax payable or repayable

Definition

Tax payable or repayable: The amount of income tax payable by a taxpayer (or repayable by HMRC) under self assessment after taking into account tax deducted at source.

The final stage that you may be asked to undertake is to compute the tax payable or repayable to the taxpayer under the self assessment system. Details of this system are covered later in this text.

The tax actually payable by the taxpayer must take into account:

- Tax credits received with dividends
- Tax deducted at source

Tax credits on dividends are set against the tax liability first (restricted to the tax credits on the taxable dividend). This is because dividend tax credits can only be used to reduce a taxpayer's tax liability. Any excess tax credits cannot be repaid.

Tax deducted at source on employment income and interest is used to reduce a taxpayer's tax liability and any excess tax deducted at source can be repaid to the taxpayer.

Worked example: Tax payable or repayable

Joe received the following income in 2012/13:

Property income	£3,400
Bank interest	£5,944
Dividends from UK companies	£549

Requirement

What is the tax payable by or repayable to Joe for 2012/13?

Solution

Joe

Tax payable/repayable

	Non-savings income £	Savings income £	Dividend income £	Total £
Property income	3,400			
Bank interest				
£5,944 × 100/80		7,430		
Dividends				
£549 × 100/90			610	
Net income	3,400	7,430	610	11,440
Less personal allowance	(3,400)	(4,705)		(8,105)
Taxable income	Nil	2,725	610	3,335

	£			£
Tax on savings income:				
– in starting rate band	2,710	× 10%		271
– in basic rate band	15	× 20%		3
	2,725			
Tax on dividend income:				
– in basic rate band	610	× 10%		61
	3,335			
Income tax liability				335
Less tax deducted at source:				
Dividend tax credit	£610	× 10%		(61)
Tax on bank interest	£7,430	× 20%		(1,486)
Income tax repayable				(1,212)

The dividend tax credit is used first to reduce the liability.

3.3 Gift Aid

The Gift Aid Scheme gives tax relief for cash donations to charities.

In order to qualify for Gift Aid, the donation must satisfy the following conditions:

- The gift must be a payment of money (not assets)

- The gift must be an outright gift and not subject to repayment

- Neither the donor nor any of his close relatives must receive a benefit in consequence of making the gift (apart from small benefits)

- The donor must give the charity a Gift Aid declaration (in writing, by telephone or via the internet).

Basic rate tax relief is given by deeming the Gift Aid donation to be made net of basic rate tax. The charity will be able to recover this tax from HMRC. For example, if a taxpayer makes a Gift Aid donation of £160, the gross donation will be £160 × 100/80 = £200.

The charity will receive the actual tax credit of £200 × 20% = £40. There is no further tax consequence for the taxpayer if he pays tax at the basic rate. Gift Aid donations can therefore be ignored in computing the tax liability of a basic rate taxpayer.

If the taxpayer is liable to income tax at the higher rate or additional rate, further tax relief is given to the individual. This is done by extending the basic rate band and the higher rate band by the amount of the grossed up Gift Aid donation. For a higher rate tax payer, this will give a maximum additional (40% – 20%) 20% relief by reducing the amount of income taxable at the higher rate. For an additional rate taxpayer, this will give a maximum additional (50% – 20%) 30% relief by reducing the amount of income taxable at the additional rate.

Worked example: Gift Aid

In 2012/13, Roz has taxable income (all non-savings income) of £40,395 and makes a cash donation of £1,000 to charity under the Gift Aid Scheme.

Requirement

What is Roz's income tax liability for 2012/13?

Solution

Roz

Taxable income (all non-savings)	£40,395

Tax

	£
£34,370 × 20%	6,874
£1,250 (£1,000 × 100/80) × 20% (extended band)	250
£4,775 × 40%	1,910
£40,395	
Income tax liability	9,034

A taxpayer who makes a Gift Aid donation in 2012/13 can elect to treat the payment as if it had been made in 2011/12. This might be beneficial if the taxpayer was liable to higher rate tax in the previous year but not in the current year. The election must be made to HMRC no later than the date when the taxpayer files his tax return for the year for which the relief is claimed. If the taxpayer elects to treat the payment as if it had been made in 2011/12 then the election must be made by no later than 31 January 2013. This election does not affect the position of the charity.

4 Allowances for taxpayers aged 65 and over

Section overview

- Taxpayers aged 65 or over are entitled to a personal age allowance (PAA).

- PAA is reduced once a taxpayer's net income reaches a certain level, but cannot be less than the basic PA unless net income exceeds £100,000.

- Married couples allowance (MCA) is available to married couples and civil partners where either one of the parties is aged 78 or over at 5 April 2013 (ie at least one spouse or civil partner must have been born before 6 April 1935).

- MCA is a tax reducer at the rate of 10%.

4.1 Personal age allowance (PAA)

There is a higher personal allowance available to older taxpayers, instead of the basic personal allowance.

The amount of the allowance is dependent on both the taxpayer's age at the end of the tax year and on the level of his net income.

A taxpayer who is aged between 65 years and 74 years at 5 April 2013 (or would have been that age, but did not live to the end of the tax year) is entitled to a personal age allowance of £10,500.

A taxpayer who is aged 75 or over at 5 April 2013 (or would have been that age, but did not live to the end of the tax year) is entitled to a personal age allowance of £10,660.

Where the taxpayer's net income exceeds £25,400 in 2012/13, the personal age allowance is reduced by £1 for every £2 that the net income exceeds £25,400 until the amount of the basic personal allowance is reached. The PAA cannot fall below £8,105 unless adjusted net income exceeds £100,000, in which case it can be reduced to £nil – see above.

You should assume a taxpayer is under 65 years of age unless told otherwise.

Worked example: Personal age allowance

Robert was born on 23 August 1937. His net income for 2012/13 is £26,060.

Requirement

What is Robert's personal age allowance?

Solution

Robert is aged 75 by 5 April 2013.

	£
Personal age allowance	10,660
Less (£26,060 – £25,400) = £660 × ½	(330)
Reduced personal age allowance	10,330

Interactive question 4: Personal age allowance   [Difficulty level: Exam standard]

Pratish was born on 30 September 1947. His net income for 2012/13 is £25,760.

Using the standard format below, compute Pratish's personal age allowance.

Pratish is aged .... by 5 April 2013.

	£
Personal age allowance	
Less (£.................... – ....) = £.................... × ½	( )
Reduced personal age allowance	══

See **Answer** at the end of this chapter.

4.2   Married couple's allowance (MCA)

There is an additional allowance available for older married couples and registered civil partners. The married couple's allowance (MCA) is not deducted from net income to arrive at taxable income like the personal allowance. Instead the MCA reduces an individual's income tax liability and is called a **tax reducer**. The MCA tax reducer is calculated at a fixed rate of 10% of the relevant MCA amount.

For civil partners and couples who married on or after 5 December 2005, the MCA is claimed by the spouse or civil partner who has the higher net income. The amount of the MCA depends on the net income of that spouse or civil partner. The exam will not test marriages before 5 December 2005.

The taxpayer is entitled to make a claim for the MCA if either spouse or civil partner was born before 6 April 1935 (in other words aged 78 by 5 April 2013).

The amount of the MCA is £7,705.

Worked example: Married couple's allowance

Angus was married to Edna in January 2006. On 5 April 2013, Angus is aged 78 and Edna is aged 72. Angus has net income of £15,590 in 2012/13 (all non-savings income). Edna has no taxable income.

Requirement

What is Angus' income tax liability for 2012/13?

Solution

Angus

Income tax liability

	Non-savings income
	£
Net income	15,590
Less PAA	(10,660)
Taxable income	4,930
Tax	£
£4,930 × 20%	986
Less: MCA tax reducer	
£7,705 × 10%	(771)
Income tax liability	215

In the year of marriage/civil partnership, the MCA is reduced by 1/12 for each complete tax month (running from the 6th of one month to the 5th of the following month) which has passed before the marriage/registration of the civil partnership.

Worked example: Year of marriage/civil partnership

Lucinda was born on 22 August 1937. Her net income for 2012/13 is £18,100. She entered into a civil partnership with Helen, who was born on 19 July 1933, on 10 December 2012. Helen has net income for 2012/13 of £12,380.

Requirement

What is the married couple's allowance for Lucinda in 2012/13?

Solution

Lucinda is aged 75 on 5 April 2013. Helen is aged 79 on 5 April 2013. The MCA is available because Helen was born before 6 April 1935. However, Lucinda is the taxpayer entitled to claim the MCA since she has the higher net income in 2012/13.

There are eight complete tax months between 6 April 2012 and 5 December 2012.

The MCA is therefore £7,705 × 4/12   £2,568

Note: The MCA tax reducer is £2,568 × 10% = £257.

Summary and Self-test

Summary

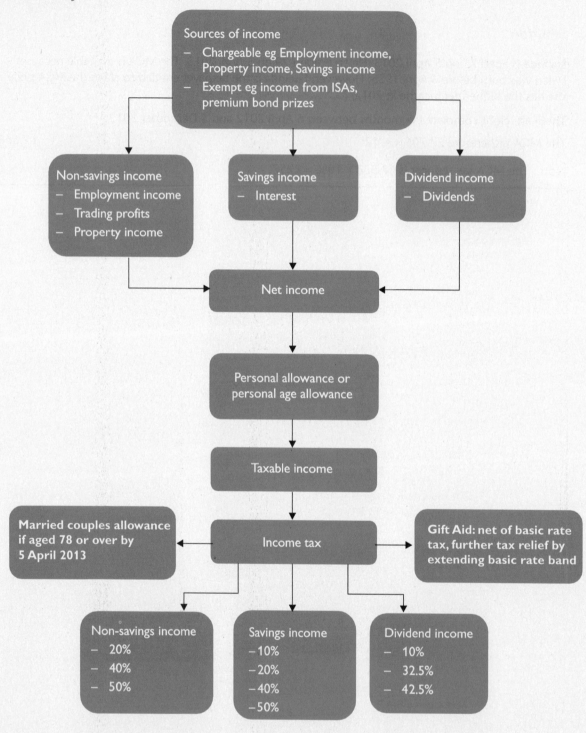

Self-test

Answer the following questions.

1 Which of the following are chargeable to income tax?

    A   Interest from a NS&I investment account
    B   Income received from an Individual Savings Account
    C   £10 Lottery winnings
    D   Scholarship awarded by a university

2 Which **two** of the following sources of income are non-savings income?

    A   Interest from a building society
    B   Property income
    C   Dividend from a UK company
    D   Trading profits

3 At what rates is tax charged on savings income?

    A   10%, 32.5%, 42.5%
    B   10%, 20%, 40%, 50%
    C   10%, 20%, 32.5%
    D   20%, 32.5%, 40%, 50%

4 How is higher rate tax relief given for a Gift Aid donation?

    A   Deducted from net income
    B   Treated as paid net of higher rate tax
    C   Basic rate band extended by grossed up donation
    D   No higher rate tax relief given

5 A taxpayer aged 67 has net income of £26,300 in 2012/13. What personal age allowance is he entitled to?

    A   £10,500
    B   £10,050
    C   £9,600
    D   £8,105

6 A taxpayer aged 45 has employment income of £176,000 in 2012/13. This is her only source of income in this tax year. What is the income tax liability for 2012/13?

    A   £60,284
    B   £63,526
    C   £62,074
    D   £66,126

Now go back to the Learning outcomes in the Introduction. If you are satisfied you have achieved these objectives, please tick them off.

Legislation

Income Tax (Earnings and Pensions) Act 2003 *(ITEPA 2003)*
Income Tax (Trading and Other Income) Act 2005 *(ITTOIA 2005)*
Income Tax Act 2007 *(ITA 2007)*

Employment income – definitions	ITEPA 2003 ss. 3 – 13
Trading income – definitions	ITTOIA 2005 ss. 3 – 8
Property income – definitions	ITTOIA 2005 ss. 263 – 265
Savings income – definitions	ITTOIA ss. 365 – 368
Miscellaneous income – definitions	ITTOIA ss. 574 – 577
Types of income and rates of tax	ITA 2007 ss. 3 –10, 12, 13, 16 – 20
Gift Aid	ITA 2007 ss.414 – 415,426
Personal allowances	ITA 2007 ss. 35 – 37
Married couples allowance	ITA 2007 s.46

This technical reference section is designed to assist you when you are working in the office. It should help you to know where to look for further information on the topics covered in this chapter. **You will not be examined on the contents of this section in your examination.**

Answer to Interactive question 1

(a) Bank interest received from HSBC of £600

Savings income, taxable amount £600 × 100/80 = £750

(b) Property income of £1,000

Non-savings income, taxable amount £1,000

(c) Dividend received from UK company of £495

Dividend income, taxable amount £495 × 100/90 = £550

(d) Interest received on Treasury Stock of £525

Savings income, taxable amount £525

(e) Trading profits of £5,000

Non-savings income, taxable amount £5,000

(f) Interest received on NS&I investment account of £600

Savings income, taxable amount £600

Answer to Interactive question 2

Max

Taxable income

	Non-savings income £	Savings income £	Dividend income £	Total £
Employment income	20,000			
Bank interest				
£280 × 100/80		350		
Dividends				
£990 × 100/90			1,100	
Net income	20,000	350	1,100	21,450
Less personal allowance	(8,105)			(8,105)
Taxable income	11,895	350	1,100	13,345

Interest arising on an Individual Savings Account is exempt income and, therefore, not included in the above computation.

Answer to Interactive question 3

Henry

Income tax liability

	Non-savings income £
Net income	45,465
Less personal allowance	(8,105)
Taxable income	37,360

Tax

	Non-savings income £
£34,370 × 20%	6,874
£2,990 × 40%	1,196
£37,360	
Income tax liability	8,070

Answer to Interactive question 4

Pratish

Pratish is aged 65 by 5 April 2013.

	£
Personal age allowance	10,500
Less (£25,760 – £25,400) = £360 × ½	(180)
Reduced personal age allowance	10,320

1   A – interest from a NS&I investment account – chargeable. All the rest are exempt from income tax.

2   B and D – property income and trading profits are non-savings income.

Interest from a building society is savings income.

Dividend from a UK company is dividend income.

3   B – the rates at which tax is charged on savings income are 10% (starting rate band), 20% (basic rate band), 40% (higher rate band) and 50% (additional rate band).

4   C – higher rate tax relief is given by extending the basic rate band by the grossed up donation.

5   B – £10,050

	£
Personal age allowance	10,500
Less (£26,300 – £25,400) = £900 × 1/2	(450)
Reduced personal age allowance	10,050

6   D – £66,126

	Non-savings income £
Employment income/Net income	176,000
Less personal allowance	–
Taxable income	176,000
Tax	
£34,370 × 20%	6,874
£115,630 × 40%	46,252
£150,000	
£26,000 × 50%	13,000
£176,000	
Income tax liability	66,126

CHAPTER 3

Employment income

Introduction

Examination context

Topic List

    1   Calculation of assessable employment income

    2   Taxable and exempt benefits

    3   Pay As You Earn (PAYE) system

Summary and Self-test

Technical reference

Answers to Interactive questions

Answers to Self-test

Learning outcomes

- Calculate assessable employment income for an employee or director, including taxable and exempt benefits ☐

- Identify the key features of the PAYE system and calculate PAYE tax codes for employees ☐

- Determine, in straightforward cases, due dates for employers' PAYE and national insurance payments ☐

Specific syllabus references for this chapter are: 2b, d, 3c.

Syllabus links

You will meet taxation of employees again in the Application paper, so you need to be very familiar with the topics in parts 1 and 2 of this chapter to prepare you for the progression to the next level of your studies.

However, it is unlikely that the PAYE system (described in part 3 of this chapter) would be examined in the Application paper. You should therefore expect it to be tested in detail in the Principles of Taxation paper.

Examination context

In the examination candidates may be required to:

- Determine how benefits are taxable on P11D employees
- Determine how benefits are taxable on P9D employees
- Identify which benefits are exempt
- Calculate an employee's coding
- Understand the operation of the PAYE system.

For extra question practice on these topics go to the section of the Question Bank covering this chapter.

Candidates need to take great care when calculating the value of a benefit, as often one important piece of information is missed when working this out.

1 Calculation of assessable employment income

Section overview

- Employment income is income received by an employee or director.

- General earnings consist of money and non-monetary benefits received as a result of the employment.

1.1 What is employment income?

Employment income includes income arising from an employment and the income of an office holder such as a director. We will use the term 'employee' to cover anyone who receives employment income.

There are two types of employment income:

- General earnings
- Specific employment income (not in your syllabus)

Definition

General earnings: Any salary, wages or fee, any gratuity or other profit or incidental benefit of any kind obtained by an employee consisting of money or money's worth, and anything else constituting an emolument of the employment, together with anything treated under any statutory provision as earnings (eg benefits).

General earnings therefore include bonuses, commissions, reimbursed expenses, expense allowances, inducements, tips and gratuities (even if received unsolicited from third parties).

1.2 Basis of assessment

The basis of assessment of general earnings is the **receipts basis**. This means that the actual amounts received between 6 April 2012 and 5 April 2013 are taxable in 2012/13.

General earnings consisting of money are treated as received on the earlier of:

- The time when payment is made
- The time when a person becomes entitled to payment

Worked example: Receipt of general earnings

Thomas is employed as a car salesman at a monthly salary of £2,100. In addition to his basic salary, he receives a bonus which is paid in May each year and relates to the sales made by Thomas in the year to the previous 31 October.

His recent bonuses are as follows:

y/e 31 October 2011	Paid 1 May 2012	£2,250
y/e 31 October 2012	Paid 1 May 2013	£4,850

Requirement

What are the taxable earnings of Thomas for 2012/13?

Solution

	£
Salary (£2,100 × 12)	25,200
Bonus (received May 2012)	2,250
Taxable earnings 2012/13	27,450

General earnings not in the form of money (ie benefits) are taxable when they are received by the employee.

2 Taxable and exempt benefits

Section overview

- The benefits code deals with taxable benefits and applies in full to most employees.
- Certain parts of the benefits code do not apply to employees in 'excluded employment'.
- All employees are taxable on the receipt of vouchers and the provision of living accommodation.
- Employees not in excluded employment are also taxable on other benefits such as cars, fuel, vans and use of assets.
- There are a number of benefits which are exempt from the charge to income tax.

2.1 The benefits code

Taxable benefits are set down in legislation called the benefits code.

The benefits code generally applies to all employees. However, only certain parts of it apply to employees in 'excluded employment'.

Definition

Excluded employment:

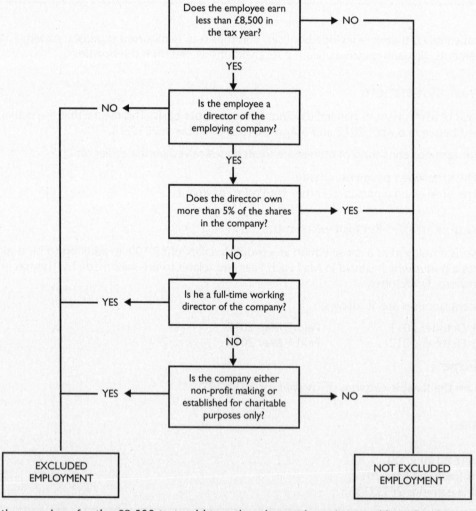

In calculating earnings for the £8,500 test, add together the total earnings and benefits that would be assessable if the employee were paid over £8,500. Do not deduct any expenses. (Allowable expenses are covered in the Application paper.)

2.2 Employees in excluded employment

Employees in excluded employment are only taxable on benefits as follows:

- Benefits convertible into cash on the amount of cash that the benefit could be converted into: this is sometimes called the **second hand value**

- Vouchers

- Living accommodation (but not any associated expenses)

Employees in excluded employment are sometimes called 'P9D' employees. This is because their employers are required to submit form P9D to HMRC under the PAYE system giving details of their taxable benefits.

2.3 Employees not in excluded employment

Most employees are not in excluded employment. Such employees are sometimes called 'P11D' employees. This is because their employers are required to submit a form P11D to HMRC under the PAYE system giving details of their taxable benefits.

Employees not in excluded employment are subject to all the benefits in the benefits code including:

- Vouchers
- Living accommodation
- Expenses connected with the provision of living accommodation
- Cars and fuel provided for private use
- Vans provided for private use
- Assets made available for private use
- Any other non-monetary benefit provided by reason of the employment

2.4 Vouchers

All employees, including those in excluded employments, are taxable on the provision of:

- Cash vouchers (vouchers exchangeable for cash) – the taxable amount is the sum of money for which the voucher is capable of being exchanged

- Credit tokens (eg a credit card) used to obtain money, goods or services – the taxable amount is the cost to the employer of providing the benefit, less any amount paid by the employee

- Vouchers exchangeable for goods and services (eg book tokens) taxable amount is the cost to the employer of providing the benefit, less any amount paid by the employee

There is an exemption for the first 15p per day of meal vouchers.

2.5 Living accommodation

All employees, including those in excluded employment, are taxable on the provision of living accommodation unless it is 'job related accommodation'.

Definition

Job related accommodation: Accommodation is job related if:

(a) the accommodation is necessary for the proper performance of the employee's duties (eg caretaker); or

(b) the accommodation is provided for the better performance of the employee's duties and the employment is of a kind in which it is customary for accommodation to be provided (eg police officers); or

(c) the accommodation is provided as part of arrangements in force because of a special threat to the employee's security (eg members of the government).

A director can only claim one of the first two exemptions if he owns 5% or less of the shares in the employer company and either he is a full-time working director or the company is non-profit making or is a charity.

There are two potential benefits on the provision of living accommodation:

Basic rental benefit

If the living accommodation is owned by the employer, the amount of the benefit is the rent that would have been paid if it had been let at its annual value (taken to be the rateable value).

The annual value will be given to you in the question.

If the living accommodation is rented by the employer, the amount of the benefit is the higher of the annual value and the rent actually paid by the employer.

If the employee makes a payment to the employer for his occupation of the property, this reduces the taxable benefit.

Additional yearly rent

This only applies to **expensive accommodation**. Expensive accommodation is accommodation which cost the employer more than £75,000 to provide. The amount of the additional yearly rent is calculated as:

(Cost of providing the living accommodation less £75,000) × the official rate of interest at the start of the tax year

The cost of providing the accommodation is the total of the original cost of the living accommodation plus any capital improvements made before the start of the tax year in which the benefit is charged.

Again, if the employee makes a payment to the employer for his occupation of the property, any excess not set against the basic rental benefit will be used to reduce the additional yearly rent benefit.

Worked example: Living accommodation

Kyle's employer provides him on 1 February 2012 with living accommodation consisting of a house owned by the employer. The annual value of the house is £7,500. The house originally cost the employer £150,000 and a conservatory was added at a cost of £15,000 in March 2012.

Kyle pays rent of £700 a month to his employer for use of the accommodation and occupies the house throughout 2012/13. The official rate of interest on 6 April 2012 is 4%.

Requirement

What are Kyle's taxable benefits in respect of the living accommodation in 2012/13?

Solution

Basic rental benefit

	£
Annual value	7,500
Less: rent paid by Kyle	(7,500)
Taxable benefit	NIL

Additional yearly rental benefit

	£
Cost of provision (£150,000 + £15,000)	165,000
Less: lower limit	(75,000)
	90,000
£90,000 × 4%	3,600
Less: rental paid by Kyle (£700 × 12) = £8,400 – £7,500	(900)
Taxable benefit	2,700

If the accommodation is only available for part of the tax year, the benefit is time apportioned (for exam purposes, on a monthly basis).

If the property was acquired by the employer more than six years before it is first provided to the employee, use the market value of the property when it was first provided plus the cost of subsequent improvements to calculate the additional yearly rent charge, instead of the original cost plus improvements. However, unless the original cost plus improvements exceeds £75,000, the additional yearly rent charge cannot be imposed, however high the market value.

 Interactive question 1: Living accommodation [Difficulty level: Exam standard]

Susan is provided with living accommodation by her employer on 6 October 2012. The annual value of the accommodation is £2,500.

The original cost of the accommodation to the employer in 2000 was £80,000. The market value of the accommodation on 6 October 2012 is £190,000. The official rate of interest on 6 April 2012 is 4%.

Susan does not make any payment to her employer for the use of the accommodation.

Requirement

Using the standard format below, show the taxable benefit for Susan in respect of the provision of living accommodation for 2012/13.

Basic rental benefit

£

Additional yearly rental benefit

£

Cost of provision
Less: lower limit

(   )

Apply official rate of interest

....

Time-apportionment

....

Taxable benefit is £

....

See **Answer** at the end of this chapter.

2.6 Expenses connected with the provision of living accommodation

In addition to the living accommodation benefits described above, P11D employees are also taxed on related expenses paid by the employer such as:

- Heat and lighting – taxable benefit is the cost to employer less any employee contribution

- Cleaning, repairs, maintenance and decoration – the taxable benefit is the cost to employer less any employee contribution

Where an employee is provided with furnished living accommodation, the employee will also have a taxable benefit for the private use of the furniture provided by his employer (see later in this chapter).

2.7 Cars and fuel for private use

There is a taxable benefit for P11D employees on the provision of a car which is available for private use by the employee. Private use includes home-to-work travel.

There is no taxable benefit for incidental private use of a 'pool' car which is available for use by any employee and which is not normally kept overnight at or near an employee's residence.

The basis of the charge is the list price of the car plus any optional accessories originally provided with the car and any further accessories costing £100 or more which are provided at a later date.

Having worked out the list price of the car, the benefit is then calculated by applying a percentage to that price. The percentage depends on the carbon dioxide (CO_2) emissions of the car expressed in grams per kilometre (g/km). The CO_2 emissions figure will be given to you in the question.

The emissions thresholds are as follows:

- For cars with zero emissions there is no taxable benefit.
- For cars classed as 'ultra- low emission cars', the percentage is 5% for cars with emissions between one g/km and 75g/km.
- For cars with CO_2 emissions above 75g/km but less than 100g/km, the percentage is 10%.
- For cars with CO_2 emissions of 100g/km, the relevant threshold for the year, the percentage is 11%
- For every 5kg/km over the 100g/km threshold (rounded down to the nearest 5g/km), an additional 1% is added, up to a maximum of 35%.

If the employee makes a contribution to the employer for the private use of the car, this contribution reduces the taxable benefit.

Where the car uses diesel instead of petrol, the percentage is increased by 3%, subject to the overall maximum of 35%.

If a car is not available for private use for the whole of a tax year, the benefit is time apportioned (for exam purposes on a monthly basis).

Worked example: Car benefit

Darren is employed on a salary of £25,000 per annum. He is provided with a car available for private use during the whole of 2012/13. The car has a petrol engine and CO_2 emissions of 141g/km. The car has a list price of £13,395, but the employer only paid £10,395 for it after discounts.

Darren contributes £50 per month for its private use.

Requirement

What is Darren's taxable benefit in respect of the car?

Solution

CO_2 emissions are 141g/km, round down to 140g/km

Appropriate percentage:

(140 – 100) = 40g/km in excess of threshold

40 ÷ 5 = 8%

11% + 8% = 19%

	£
List price £13,395 × 19%	2,545
Less: contribution for use £50 × 12	(600)
Taxable benefit	1,945

The price actually paid by the employer of £10,395 is irrelevant.

Interactive question 2: Car benefit   [Difficulty level: Exam standard]

Pedro is employed on a salary of £40,000 per annum. He is provided with a car for private use from 6 January 2013. The car had a list price of £17,820 and CO_2 emissions of 176g/km. It runs on diesel. Pedro makes no contributions towards the running costs of the car.

Requirement

Using the standard format below, calculate Pedro's taxable benefit in respect of the car.

CO$_2$ emissions are .... g/km, round down to .... g/km

Appropriate percentage:
(............. – 100) = ... g/km in excess of threshold

.... ÷ 5 = ... %

11% +....... % +....... % (diesel) = ... %

List price is £
£ .... × .... % = £ ....

Time-apportionment

....

Taxable benefit

....

See **Answer** at the end of this chapter.

The car benefit charge is designed to cover the cost of running the car such as repairs, vehicle excise duty and insurance.

However, there is a separate charge for the provision by the employer of fuel for private use for a car provided by the employer with private use.

The benefit uses the same percentage calculated for the car benefit. This is then applied to a fixed amount which is £20,200 in 2012/13.

There is no reduction in the benefit if the employee makes a partial contribution to the cost of private fuel. There is a taxable benefit unless the employee reimburses the employer with the full cost of private fuel. If the car for which the fuel is provided is not available for part of the tax year, the fuel benefit is time apportioned on the same basis as the car benefit.

Worked example: Fuel benefit

Dilip is a P11D employee who is provided by his employer with a car for private use. The CO$_2$ emissions of the car are 212g/km and the car uses diesel. Dilip is required to pay a nominal amount of £30 per month towards the cost of private fuel.

Requirement

What is Dilip's fuel benefit?

Solution

CO$_2$ emissions are 212g/km, round down to 210g/km
Appropriate percentage:
(210 – 100) = 110g/km in excess of threshold
110 ÷ 5 = 22%
11% + 22% + 3% (diesel) = 35% (maximum)
£20,200 × 35% =   <u>£7,070</u>
No reduction for partial contribution for private fuel.

2.8 Vans for private use

P11D employees have a taxable benefit on the provision of a van available for private use. In this case, private use does not include travel from home to work, as long as the employee is not allowed any other private use that is more than insignificant.

The benefit is an annual amount of £3,000. The benefit is time-apportioned if the van is not available for the whole of the tax year. The benefit is reduced by any amount paid by the employee for the private use of the van.

There is a separate charge for the provision by the employer of fuel for private use of the van. The benefit is an annual amount of £550. If the van for which the fuel is provided is not available for part of the tax year, the fuel benefit is time-apportioned on the same basis as the van benefit.

There is no reduction in the van fuel benefit if the employee makes a partial contribution to the cost of private fuel.

There is no taxable benefit on the provision of a van for private use where the van has zero CO_2 emissions.

2.9 Assets available for private use

2.9.1 General rule

A taxable benefit arises to a P11D employee who is provided by the employer with an asset available for private use, including use by the taxpayer's family.

The amount of the taxable benefit is the higher of the annual value of the asset or any rent or hire charge payable by the employer. In both cases any expenses relating to the provision of the asset are also added to the taxable benefit.

The annual value is 20% of the market value of the asset when first provided for private use to any employee.

If the asset is only provided for part of the year, the benefit is time-apportioned (on a monthly basis for exam purposes).

The taxable benefit is reduced by any contribution made by the employee for private use.

2.9.2 Computers

There is no taxable benefit on the provision of a computer to an employee where the private use of it by the employee is not significant.

Where the private use of the computer is significant the benefit is calculated as under the general rule above, but then reduced by the percentage of business use. HMRC guidance suggests 40% private use would be deemed significant.

Worked example: Private use assets

Maria is provided with the following assets by her employer which are available for private use:

Television (provided on 6 October 2012) costing	£1,100
Computer (provided on 6 April 2012) costing	£2,700

Maria makes a contribution of £10 a month for private use of the television.

Requirement

(a) What are the benefits taxable on Maria for 2012/13 for private use of these assets, assuming private use of the computer is insignificant?

(b) What is the taxable benefit of the computer on Maria for 2012/13 if private use of the computer is agreed to be 45%?

Solution

(a)

Television
Annual value
20% × £1,100   £220

Available for six months in tax year

	£
£220 × 6/12	110
Less: employee contribution £10 × 6	(60)
Taxable benefit	50

Computer
Insignificant private use therefore no taxable benefit   £nil

(b)

Computer	£
Annual value	
20% × £2,700	540
Business use (55%)	(297)
Taxable benefit	243

2.10 Other benefits

If a P11D employee (or member of the employee's family or household) receives any other non-monetary benefit by reason of employment and there is no specific provision covering this type of benefit in the benefits code, the taxable benefit is the cost to the employer of providing the benefit less any amount paid by the employee for the benefit. Where benefits are provided in-house, the cost of the benefit is the marginal cost.

Worked example: Marginal cost

Leonard is a teacher at a public school. He pays a reduced fee of £2,000 in 2012/13 for his son to attend the school.

In 2012/13 the following figures relate to students attending the school.

	£
Normal fee payable per student	3,500
Average cost per student, including a proportion of fixed overheads	2,800
Additional cost of an extra student, including extra writing books, food etc	1,500

Leonard's son is taking up a place that would otherwise not be filled.

Requirement

What is the taxable benefit for Leonard for 2012/13 in respect of the school place?

Solution

First determine which fee cost is relevant.

The marginal cost of providing the place is the equivalent to the additional cost, ie £1,500.

Then deduct the contribution paid by Leonard ie £2,000

This cannot give rise to a negative benefit, so the benefit is nil.

2.11 Exempt benefits

There are a number of benefits which are specifically exempt from the charge on employment income. Exempt benefits include:

- Contributions by an employer to a registered pension scheme

- Pension advice available to all employees up to £150 per tax year

- Childcare facilities run by or on behalf of an employer

- Childcare payments of up to £55 per week under a contract entered into before 6 April 2011 between the employer and an approved child carer or by childcare vouchers, provided that childcare payments are available to all employees, with some exclusions for those earning close to the national minimum wage.

  For those joining an approved childcare scheme from 6 April 2011 the amount that is exempt per week depends on the employee's basic earnings assessment.

  The basic earnings assessment is the individual's expected earnings for the current tax year. It is calculated by adding together the employee's basic earnings and taxable benefits and then deducting excluded income which includes occupational pension contributions, allowable expense payments and the personal allowance.

  The exemption is as follows:

  - Basic rate taxpayer – £55 per week

  - Higher rate taxpayer – £28 per week

  - Additional rate taxpayer – £22 per week.

  For anyone already in a scheme at 6 April 2011 the £55 per week exemption continues to apply irrespective of their level of earnings.

- One mobile telephone available for private use by an employee

- Free or subsidised meals in a canteen where such meals are available to all staff

- Meal vouchers up to 15p per day

- Social events paid for by the employer up to £150 per head per tax year

- Entertainment provided by a third party (eg seats at sporting/cultural events)

- Non-cash gifts from third parties up to £250 per tax year from the same donor

- Provision of a parking space at or near the employee's place of work

- Awards of up to £5,000 made under a staff suggestion scheme

- Work-related training courses

- Sports and recreation facilities available to employees generally but not to the general public

- Payments towards the additional costs of an employee working from home (up to £4 per week without supporting evidence, payments in excess of £4 per week require documentary evidence that the payment is wholly in respect of such additional costs)

- Personal incidental expenses (eg cost of telephone calls home) whilst the employee is required to stay away overnight on business up to £5 per night in the UK, £10 per night abroad. If reimbursement by the employer exceeds these daily limits the total amount reimbursed is taxable.

- Works buses and subsidies to public bus services

- Travel expenses when public transport disrupted, late night journeys and where car sharing arrangements break down

- Use of bicycles or cyclists safety equipment if made available to all employees

- Reasonable removal expenses (maximum £8,000) paid for by an employer for a new employment position or on relocation

- Non-cash long service awards in respect of at least 20 years service, not exceeding £50 per year of service

- Eye tests and glasses provided for employees who use VDU equipment

- Health-screening assessment or medical check up provided for an employee, by the employer (maximum of one of each per tax year).

3 Pay As You Earn (PAYE) system

Section overview

- The PAYE system ensures that tax and NICs are paid on employment income.
- Amounts deducted under PAYE must usually be paid to HMRC by the 19th of each calendar month.
- HMRC can require security payments from employers who are at risk of deliberately not paying PAYE.
- The amount of tax deducted under PAYE depends on the employee's tax code.
- HMRC are introducing the Real Time Information (RTI) reporting system.

3.1 What is the PAYE system?

The aim of the PAYE system is to ensure that the correct amounts of income tax and national insurance contributions are paid on cash payments to employees. The system also ensures that taxable non-cash benefits are reported by the employer to HMRC.

The PAYE system applies to all cash payments made to employees (eg salaries, bonuses) and also to certain assets which can be readily converted into cash (eg gold bars, wine).

Income tax and national insurance contributions deducted under the PAYE system must usually be paid to HMRC 14 days after the end of the tax month to which they relate. The tax month runs from the 6th day of one month to the following 5th day of the next month. Therefore, payment is required by the 19th of each calendar month.

Large employers (more than 250 employees) must pay electronically. Any other employer can pay electronically by choice. If payment is made electronically the payment deadline is extended to the 22nd of each calendar month.

Payments can be made quarterly instead of monthly where the average monthly total of the PAYE income tax and national insurance contributions does not exceed £1,500.

3.2 Security for payment of PAYE

This section is new.

HMRC can require employers to provide a security where amounts due under PAYE or NIC obligations are seriously at risk.

HMRC will require a security from employers who try to defraud the government by deliberately choosing not to pay PAYE and NIC, building up large PAYE or NIC debts (including penalties), or who do not respond to HMRC's attempts to contact them.

HMRC calculates the amount of the security on a case by case basis, depending on the amount of tax at risk and the previous behaviour of the employer. The form of the security is usually either a cash deposit from the business or director, held solely by HMRC or in a joint account with the taxpayer, or a bond from an approved financial institution.

The employer can appeal against either the notice requiring the security or the amount.

It is a criminal offence if a person required to give a security fails to do so. If that person is found guilty of the offence a fine of up to £5,000 may be imposed.

3.3 PAYE codes

The calculation of the PAYE income tax deduction is based on 'tax codes'.

For each tax year, the employee receives a PAYE coding notice (Form P2) setting out the allowances and deductions available to the employee in that year and the resultant tax code. The employer is informed of the PAYE code (Form P6), but not the details of how it is calculated.

The tax code computation is as follows:

Allowances	£	Deductions	£
Personal allowance	X	Taxable benefits	X
Allowable expenses	X	Adjustment for underpaid tax	X
Adjustment for overpaid tax	X		
	X		X

If total allowances less total deductions gives a positive figure, the tax code is created by removing the last digit in the computation and adding a letter at the end. This is usually the letter L showing that the employee is entitled to the basic personal allowance. If the employee is entitled to a full age personal allowance the letter to add is P for those aged 65-74 and Y for those aged 75 or older.

Worked example: PAYE code

Katie earns £24,000 a year. She is entitled to a basic personal allowance. She also receives taxable benefits of £4,235.

Requirement

What is Katie's PAYE code for 2012/13?

Solution

	£
Allowance: Personal allowance	8,105
Less: Deduction (taxable benefits)	(4,235)
Net allowances	3,870

Katie's tax code is therefore 387L.

If total allowances less total deductions give a negative figure, the tax code will have a letter K at the beginning. The application of a K code will mean that the taxable pay of the employee will be increased rather than decreased. A K code is calculated in the same way as an L code except that the code is decreased by 1.

Worked example: K code

Zack earns £18,000 a year. He is entitled to a basic personal allowance. He also receives taxable benefits of £9,312.

Requirement

What is Zack's PAYE code for 2012/13?

Solution

	£
Allowances: Personal allowance	8,105
Less: Deduction (taxable benefits)	(9,312)
Net allowances	(1,207)

Deduct the last digit (gives 120) and deduct 1.

Zack's tax code is therefore K119.

The tax deducted using a K code cannot exceed 50% of the amount of actual remuneration on that pay day, so as not to cause hardship to the employee.

The code number can also reflect unpaid tax on income from earlier years. In this case, gross up the unpaid tax using the taxpayer's estimated marginal rate of income tax and deduct the grossed up unpaid tax from total allowances.

Worked example: Unpaid tax

Brandon earns £10,000 a year and has no other sources of income. He is entitled to a basic personal allowance. He has unpaid tax of £300 from 2011/12 which is to be paid through the PAYE system.

Requirement

What is Brandon's PAYE code for 2012/13?

Solution

Brandon is a basic rate taxpayer

	£
Allowances: Personal allowance	8,105
Less: Deduction (unpaid tax) £300 × 100/20	(1,500)
Net allowances	6,605

Brandon's tax code is therefore 660L.

3.4 Operation of PAYE system

Most payroll systems now operate electronically. Software packages calculate income tax and NICs due at each pay day, given an employee's income and PAYE code.

Tax tables are issued to employers with manual payroll systems, which enable them to calculate income tax due on each payment date.

The key tables used are:

- Table A – Pay Adjustment Tables

    Spread an employee's allowances evenly over the tax year. The tables show the tax-free pay for every tax code, for each payment period, on a weekly or monthly basis.

- Table B – Taxable Pay Tables

    These show an employee's income tax liability to date, after taking into account tax-free pay, for each payment period.

Similar tables exist to help calculations of NICs due.

3.5 Real Time Information

This section is new.

Real Time Information (RTI) reporting is aimed at improving the PAYE system, making it easier for employers and HMRC to operate. Under RTI, employers will be required to inform HMRC about tax, NICs and other deductions every time a payment is made to an employee, rather than after the end of each tax year.

This information will be sent online, integrated with employer payroll software, and will enable HMRC to ensure the employee pays the correct amount of tax and NIC during the year.

RTI will remove the need for employers to send end of year PAYE forms (P14 and P35) and leaver and joiner forms (P45 and P46) to HMRC.

The scheme will be piloted with volunteer employers for a year from April 2012. Most employers will join the scheme in April 2013, with all employers required to join by October 2013.

Summary

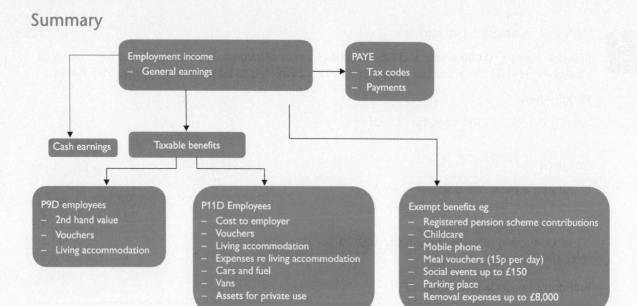

Self-test

Answer the following questions.

1   Sandra works for Julian (a sole trader) as a part-time salesperson at a salary of £6,000 a year. On 31 December 2012, she received a bonus of £2,000 in respect of Julian's trading results for the year ended 30 September 2012. She expects to receive a bonus of £2,500 in December 2013 in respect of the year ended 30 September 2013.

What are Sandra's assessable earnings for 2012/13?

A   £6,000
B   £7,250
C   £8,000
D   £8,250

2   Peter and Jane both work for Apple Ltd (a trading company).

Peter is a director of Apple Ltd. He has no shares in Apple Ltd and works one day a week for a salary of £8,400.

Jane is an employee and earns £8,600 working two days a week for Apple Ltd.

Which of them is in an 'excluded employment'?

A   Both of them
B   Neither of them
C   Peter
D   Jane

3   Oliver is employed by Munton plc and earns £20,000 a year. He also receives the following benefits during 2012/13:

Meal vouchers of £2 per day (240 working days in year)

Pension advice costing £100

Ticket to sporting event from a customer of Munton plc worth £50

What are Oliver's taxable benefits for 2012/13?

A   £0
B   £444
C   £544
D   £594

4   Gerald is employed by Zoom plc at a salary of £30,000 a year. He is provided with a car available for private use from 1 November 2012. The car has CO_2 emissions of 142g/km and a list price of £18,000. The car has a diesel engine.

What is the taxable car benefit?

A   £3,960
B   £3,420
C   £1,650
D   £1,425

5   Tricia (aged 30) is employed by Wilton Ltd at a salary of £10,000 per year. She is also entitled to taxable benefits of £1,800. She has no tax overpaid or underpaid from previous tax years.

What is Tricia's tax code for 2012/13?

A   810L
B   631L
C   630L
D   629L

6   David earns £60,000 a year. He is entitled to a basic personal allowance. He has unpaid tax of £920 from 2011/12 which is to be paid through the PAYE system.

David's tax code for 2012/13 is ....

Now go back to the Learning outcomes in the Introduction. If you are satisfied you have achieved these objectives, please tick them off.

Technical reference

Legislation

References relate to Income Tax (Earnings and Pensions) Act 2003 (*ITEPA 2003*) unless otherwise stated

Tax on employment income	ss.6-8
When general earnings are received	ss.18-19
The benefits code (general)	s.63
Excluded employment	ss.216-220
Vouchers	ss.73-96A
Living accommodation	ss.97-113
Expenses connected with provision of living accommodation	ss.313-315
Cars and fuel for private use	ss.114-153, 167
Vans for private use	ss.154-164
Assets available for private use/transfer	ss.204-210
Other benefits	ss.201-203
Exempt benefits	ss.227-326
PAYE codes	Income tax (Pay As You Earn) Regulations 2003 paras 13-17
PAYE payment of tax	Income tax (Pay As You Earn) Regulations 2003 paras 68-70

HMRC manuals

Employment Income Manual (Found at http://www.hmrc.gov.uk/manuals/eimanual/index.htm)

Employment income: introduction	EIM00510
Employment income: basis of assessment for general earnings	EIM42200
Employment income: general earnings: amounts treated as earnings	EIM00513

This gives an overview of the benefits code and provides links to further guidance on individual types of benefit.

Employment income: alphabetical list of particular items   EIM01005

This gives links to more unusual types of benefit from employment, including those which are not taxable.

PAYE Manual can be found at http://www.hmrc.gov.uk/manuals/pommanual/index.htm

> This technical reference section is designed to assist you when you are working in the office. It should help you to know where to look for further information on the topics covered in this chapter. **You will not be examined on the contents of this section in your examination.**

Answer to Interactive question 1

	£
Basic rental benefit	
Annual value	2,500
Additional yearly rental benefit	
Cost of provision (MV at provision)	190,000
Less: lower limit	(75,000)
	115,000
Apply official rate of interest	
£115,000 × 4%	4,600
Time-apportionment	
(£2,500 + £4,600) = £7,100 × 6/12	
Taxable benefit is	3,550

Answer to Interactive question 2

CO_2 emissions are 176g/km, round down to 175g/km

Appropriate percentage:

(175 – 100) = 75g/km in excess of threshold

75 ÷ 5 = 15%

11% + 15% + 3% (diesel) = 29%

List price is £17,820

£17,820 × 29% = £5,168

Time-apportionment

£5,168 × 3/12

Taxable benefit is £1,292

1   C – £8,000

Sandra's basic salary is £6,000. She is also taxed on the bonus of £2,000 received in the tax year 2012/13. Note that in terms of any benefits, Sandra is a P9D, or excluded, employee.

2   B – Neither of them

Peter earns less than £8,500, but he is a director who does not work full-time and the company is not non-profit making nor charitable. Therefore Peter is not in excluded employment.

Jane earns over £8,500 a year and so is not in excluded employment.

3   B – £444

Meal vouchers (£2 less 15p per day exempt) = £1.85 × 240 = £444

Pension advice up to £150 is exempt (assume available to all employees)

Entertainment provided by third party is exempt

4   C – £1,650

CO_2 emissions are 142g/km, round down to 140g/km

Appropriate percentage:

(140 – 100) = 40g/km in excess of threshold

40 ÷ 5 = 8%

11% + 8% + 3% (diesel) = 22%

List price is £18,000

£18,000 × 22% = £3,960

Available for 5 months in tax year

£3,960 × 5/12 = £1,650

5   C – 630L

	£
Allowance: Personal allowance	8,105
Less: Deduction (taxable benefits)	(1,800)
Net allowances	6,305

Tricia's tax code is therefore 630L.

6   580L

	£
Allowance: Personal allowance	8,105
Less: Deduction (unpaid tax) £920 × 100/40 – higher rate tax payer	(2,300)
Net allowances	5,805

David's tax code is therefore 580L.

CHAPTER 4

Trading profits

Introduction

Examination context

Topic List

    1   Badges of trade

    2   Adjustment to profits

    3   Allowable and disallowable expenditure

    4   Other adjustments

Summary and Self-test

Technical reference

Answer to Interactive question

Answers to Self-test

Learning outcomes

- Recognise the badges of trade

- Allocate given items of business expenditure as allowable or disallowable for tax purposes and calculate adjusted trading profits of a sole trader or partnership

Specific syllabus references for this chapter are: 3d, e.

Syllabus links

The material in this chapter forms the basis of the charge to tax on business profits.

You will be expected to know the main adjustments to profit in the Application paper later on in the Professional Stage and also as technical background at the Advanced Stage.

Examination context

In the examination candidates may be required to:

- Identify and use the badges of trade in a given scenario
- Determine whether expenditure incurred is allowable or disallowable in calculating trading profits
- Correctly deal with other adjustments required to calculate adjusted trading profits

For extra question practice on these topics go to the section of the Question Bank covering this chapter.

1 Badges of trade

Section overview

- Taxable trading profits arise from a trade.

- It is not always clear whether activities constitute a trade.

- The badges of trade are key factors which indicate whether a trade is being carried on.

- All the circumstances need to be taken into account to decide whether a taxpayer is carrying on a trade.

1.1 Is a trade being carried on?

Before considering the details of how to compute taxable trading profits, you need to ask whether a trade is being carried on. This is important in deciding how the profits or losses on a transaction are taxed. For example, the disposal of an asset might result in a trading profit or a capital gain; income received might be trading income or investment income.

A trade is defined in tax legislation as 'every trade, manufacture, adventure or concern in the nature of trade'. In practice, it is not always clear whether the activities of a taxpayer constitute a trading activity.

It has been left to the courts to interpret this definition and there are a number of decided cases identifying a number of key factors in deciding whether an activity constitutes a trade. These are known as the **badges of trade**. You will be expected to know the badges of trade and the facts of the cases described below. The case names are not examinable.

It is important to understand that no one factor is decisive. The badges of trade merely provide guidance to be used in conjunction with all the facts surrounding the transaction and with common sense.

1.2 Intention to make a profit

Trading requires a profit motive to exist when the asset is acquired. If it can be established that an asset was bought with the intention of reselling it at a profit, this would normally be regarded as an indicator that there is a trading activity.

An example was the purchase and resale of £20,000 of silver bullion as protection against the devaluation of sterling. The transaction was treated as a trading activity (*Wisdom v Chamberlain 1969*).

1.3 Number of similar transactions

A transaction which, by itself, might be regarded as of a capital nature, may be treated as a trading activity if a number of similar transactions are entered into.

An example was the purchase of a mill-owning company and the subsequent stripping of its assets (*Pickford v Quirke 1927*). Since this was the fourth such transaction, it was decided that a trade was being carried on.

1.4 Nature of the asset

The subject matter of the transaction may indicate whether a trade is being carried on.

There are three reasons for purchasing an asset:

- For personal use

- As an investment for its aesthetic value or to yield an income and/or a longer-term gain on the sale of the investment (examples include shares, land, works of art)

- For resale at a profit (which constitutes trading)

Examples of subject matter held to be for resale at a profit are 34,000,000 yards of aircraft linen (*Martin v Lowry 1927*) and 1,000,000 rolls of toilet paper (*Rutledge v Commissioners of Inland Revenue 1929*).

1.5 Connection with existing trade

The other activities of the taxpayer should be considered to see whether any similarities exist. For example, if an accountant sold a car it is unlikely that the accountant would be deemed to be trading. If however a car mechanic in business as a sole trader sold a car, there is a direct link between repairing and selling cars. HMRC may seek to tax the profit on the car sale as trading income.

1.6 Changes to the asset

If an asset is purchased and then subjected to a process before resale to enhance its marketability, the sale is more likely to be regarded as a trading activity.

An example was the purchase of a quantity of brandy which was blended and recasked before sale. The sale was treated as a trading activity (*Cape Brandy Syndicate 1921*).

Active marketing and advertising are also likely to lead to the conclusion that there is a trading activity.

1.7 Reasons for sale

The circumstances leading to the sale of the asset can be an important factor. A person who is forced to sell an asset due to financial problems is unlikely to be trading.

However, if a sale is made to clear a short-term loan taken out to finance the purchase or to improve the asset, this indicates a trading activity.

1.8 Source of finance

If money was borrowed short-term to buy or improve the asset, this indicates a trading activity, especially if the loan could only be repaid by selling the asset.

1.9 Interval of time between purchase and sale

If an asset is bought and then resold shortly afterwards, this may indicate a trading activity.

1.10 Method of acquisition

An asset that is acquired by inheritance, or as a gift, is less likely to be the subject of trade.

2 Adjustment to profits

Section overview

- Trading profits cover income from a trade, profession or vocation.

- Profit and loss accounts must be drawn up under recognised accounting principles.

- The accounting profit or loss must be adjusted for tax purposes.

2.1 Introduction

Having established that a taxpayer is carrying on a trade, it is necessary to work out what the taxpayer's **taxable trading profits** are. The same rules apply to income from professions (eg accountants) so we will simply refer to trading profits in this text. A taxpayer may carry on a trade as a sole trader or as a partner in a partnership.

2.2 Profit and loss account

UK tax law requires the use of accounts drawn up under recognised accounting principles. This will usually be in accordance with UK accepted accounting practice (UK GAAP). In some cases, accounts may be prepared in accordance with International Accounting Standards (IAS) and International Financial Reporting Standards (IFRS).

2.3 Computing taxable trading profits

Whichever accounting method is used, the profit and loss account will show a figure for the accounting profit or loss for a period of account. However, this figure needs to be adjusted to accord with tax law. This process is called the **adjustment to profits** and we will deal with the main adjustments in the rest of this chapter. The adjustments are those which apply to sole traders and partnerships. Broadly similar adjustments are required to compute tax adjusted trading profits for companies and we will deal with the differences when we look at tax on companies later in this text.

Once the tax adjusted profit or loss has been computed, capital allowances need to be taken into account to find taxable trading profits. We will deal with capital allowances in the next chapter.

Overview of the trading profits computation

Per accounting period:

	£
Net profit per financial accounts	X
Add disallowable expenditure/income not shown in accounts	X
Less non-trade income in accounts/expenditure not in accounts	(X)
Tax adjusted profits before capital allowances	X
Less capital allowances	(X)
Tax adjusted profits after capital allowances	X

3 Allowable and disallowable expenditure

Section overview

- Expenditure is generally allowable if it is incurred wholly and exclusively for the purposes of the trade.
- Capital expenditure, appropriations of profit, general provisions, non-trade debts, most entertaining and gifts, and fines and penalties are disallowable.
- Some expenditure is specifically allowable such as legal costs on the renewal of a short lease.
- Leasing costs on expensive cars are restricted.

3.1 General principles

Definition

Allowable expenditure: Expenditure incurred wholly and exclusively for the purposes of the trade, not specifically disallowed by legislation.

In theory, if there is a dual purpose for expenditure (eg expenditure for both business and private use), the whole of the expenditure should be disallowed. In practice, however, HMRC will allow a reasonable apportionment between business (allowable) and private (disallowable) use.

Expenditure will also be disallowable if it is too remote from the purposes of the trade.

Some expenditure is allowable for accounting purposes, but not for tax purposes. Such expenditure is **disallowable** and must be *added back* to the accounting profit or loss.

3.2 Capital expenditure

Capital expenditure is disallowable. Usually, accounting practice would not include capital expenditure in the profit and loss account in any case. However, repairs and maintenance expenditure often requires careful review.

Maintenance (eg redecoration) and repair (returning the asset to its original condition) are allowable.

Improvement or enhancement of the asset, however, is a capital expense and must be disallowed. This would include expenditure on an asset newly acquired in a dilapidated state, where expenditure is required to bring the asset into use in the business.

Depreciation of capital assets is also disallowable as are any profits or losses on the sale of fixed assets. For tax purposes depreciation and losses on disposals of fixed assets are added back to the net profit in the accounts, while profits on disposals of fixed assets are deducted from the net profit in the accounts.

3.3 Appropriations of profit

Appropriations of profit (such as the payment of a 'salary' to a sole trader or partner) are disallowable.

Payment of a salary to a family member which is not reasonable remuneration for the services provided to the business may also be treated as an appropriation of profit.

If a business pays the owner's personal income tax and national insurance contributions or any other personal expense on his behalf, these are also appropriations of profit and are disallowable.

3.4 General provisions

The accounts may include a general provision for bad debts or a general stock provision.

The creation of, or increase in, a general provision is disallowable and must be added back to the accounting profit. Conversely, a decrease in a general provision must be deducted from the accounting profit.

The creation of, or increase in, a specific provision, for example relating to a specific debt, is allowable and does not require adjustment. A reduction in a specific bad debt provision is trading profit and so does not require adjustment.

3.5 Bad debts

Trade bad debts are allowable. Trade debts recovered are trading profit and do not require adjustment.

Non-trade bad debts are disallowable. These would include loans to employees unless either made in the course of trade or if the write-off is taxable as employment income for the employee.

Worked example: Bad debts

Jack's bad debts for the year to 30 April 2012 appear as follows:

	£		£
Written off		Balance b/f	
Trade debts	1,274	Specific provision	1,185
Loan to former employee	180	General provision	1,225
		Trade debts recovered	123
Specific provision	1,194		
General provision	1,260	Profit and loss a/c	1,375
	3,908		3,908

Requirement

What adjustments are required to arrive at Jack's taxable trading profits?

Solution

Loan to former employee written off – disallowable, add back £180

Increase in general bad debt provision – disallowable, add back (£1,260 – £1,225) = £35

Following changes in accounting standards, all reductions in the value of debtors are supposed to be specific in nature. This means that going forward, general provisions are less likely to be seen in practice. Instead of writing off or providing against a specific debt, debts will now be 'impaired'.

3.6 Entertainment and gifts

Expenditure on entertaining staff is allowable. All other entertaining expenditure (eg customer entertaining) is disallowable.

The following gifts are allowable:

- Gifts to employees

- Gifts of trade samples (not for resale), limited to one per customer per year

- Gifts to customers if they incorporate a conspicuous advertisement for the business, are not food, drink, tobacco or vouchers exchangeable for goods, and the total cost per customer is no more than £50

All other gifts are disallowable.

3.7 Donations and subscriptions

Reasonably small donations to local charities are allowable if the gift enhances the public image of the trade.

Donations to national charities are disallowable.

Any charitable donations made within the Gift Aid Scheme are given tax relief in the income tax computation by extending the taxpayer's basic rate band (see earlier in this text).

To ensure that tax relief is not given for these donations twice, any donations made with a Gift Aid declaration are disallowable in arriving at trading profits and must be added back to the net profit in the accounts.

Gifts of trading stock or used plant and machinery to charities or UK educational establishments are specifically allowable.

Political donations are generally disallowable.

Subscriptions to trade and professional associations are generally allowable.

3.8 Fines and penalties

The general rule is that fines and penalties are disallowable. Examples include parking fines incurred by a sole trader or partner and penalties for late payment of tax.

Parking fines incurred by an employee on a business activity are generally allowable by HMRC.

3.9 Interest

Interest paid on money borrowed for business purposes is allowable.

Interest on late payment of tax is disallowable.

3.10 Legal and professional fees

Legal and professional fees relating to income are allowable. Examples include collection of trade debts, employment issues, action for breach of contract, preservation of trading rights and preparation of accounts.

Legal and professional fees relating to capital expenditure are generally disallowable. Examples include costs of acquiring capital assets and drawing up a partnership agreement. However the following expenses relating to capital assets are specifically allowable:

- Legal costs relating to the *renewal* of a short lease (50 years or less)
- Costs of registration of a patent or copyright for trade use
- Incidental costs of raising long-term finance

3.11 Irrecoverable value added tax

Irrecoverable VAT is allowable for trading purposes only if the item of expenditure to which it relates is allowable.

3.12 Employment payments and pensions

Earnings paid to employees are generally allowable. If earnings are charged in the accounts but not paid within nine months of the end of the period of account, the cost is only allowable in the period in which the earnings are paid.

Redundancy payments and compensation for loss of office are generally allowable. However, on the cessation of trade, the deduction is restricted to additional payments of up to three times the amount of statutory redundancy pay.

The cost of educational courses for employees is allowable if incurred for trade purposes.

Employers' contributions to a registered pension scheme are allowable in the accounting period of payment, not when accrued.

Payments of employers' national insurance contributions in respect of employees are allowable.

3.13 Car leasing and rental costs

In principle, the costs of hiring, leasing or renting plant and equipment are allowable.

However for leases taken out on cars (not motorcycles) a flat rate disallowance of 15% of the lease payments applies for cars with CO_2 emissions above 160g/km. Thus there is no disallowance if CO_2 emissions are less than or equal to 160g/km.

 Worked example: Leased car

Douglas leases a car with a retail price of £14,200 and CO_2 emissions of 171g/km on 1 June 2012. The leasing cost is £1,960 up to 31 December 2012.

Douglas prepares accounts to 31 December 2012.

Requirement

What is the disallowable amount which needs to be added back?

Solution

As the CO_2 emissions exceed 160g/km there is a flat rate disallowance.

Disallowable amount 15% × £1,960 £294

If the sole trader or partner then uses the leased car partly for business and partly for private purposes a further adjustment would be required to disallow the private usage of the leased car.

Worked example: Leased car and private use by sole trader

Jane leases a car with a retail price of £16,000 and CO_2 emissions of 200g/km on 1 May 2012.

Jane uses the car partly for business and partly for private purposes. Business usage of 60% has been agreed with HMRC.

Jane prepares accounts to 31 December each year. The leasing cost up to 31 December 2012 was £1,600.

Requirement

What is the disallowed amount which needs to be added back?

Solution

Allowable amount

85% × £1,600 × 60% (business use) =	£816
Disallowable amount (£1,600 – £816) =	£784

Interactive question 1: Allowable or disallowable?   [Difficulty level: Exam standard]

Classify the following expenditure as allowable or disallowable and state how you would deal with it in the adjustment of profits computation.

Question	Fill in your answer
£1,000 on party for five employees	
Gift of desk diary to ten customers with trade logo costing £35 each	
£5,000 on new roof for workshop	
£500 increase in general bad debt provision	
£50 to local hospital, a registered charity, as sponsor for new scanner	
£150 debt to former employee written off	
£35 parking fines incurred by salesman on business	
£5,000 contribution to registered pension scheme	
Gift of bottle of wine to twenty customers with trade logo costing £25 each	
£1,000 donation to the Conservative Party, a political party	
£1,500 accountancy fees for preparing accounts	
£2,500 on redecoration of office	
£100 interest on late payment of tax	
£6,000 depreciation on capital assets	
£500 legal fees on grant of a new 25 year lease of shop	

See **Answer** at the end of this chapter.

4 Other adjustments

Section overview

- The sale price of goods taken from the business by the owner is trading profit.
- Non-trading income must be deducted.
- Business expenditure not shown in the accounts is deductible as an allowable expense.

4.1 Trading profits not shown in accounts

The main example of trading profit not shown in the accounts of the business arises when goods are taken from the business by the owner for personal use without reimbursing the business with the full value.

The owner must be taxed on the profit he would have made if the goods had been sold at market value.

The adjustment will depend on how the transaction has been shown in the accounts:

- If nothing is recorded in the accounts, add back the selling price
- If treated as drawings at cost, add back profit

Worked example: Goods taken for own use

Max took some goods from his business with a selling price of £160.

The cost of the goods was £90.

Requirement

What adjustments are required if:

(a) the transaction is not recorded in the accounts, or
(b) the transaction has been treated as drawings of £90?

Solution

(a) Add back selling price of £160
(b) Add back profit (£160 – £90) = £70

4.2 Non-trading income in accounts

Any non-trade income in the accounts must be deducted.

Examples include rental income, profits on the disposal of fixed assets and investment income.

4.3 Expenditure not shown in the accounts

The most common expenditure not shown in the accounts is business expenditure paid personally by the owner.

Such expenditure is allowable and should be deducted.

Summary

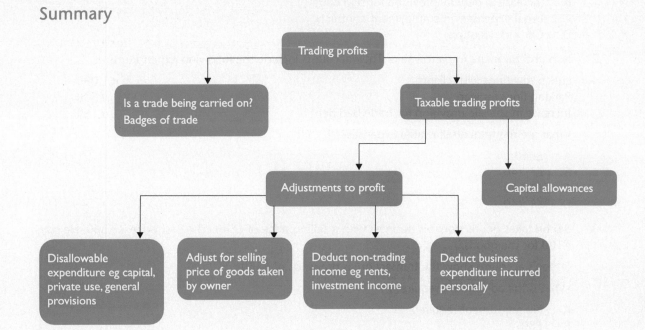

Answer the following questions.

1   Which of the following is an allowable expense?

   A   Gift of fleece jackets to customers with trade logo costing £55 each
   B   Increase in general provision for bad debts
   C   Legal expenses on employment contracts
   D   Gift Aid donation

2   Ivan and Ewan are in partnership. Their accounts include the following expenditure:

   Lunch meetings with clients   £1,090
   Parking fines for Ivan   £500
   Increase in specific provision for trade bad debt   £150

   What are the total disallowable expenses?

   A   £650
   B   £1,240
   C   £1,590
   D   £1,740

3   Simon takes goods from his business with a selling price of £540. The cost price is £360. He pays £100 for the goods.

   Simon's accounts show the transaction as drawings of £360.

   What is the adjustment required?

   A   No adjustment required
   B   £80
   C   £180
   D   £540

4   Henry leases a car with a retail price of £20,000 and CO_2 emissions of 184g/km on 1 November 2011. The annual leasing charge is £5,000.

   What adjustment needs to be made in his accounts for the year ended 31 October 2012?

   A   No adjustment required
   B   £750 added back
   C   £4,250 added back
   D   £5,000 added back

5   Patrick's accounts show £16,550 on repairs and maintenance during the year to 30 September 2012.

   Demolishing out-house and building new toilets   £5,950
   Repainting offices   £3,600
   Installing new heating system   £7,000

   How much should be added back to the accounting profit?

   A   £9,550
   B   £10,600
   C   £12,950
   D   £16,550

6   Janice leases a car with a retail price of £36,000 and CO_2 emissions of 150g/km on 1 July 2012. The annual leasing charge is £4,700. The car is for business use only.

   What adjustment needs to be made in her accounts for the year ended 31 December 2012?

   A   £1,998
   B   £705
   C   £353
   D   nil

Now, go back to the Learning outcomes in the Introduction. If you are satisfied you have achieved these objectives, please tick them off.

Technical reference

Legislation

References relate to Income Tax (Trading and Other Income) Act 2005 (*ITTOIA 2005*)

Charge to tax on trade profits	s.5
Accounting practice	s.25

Disallowable expenditure

• Capital	s.33
• Wholly and exclusively	s.34
• Bad debts	s.35
• Unpaid remuneration	s.36
• Employee benefits	ss.38-44
• Business entertainment and gifts	ss.45-47
• Car hire	ss.48-50
• Penalties etc	s.54

Allowable expenditure

• Incidental costs of finance	s.58
• Redundancy payments	ss.76-80
• Incidental expenses re patents	s.89
• Gifts to charities etc of stock	s.108

HMRC manuals

Business income manual (Found at http://www.hmrc.gov.uk/manuals/bimmanual/index.htm)

Trade: badges of trade: summary	BIM20205
Measuring the profits (general rules)	BIM30000
The relationship between tax and accountancy	BIM 31000
Capital/revenue divide: introduction: overview of the guidance	BIM35001
Wholly & exclusively	BIM37000

This technical reference section is designed to assist you when you are working in the office. It should help you to know where to look for further information on the topics covered in this chapter. **You will not be examined on the contents of this section in your examination.**

Answer to Interactive question

Answer to Interactive question 1

Question	Fill in your answer
£1,000 on party for five employees	Allowable as the £150 limit applies to employment income not trading profits (NB taxable benefit for employees)
Gift of desk diary to ten customers with trade logo costing £35 each	Allowable (advert, £50 or less)
£5,000 on new roof for workshop	Disallowable (capital), add back £5,000
£500 increase in general bad debt provision	Disallowable, add back £500
£50 to local hospital, a registered charity, as sponsor for new scanner	Allowable (small, local, public image)
£150 debt to former employee written off	Disallowable, add back £150
£35 parking fines incurred by salesman on business	Allowable
£5,000 contribution to registered pension scheme	Allowable
Gift of bottle of wine to twenty customers with trade logo costing £25 each	Disallowable (drink), add back £500 (20 × £25)
£1,000 donation to the Conservative Party, a political party	Disallowable (political donation), add back £1,000
£1,500 accountancy fees for preparing accounts	Allowable
£2,500 on redecoration of office	Allowable (maintenance)
£100 interest on late payment of tax	Disallowable, add back £100
£6,000 depreciation on capital assets	Disallowable add back £6,000
£500 legal fees on grant of a new 25 year lease of shop	Disallowable (not renewal), add back £500

1   C – legal expenses on employment contracts – allowable

Gift of fleece jackets to customers with trade logo costing £55 each – disallowable as exceeds £50 per customer

General provision for bad debts – disallowable

Gift Aid donation – disallowable, take into account in income tax computation

2   C – £1,590

Lunch meetings with clients – disallowable as entertaining

Parking fines for Ivan – disallowable as incurred by partner

Specific provision for trade bad debt – allowable as specific and for trade debt

3   B – £80

Add back profit (£540 – £360) = £180 – £100 (paid by Simon) = £80

4   B – £750 added back

Disallowable amount (15% × £5,000)   £750

5   C – £12,950

Demolishing out-house and building new toilets: disallowable, capital

Repainting offices: allowable

Installing new heating system: disallowable, capital

6   D – nil

As the CO_2 emissions are below 160g/km there is no disallowance.

Note: Only (6/12 × £4,700) £2,350 leasing charge would be in the accounts for the year ended 31 December 2012.

CHAPTER 5

Capital allowances

Introduction

Examination context

Topic List

Summary and Self-test

Technical reference

Answers to Interactive questions

Answers to Self-test

Learning outcome

- Calculate the adjusted trading profits after capital allowances on plant and machinery of a sole trader or partnership

The specific syllabus reference for this chapter is 3e.

Syllabus links

Capital allowances are an important area of taxation and are examinable at all levels.

You will be expected to be thoroughly conversant with the topics covered in this chapter in the Application paper and at the Advanced Stage, so it is vital that you make sure you learn the material in this chapter very well.

Examination context

In the examination candidates may be required to:

- Calculate writing down allowances for short or long periods of account
- Identify which assets are eligible for first year allowances
- Correctly apply the annual investment allowance
- Correctly treat cars and other assets with private use by the sole trader or partner
- Determine the amount of any balancing adjustment

For extra question practice on these topics go to the section of the Question Bank covering this chapter.

A methodical approach is required to calculate capital allowances. This can be an unnecessarily time-consuming area if such an approach is not adopted.

1 Introduction

Section overview

- Capital allowances give tax relief for expenditure on capital assets such as plant and machinery.

- Plant includes assets which perform an active (not passive) function in a business and some expenditure specified in legislation.

- Sole traders, partners and companies qualify for capital allowances on assets used in their businesses.

- The acquisition cost of an asset is usually the cost of the asset to the business.

- The disposal value of assets in the capital allowances computation cannot exceed original cost.

1.1 What are capital allowances?

This chapter covers the second step in computing taxable trading profits which is the calculation of capital allowances. These are deducted from the adjusted accounting profit as described in the previous chapter.

Capital allowances are tax allowances for certain types of capital expenditure. Depreciation on assets is not allowable for tax purposes. Instead, capital allowances give tax relief by allowing part of the cost of capital assets each year.

Capital allowances must be claimed by a taxpayer. A taxpayer may claim less than the full amount of the capital allowances, for example if trading profits are not sufficient to absorb the full allowances. This will mean that larger allowances will be available in future periods of account.

In your examination, you are only required to deal with one type of capital allowance which is the allowance for expenditure on plant and machinery.

Machinery includes all machines, motor vehicles and computers. Plant includes such things as office furniture and equipment.

The definition of plant can be problematic. In general, if an asset performs an active function in the business it is considered to be plant whereas if an asset is merely part of the setting in which the business is carried on it does not qualify as plant.

This definition can cause difficulties with expenditure related to buildings. For example, moveable partitions are deemed to be plant since they perform an active function in the business whereas fixed partitions are not deemed to be plant since they are just part of the business setting.

There are also some types of expenditure which are specified in legislation as qualifying for capital allowances on plant and machinery. These include:

- Building alterations incidental to the installation of plant and machinery
- Licence to use computer software.

1.2 Who is entitled to capital allowances?

Capital allowances are available to a taxable person who incurs capital expenditure on assets to be used for the purposes of a trade carried on by that person.

Taxable person here means a sole trader, a partner in a partnership, or a company. In this chapter, we will concentrate on trades carried on by a sole trader or a partnership. Companies are dealt with later in this text, but the rules in this chapter apply in a similar way for companies.

It is important to remember that capital allowances for a sole trader or a partnership are calculated for each period of account, not for each tax year.

1.3 Acquisition cost

You will need to identify the acquisition cost of assets qualifying for capital allowances as the allowances will be based on this amount.

In most cases, you will simply be given a figure for the cost of the asset and will use this in your computation.

The owner may bring personally-owned assets into the business. This may happen when a business starts. Here, the acquisition cost for capital allowances is the market value of the asset when it is brought into the business.

1.4 Disposal value

You may also need to know the disposal value of an asset to work out capital allowances.

The general rule is that the disposal value is the sale proceeds of the asset. However, this cannot exceed the original cost of the asset.

If the asset is given away or sold for less than market value, the disposal value will be the market value on the date of disposal.

If the asset is scrapped or destroyed, the disposal value is the scrap value or the compensation received, as appropriate.

If a business ceases, a disposal value must be brought into the capital allowances calculation and balancing adjustments calculated (see later in this chapter). The disposal value will be the proceeds received or the scrap value (which may be nil).

1.5 Overview of capital allowances on plant and machinery

Per accounting period

	FYA £	Main pool £	Each expensive car £	Each private use asset £	Allowances £
Per period of account					
TWDV b/f		X	X	X	
Acquisitions – low emission car	X				
FYA @ 100%	(X)				X
	—				
Acquisitions – ECA	X				
FYA @ 100%	(X)				X
	—				
Disposals		(X)	(X)		
Balancing allowance/(charge)			X/(X)		X/(X)
Acquisitions (AIA)		X			
AIA		(X)			X
Acquisitions (non AIA & FYA) cars		X			
		X			
WDA @ 18%		(X)		(X)	X*
TWDV c/f		X		X	
Total allowances					X

* Only the business use percentage of the WDA on private use assets is taken to the capital allowances column.

AIA:	annual investment allowance
FYA:	first year allowance
Expensive car:	car which cost over £12,000 pre April 2009 and is not a qualifying low emission car
Private use asset:	used partly for non-business purposes by a sole trader or partner

2 Main pool: writing down allowances

Section overview

- Most expenditure on assets is pooled in the main pool.

- For each period of account, acquisition costs are added to the pool and disposal costs deducted from the pool.

- A writing down allowance (WDA) is given on the balance of the pool at the end of the period of account.

- The tax written down value (TWDV) of the pool is carried forward to the start of the next period of account.

2.1 Assets in the main pool

In most cases, capital allowances are not calculated for expenditure on a single asset, but on a pool of expenditure, ie on a number of assets. For each period of account, the cost of assets acquired is added to the pool and the value of any disposals deducted from the pool.

Expenditure on assets in the main pool includes:

- All machinery, fixtures and fittings and equipment

- Vans, forklift trucks, lorries, motorcycles

- Cars costing £12,000 or less purchased prior to 6 April 2009

- Cars with CO_2 emissions of not more than 160g/km purchased on or after 6 April 2009. See section 3.2 for first year allowances on cars.

2.2 Writing down allowance

A **writing down allowance** (WDA) is given on the balance of the main pool at the end of the period of account.

The WDA is a percentage of the pool balance for a period of account.

The WDA is 18% per annum from 6 April 2012 (1 April for companies). Prior to 6 April 2012 (1 April for companies) the WDA was 20% per annum.

For accounting periods that straddle 6 April 2012 (1 April for companies) a hybrid WDA must be calculated for the accounting period on a pro rata basis. This rate is arrived at by applying the WDA of 20% to the portion of the accounting period that falls before the change date and the WDA of 18% to the portion of the accounting period after the change date, then adding them together to find the rate for the accounting period as a whole. The hybrid rate is rounded to two decimal places.

If the period of account is longer or shorter than 12 months, the WDA is increased or decreased accordingly.

Once the WDA has been deducted from the pool balance, the remainder of the value of the pool is then carried forward to the start of the next period of account. This amount is called the **tax written down value** (TWDV). It continues to be written down on a reducing balance basis.

CHAPTER

5

Worked example: Writing down allowances

Trump started in business on 1 June 2011. He decided to make up his accounts to 31 December each year.

He makes the following acquisitions:

1.6.11   Brings Volvo car into business, market value £5,500 (actual cost £7,000) with CO_2 emissions of 145 g/km

1.9.11   Buys Nissan car costing £6,500, with CO_2 emissions of 153g/km

He makes the following disposals:

1.9.12   Sells Volvo for £4,000

1.11.12   Nissan car is involved in an accident and is scrapped. Trump receives compensation of £250.

Neither car is used for Trump's non-business journeys and neither car is a qualifying low emission car.

Requirement

Show the maximum capital allowances available for Trump's first two periods of account.

Solution

	Main pool £	Allowances £
Period of account – 1.6.11 to 31.12.11 (7 months)		
Acquisitions		
1.6.11 Volvo (MV)	5,500	
1.9.11 Nissan	6,500	
	12,000	
No disposals		
WDA: £12,000 × 20% × 7/12 (time apportioned for 7 month period)	(1,400)	1,400
TWDV c/f	10,600	
Period of account – 1.1.12 to 31.12.12 (12 months)		
Acquisitions		
No acquisitions		
Disposals		
1.9.12 Volvo	(4,000)	
1.11.12 Nissan	(250)	
	6,350	
WDA £6,350 × 18.5% (ie (3/12 × 20%) + (9/12 × 18%))	(1,175)	1,175
TWDV c/f	5,175	

3 Main pool: first year allowances

Section overview

- First year allowances (FYAs) may be given in the period of account in which expenditure is incurred.

- All businesses may claim a 100% FYA on certain energy-saving expenditure, low emission cars and zero emission goods vehicles.

3.1 What are first year allowances?

As its name suggests, a first year allowance (FYA) is given in the period of account in which the expenditure is incurred.

A FYA is always given in full, regardless of the length of the period of account. Where the full 100% FYA is claimed, there are no further WDAs on such expenditure.

3.2 100% first year allowances

There is a 100% FYA for expenditure on designated energy saving technologies, such as equipment that generates heat and power.

A 100% FYA also applies to expenditure on qualifying low emission cars. To qualify as a low emission car it must emit not more than 110g/km of CO_2 or it must be electrically propelled.

In addition, there is a 100% FYA for expenditure on new and unused zero emission goods vehicles where expenditure is incurred on or after 6 April 2010 (1 April for companies). This is expected to apply for five years.

3.3 Disposal of assets attracting first year allowances

In the year of disposal of an asset previously qualifying for first year allowances, or in the accounting period of cessation, the disposal proceeds (limited to cost) must be deducted from the relevant pool.

4 Annual investment allowance

Section overview

- An annual investment allowance (AIA) is available for expenditure on plant and machinery, except cars.

- The AIA is given for a 12 month period of account. From 6 April 2012 (1 April for companies) the AIA is £25,000. Before this, the AIA was £100,000.

- Any balance of expenditure in excess of the AIA receives a WDA at the end of the accounting period.

4.1 Annual Investment Allowance

An Annual Investment Allowance (AIA) is available to a sole trader, partnership or company. It can be used against qualifying expenditure, which includes most plant and machinery, except cars.

The maximum allowance is £25,000 per annum for expenditure incurred on or after 6 April 2012 (1 April for companies) and £100,000 per annum for expenditure incurred before then. It must be set against expenditure in the accounting period in which it is incurred.

For accounting periods which are not 12 months long, the AIA is pro-rated up or down accordingly.

For accounting periods that straddle 6 April 2012 (1 April for companies) the maximum AIA for the accounting period must be calculated on a pro rata basis. The maximum AIA is arrived at by applying the £100,000 AIA to the portion of the accounting period that falls before the change date and the £25,000 AIA to the portion of the accounting period after the change date, then adding them together to find the AIA for the accounting period as a whole. However, the maximum actual expenditure incurred after the change date that can be covered by the AIA is restricted to the amount found by applying the £25,000 AIA to the portion of the accounting period after the change date.

If a business has an accounting period for the year ended 31 December 2012, the maximum AIA available would be £43,750, ie ((3/12 × £100,000) + (9/12 × £25,000)), which is (£25,000 + £18,750). However if the business has expenditure in the period from 6 April 2012 to 31 December 2012 the maximum amount that can be covered by the AIA is restricted to £18,750.

Any balance of expenditure incurred within an accounting period on which the AIA is not given is eligible for the WDA.

Worked example: Annual investment allowance

Jose has been trading for many years and makes up accounts to 31 December each year. His capital allowances pool brought forward at 1 January 2012 is £8,000. He makes the following acquistions and disposals:

1.3.12	Buys a printing press for £126,000
1.2.13	Sells for £480 plant which cost £900 two years earlier
24.4.13	Buys a further printing press for £40,000

Requirement

What are the maximum capital allowances available to Jose for the years ended 31 December 2012 and 2013?

Solution

	Main pool £	Allowances £
Period of account – Year ended 31 December 2012		
TWDV b/f	8,000	
Acquisitions		
1.3.12 Press	126,000	
Less AIA ((3/12 × £100,000) + (9/12 × £25,000)) (note)	(43,750)	43,750
	90,250	
WDA @ 18.5% (ie (3/12 × 20%) + (9/12 × 18%))	(16,696)	16,696
TWDV c/f	73,554	
Total allowances		60,446
Period of account – Year ended 31 December 2013		
Acquisitions		
24.4.13 Press	40,000	
Less AIA	(25,000)	25,000
Disposals		
1.2.13 Plant	(480)	
	88,074	
WDA @ 18%	(15,853)	15,853
TWDV c/f	72,221	40,853

Note: If the expenditure had been incurred on or after 1 April 2012 the AIA would have been restricted to £18,750 (9/12 × £25,000)

Interactive question 1: Annual investment allowance [Difficulty level: Exam standard]

Wolfgang commences to trade on 6 April 2012 and draws up accounts to 5 April each year. During his first year to 5 April 2013, he incurs the following expenditure:

6.4.12	Machinery	£162,000
6.7.12	Car with emissions of 105g/km	£8,000
31.10.12	Car with emissions of 155g/km	£10,500

Requirement

Using the standard format below, compute the maximum capital allowances available to Wolfgang for the year ended 5 April 2013.

	FYA £	Main pool £	Allowances £
Period of Account year ended....			
Acquisitions (FYA): FYA	_____ _____		
Acquisitions (AIA): AIA			
Acquisitions (non AIA or FYA):		_____	
WDA	_____	_____	
TWDV c/f	_____	_____	_____
Total allowances			_____

See **Answer** at the end of this chapter.

5 Small plant and machinery pools

Section overview

- Businesses may write off small balances remaining at the end of the accounting period in the main pool.

- This applies where the tax written down value at the end of the accounting period is £1,000 or less.

- The £1,000 limit is scaled up or down for long or short accounting periods.

5.1 WDA for small pools

If the balance on the main pool is less than the small pool limit at the end of the accounting period, a WDA can be claimed up to the value of the small pool limit. This means that the main pool may be written down to nil, rather than a small balance being carried forward on which allowances have to be claimed each year.

The small pool limit is £1,000 for a 12 month period of account. The limit is scaled up or down for long or short periods of account.

It is available to businesses of any size – sole traders, partnerships and companies.

The write-off does not apply to single asset pools such as cars costing more than £12,000 or private-use assets (see next section).

6 Single asset pools

Section overview

- Some assets are not put in the main pool but have a separate pool for each asset.

- This applies to cars costing more than £12,000 acquired before 6 April 2009, and assets with private use by the sole trader or partner.

6.1 Cars

The treatment of cars depends on whether they were purchased before or on or after 6 April 2009 (1 April for companies).

6.1.1 For cars purchased pre 6 April 2009

Cars costing £12,000 or less (except low emission cars) were dealt with in the main pool unless there was private use by a sole trader or partner.

Each car costing more than £12,000 (except low emission cars) continues to have its own pool. It continues to receive a WDA of 18% pa but this is restricted to a maximum of £3,000 pa.

Transitional rules mean that these old rules continue to apply to expensive cars purchased prior to 6 April 2009 until at least 2013/14.

6.1.2 For cars purchased on or after 6 April 2009

For cars purchased on or after 6 April 2009 the treatment is based on the CO_2 emissions of the car as follows:

Cars with emissions of 110g/km or less continue to be treated as low emission cars and receive a FYA of 100% (see earlier).

Cars with emissions of 111g/km up to 160g/km, irrespective of cost, go in the main pool where they receive a WDA of 18% per annum.

Cars with emissions of greater than 160g/km enter into a special rate pool where they receive a WDA of 8% per annum. These are not within your syllabus.

If the car is one with private use by a sole trader or partner it goes into a single asset pool, however the allowances received are based on the emissions of the car (as stated above).

Cars are not entitled to the annual investment allowance.

Worked example: Cars

Gordon had the following balances brought forward at 6 April 2012:

Main pool	£7,600
Expensive car (purchased pre-6 April 2009 – business use only)	£16,000

On 15 October 2012 Gordon bought a car with emissions of 150g/km at a cost of £10,300. The car was for business use only. Gordon prepares accounts to 5 April each year.

Requirement

What are the maximum capital allowances available to Gordon for the year ended 5 April 2013?

Solution

Period of account	Main pool £	Expensive car £	Allowances £
Year ended 5.4.13			
TWDV b/f	7,600	16,000	
Acquisitions (non AIA or FYA)			
car – emissions 150g/km	10,300		
	17,900	16,000	
WDA @ 18%	(3,222)	(2,880)	6,102
TWDV c/f	14,678	13,120	
Total allowances			6,102

6.2 Assets with private use by sole trader or partner

Any asset that is partly used privately by a sole trader or partner is kept in a separate pool. The AIA, the FYA or WDA is still calculated in full and deducted from the single asset pool but the trader can only claim the business element of the allowance.

Worked example: Assets with private use

Jasper has been in business for many years making up accounts to 30 April each year. The only asset he owns for capital allowances purposes is computer equipment which he uses 20% privately and has a tax written down value at 1 May 2012 of £2,000.

On 1 August 2012, he buys a car with CO_2 emissions of 142g/km for £16,000 which he uses 30% privately.

Requirement

What are the maximum capital allowances that Jasper can claim for the year to 30 April 2013?

Solution

Period of account	Computer £	Car £	Allowances £
Year ended 30.4.13			
TWDV b/f	2,000		
Acquisition (no FYA or AIA)		16,000	
WDA @ 18%	(360) × 80%		288
WDA @ 18%		(2,880) × 70%	2,016
TWDVs c/f	1,640	13,120	
Allowances			2,304

Interactive question 2: Assets with private use [Difficulty level: Exam standard]

Jolene started trading on 1 July 2012. Her first set of accounts were made up to 31 March 2013.

On 1 December 2012, Jolene purchased a car with CO_2 emissions of 155g/km for £21,000 which she uses 70% for business purposes.

Requirement

Using the standard format below, compute the maximum capital allowance for Jolene for the period ended 31 March 2013.

	Car £	Allowances £
Period of account .... to		
Acquisition		
WDA	(_____) × .....%	_____
TWDV c/f	═══════	
Allowances		═══════

See **Answer** at the end of this chapter.

7 Balancing adjustments

Section overview

- A balancing charge arises on disposal if too many capital allowances have been given.
- A balancing allowance arises on disposal if too few capital allowances have been given.

7.1 Balancing charge

If too many capital allowances have been given on an asset over its lifetime, a balancing charge arises. This might happen if an asset is sold for an amount in excess of its tax written down value.

The balancing charge will be taxed either by using it to reduce the capital allowances in the period of account or by adding it to the adjusted trading profits computation.

If the asset is one with private use, only the business use element is actually chargeable.

A balancing charge can occur on the main pool and on single asset pools at any time.

7.2 Balancing allowance

If too few capital allowances have been given on an asset over its lifetime, a balancing allowance may arise. This might happen if an asset is sold for an amount less than its tax written down value.

The balancing allowance will be added to the capital allowances otherwise available for the period of account.

If the asset is one with private use, only the business use element is allowable as for all capital allowances.

A balancing allowance can only arise on the main pool if the business comes to an end. Balancing allowances can arise on single asset pools at any time.

Worked example: Balancing adjustments

Philip has carried on a trade for many years making up accounts to 31 March.

At 1 April 2012, Philip had a main pool with a tax written down value of £6,250, and a Ford car with 20% private use with a tax written down value of £10,000.

On 1 December 2012, Philip sold office equipment for £7,200 (original cost £10,000).

On 1 February 2013, Philip sold his Ford for £7,500. On the same day Philip bought an Audi with CO_2 emissions of 145g/km for £17,500. The Audi also has 20% private use.

Requirement

What are the maximum capital allowances available to Philip for the year ended 31 March 2013?

Solution

	Main pool £	Ford £	Audi £	Allowances £
Period of account				
Year ended 31.3.13				
TWDV b/f	6,250	10,000		
Acquisition (no AIA or FYA)				
1.2.13			17,500	
Disposals				
1.12.12	(7,200)			
	(950)			
Balancing charge	950			(950)
	—			
	═══			
1.2.13		(7,500)		
		2,500		
Balancing allowance		(2,500) × 80%		2,000
		—		
		═══		
WDA @ 18%			(3,150) × 80%	2,520
TWDV c/f			14,350	
Allowances				3,570

If the balancing charge had exceeded the allowances, the excess charge would have been added to the adjusted trade profit for the year.

Summary

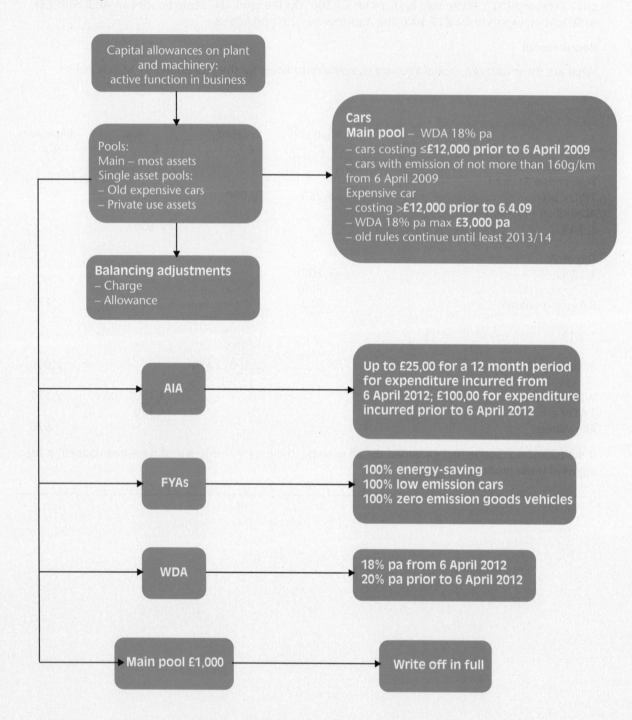

Capital allowances on plant and machinery: active function in business

Pools:
Main – most assets
Single asset pools:
– Old expensive cars
– Private use assets

Cars
Main pool – WDA 18% pa
– cars costing ≤**£12,000 prior to 6 April 2009**
– cars with emission of not more than 160g/km from 6 April 2009
Expensive car
– costing >**£12,000 prior to 6.4.09**
– WDA 18% pa max **£3,000 pa**
– old rules continue until least 2013/14

Balancing adjustments
– Charge
– Allowance

AIA

Up to £25,00 for a 12 month period for expenditure incurred from 6 April 2012; £100,00 for expenditure incurred prior to 6 April 2012

FYAs

100% energy-saving
100% low emission cars
100% zero emission goods vehicles

WDA

18% pa from 6 April 2012
20% pa prior to 6 April 2012

Main pool £1,000

Write off in full

Self-test

Answer the following questions.

1   David began trading on 1 May 2012. On that date he brought a car into the business (business use only) valued at £10,000. The car has CO_2 emissions of 150g/km

David made up his first accounts to 31 December 2012.

What is the maximum capital allowance that David can claim for the period to 31 December 2012?

A   £1,200
B   £1,800
C   £3,000
D   £10,000

2   Terry has been trading for many years making up accounts to 30 September each year.

At 1 October 2011, the tax written down value of his main pool was £8,000.

On 12 October 2011, Terry bought a van for use in the business costing £16,000.

What are the maximum capital allowances that Terry can claim for the year to 30 September 2012?

A   £4,560
B   £4,320
C   £17,440
D   £17,520

3   Marcus has been trading for many years making up accounts to 5 April.

The tax written down value of the main pool was £900 at 6 April 2012.

The only other asset in the business for capital allowances purposes was a car, which Marcus uses 75% for business purposes. The tax written down value of the car at 6 April 2012 was £7,000.

On 1 September 2012 Marcus sold the car for £7,800. The original cost was £9,500.

What are the maximum capital allowances available to Marcus for the year ended 5 April 2013?

A   £1,700
B   £1,500
C   £100
D   £300

4   Sergio buys a car at a cost of £14,000 on 7 October 2012. The CO_2 emissions of the car are 105g/km.

What, if any, first year allowance can he claim?

A   £0
B   £3,000
C   £2,520
D   £14,000

5   Nadia starts trading on 1 May 2012. On 1 November 2012 she buys a single item of machinery for £114,000. What is the maximum capital allowance Nadia can claim for the year ended 30 April 2013?

A   £20,520
B   £102,520
C   £25,000
D   £41,020

6   Aimee starts trading on 1 July 2012. On 1 July 2012 she buys a single item of plant for £80,000. What is the maximum capital allowance Aimee can claim for the 9 months to 31 March 2013?

A   £80,000
B   £18,750
C   £29,775
D   £27,019

7   Jacob has been trading for many years making up accounts to 31 December.

The tax written down values at 1 January 2012 were:

Main pool	£11,800
Expensive car (pre-6 April 2009 – 40% private use by Jacob)	£14,000

On 15 May 2012 Jacob purchased a car for use by an employee, with CO_2 emissions of 135g/km at a cost of £7,600.

What is the maximum capital allowances that Jacob can claim for the year to 31 December 2012?

A   £6,589
B   £5,143
C   £5,004
D   £5,389

Now go back to the Learning outcome in the Introduction. If you are satisfied you have achieved this objectives, please tick it off.

Legislation

References relate to Capital Allowances Act 2001 (*CAA 2001*)

Qualifying activities	ss.15 – 20
Qualifying expenditure: general	ss.21 – 38
Qualifying expenditure: first year allowances	ss.39 – 49
Pooling	ss.53 – 54
Writing down allowances	s.55
First year allowances	s.52
Cars costing more than £12,000	ss.74 – 82
Main rate cars (111-160 g/km)	s.104AA
Private use assets	ss.205 – 208
Balancing adjustments	s.56
Annual investment allowance	ss.38A – 38B ss.1A – 1N
Small pools	s.56A

HMRC manual

Capital allowances manual (Found at http://www.hmrc.gov.uk/manuals/camanual/index.htm)

PMAs: Introduction: Outline	CA20006
General: Definitions: Chargeable period, accounting period and period of account	CA11510
PMA: FYA: Expenditure on which available and rates	CA23110

> This technical reference section is designed to assist you when you are working in the office. It should help you to know where to look for further information on the topics covered in this chapter. **You will not be examined on the contents of this section in your examination**.

CHAPTER

5

Answers to Interactive questions

Answer to Interactive question 1

	FYA £	Main pool £	Allowances £
Period of account			
Year ended 5 April 2013			
Acquisitions (FYA)			
6.7.12 car (< 110g/km)	8,000		
FYA @ 100%	(8,000)		8,000
	–		
Acquisitions (AIA)			
6.4.12 Machinery		162,000	
AIA		(25,000)	25,000
Acquisitions (non AIA or FYA)			
31.10.12 car		10,500	
		147,500	
WDA @ 18%		(26,550)	26,550
TWDV c/f		120,950	
Total allowances			59,550

Answer to Interactive question 2

	Car £	Allowances £
Period of account		
1 July 2012 to 31 March 2013 (9 months)		
Acquisitions	21,000	
WDA @ 18% × 9/12	(2,835) × 70%	1,985
TWDV c/f	18,165	
Allowances		1,985

1   A – £1,200

	Main pool £	Allowances £
Period of account		
1 May 2012 to 31 December 2012 (eight months)		
1 May 2012 Acquisition	10,000	
WDA: 18% × 8/12	(1,200)	1,200
TWDV c/f	8,800	
Allowances		1,200

2   D – £17,520

	Main pool £	Allowances £
Period of account		
1 October 2011 to 30 September 2012		
TWDV b/f	8,000	
Acquisition (AIA)		
12 October 2011 Van	16,000	
AIA (max £62,500, ie (£100,000 × 6/12) + (£25,000 × 6/12))	(16,000)	16,000
WDA @ 19% (ie (20% × 6/12) + (18% × 6/12))	(1,520)	1,520
TWDV c/f	6,480	
Allowances		17,520

3   D – £300

	Main pool £	Car £	Allowances £
Period of account			
6 April 2012 to 5 April 2013			
TWDV b/f	900	7,000	
Disposal			
1 September 2012		(7,800)	
Balancing charge		(800) × 75%	(600)
WDA ≤ £1,000	(900)		900
TWDV c/f	0		
Allowances			300

The pool is written off in full as it does not exceed £1,000

4   D – £14,000

The car is a qualifying low emission car (CO_2 emissions 110g/km or less). 100% FYA for such cars.

5   D – £41,020

	£
AIA in full	25,000
WDA (£114,000 – £25,000) @ 18%	16,020
Total capital allowance	41,020

6   D – £27,019

9 month period of account.

AIA and WDA are pro rated for short period of account. Note though that a FYA is never pro rated.

	£
AIA in full (£25,000 × 9/12)	18,750
WDA (80,000 – 18,750) × 18% × 9/12	8,269
Total capital allowance	27,019

CHAPTER

5

7   B – £5,143

	Main pool £	Expensive car £	Allowances £
Period of account			
Year ended 31 December 2012			
TWDV b/f	11,800	14,000	
Acquisition – car (no FYA or AIA)	7,600		
	19,400		
WDA @ 18.5% (ie (20% × 3/12) + (18% × 9/12))	(3,589)		3,589
WDA @ 18.5% (max £3,000)		(2,590) x 60%	1,554
	15,811	11,410	
			5,143

CHAPTER 6

Trading profits – basis of assessment

Introduction

Examination context

Topic List

Summary and Self-test

Technical reference

Answers to Interactive questions

Answers to Self-test

Introduction

Learning outcomes

- Calculate the assessable trading profits for a new unincorporated business and identify the overlap profits on the commencement of trade

- Calculate the final assessable trading profits for an unincorporated business ceasing to trade

- Allocate the tax-adjusted profits of a partnership to each partner and calculate the final assessable profits for each partner for any given tax year

Specific syllabus references for this chapter are: 3f, g, h.

Syllabus links

The topics covered in this chapter are very important to your knowledge of how an unincorporated business is taxed.

When you tackle the Application paper later on in the Professional Stage, you will be expected to be very familiar with the concepts in this chapter.

Examination context

In the examination candidates may be required to:

- Correctly apply the current year basis for taxing trading profits
- Calculate the taxable trading profits in the opening years of a business, including overlap profits
- Determine the taxable trading profits in the final tax year of a business
- Understand how partnership profits are allocated to individual partners and are taxed on them individually

For extra question practice on these topics go to the section of the Question Bank covering this chapter.

A significant amount of practice is required by candidates in order to be able to deal efficiently with opening year rules for sole traders and partnerships.

1 Current year basis

Section overview

- Rules are needed to link a period of account of an unincorporated business to a tax year.

- Under the current year basis, the basis period for the tax year is the 12 month period of account ending in that tax year.

1.1 Basis periods and tax years

In the previous two chapters, you learnt how to calculate the taxable trading profits of an unincorporated business. In this chapter you will learn how the taxable trading profits for a period of account are taxed in a particular tax year.

The tax year runs from 6 April to 5 April. Many businesses do not have periods of account ending on 5 April. Rules are needed to link a period of account of a business with a tax year to find the amount of taxable trading profits for that year. The period which is taxable in a particular tax year is called a **basis period** because it is the basis of assessment for that tax year.

The basic rule is called the current year basis (CYB). Under the current year basis, the basis period for the tax year is the taxable trading profits for the 12 month period of account ending in that tax year.

Worked example: Basis period

Sasha has been trading for many years, making up accounts to 31 December each year.

Her recent taxable trading profits have been as follows:

y/e 31 December 2011	£12,000
y/e 31 December 2012	£15,000

Requirement

What is the amount of taxable trading profit assessable in 2012/13?

Solution

The basis period for 2012/13 is the period of account ending 31 December 2012.

Sasha's taxable trading profit for 2012/13 is therefore £15,000

---

2 Opening years

Section overview

- Special rules are needed in the opening years of a business.

- In the first tax year, the actual basis applies (commencement to following 5 April).

- In the second tax year, the basis period depends on the length of the period of account (if any) ending in that tax year.

- In the third tax year, the current year basis usually applies.

2.1 Introduction

Special rules are needed for the opening years of a business. This is because there will not usually be a 12 month period of account ending in the tax year in which the business starts.

For example, a business may start on 1 July 2012 preparing accounts to 30 June 2013. The first tax year in which the business operates is 2012/13, as this is the tax year in which the date of commencement falls, but there is no 12-month period of account ending in that tax year.

The opening year rules ensure that there is an amount of taxable trading profit for each tax year that the business is trading.

2.2 First tax year

The basis of assessment in the first tax year that a business operates is the **actual basis**. This means that the taxable trading profits for the first tax year are the taxable trading profits of the business from the date of commencement to the following 5 April.

It will usually be necessary to time apportion the taxable trading profits in the first (and sometimes the second) period of account to find this amount. For examination purposes, time-apportionment should be made to the nearest month. In practice, apportionment is made on a daily basis.

Worked example: First tax year

Ahmed started trading on 1 October 2012. He decided to make up his accounts to 30 September each year and his results to 30 September 2013 show taxable trading profits of £18,000.

Requirement

What is the amount of taxable trading profit taxed in 2012/13?

Solution

The first tax year is 2012/13 as 1 October 2012 falls within this tax year.

The basis period runs from 1 October 2012 to 5 April 2013 (6 months).

The taxable trading profit taxed in 2012/13 is therefore £18,000 x 6/12 =   £9,000

2.3 Second tax year

The basis of assessment in the second tax year depends on the length of the period of account ending in the second tax year. There are four possibilities:

Period of account ending in tax year	Basis period
Less than 12 months long	First 12 months of trading
12 months long	That 12-month period of account
More than 12 months long	12 months to the end of the period of account ending in the second tax year
No such period of account	Actual basis (6 April to 5 April)

Worked example: Second tax year

Ernest started trading on 1 January 2012. He decided to make up accounts to 31 December. His taxable trading profit for the period of account for the year ended 31 December 2012 is £12,000.

Requirement

What are the amounts of taxable trading profits taxed in the first two tax years of trading?

Solution

First tax year (2011/12)
Actual basis
Basis period 1 January 2012 to 5 April 2012
3/12 × £12,000   £3,000

Second tax year (2012/13)
12 month period of account ending in 2nd tax year
Basis period 1 January 2012 to 31 December 2012
y/e 31 December 2012   £12,000

Interactive question 1: First and second tax years   [Difficulty level: Exam standard]

Scott started trading on 1 November 2011. He decided to make up his accounts to 31 July. His taxable trading profit for the 9 month period of account to 31 July 2012 is £18,000 and for the year ended 31 July 2013 is £48,000.

Requirement

Using the standard format below, compute the amounts of taxable trading profit taxed in the first two tax years of trading.

First tax year (20...../.....)

Basis period .... to ....

£ _____

Second tax year (20...../.....)

Basis period .... to ....

£ _____

See the **Answer** at the end of this chapter.

2.4   Third tax year

Usually, the current year basis applies to the third tax year of trading because there will be a 12 month period of account ending in that tax year.

Occasionally, there will not be a 12 month period of account ending in the third tax year. In this case the basis period will be the 12 months to the end of the period of account ending in the third tax year.

Worked example: Third tax year

Sergio started trading on 1 February 2011. He decided to make up his accounts to 30 April each year.

Sergio has taxable trading profits of £30,000 for the 15-month period ended 30 April 2012 and £12,000 for the year ended 30 April 2013.

Requirement

What are the amounts of taxable trading profits taxed in the first three tax years of trading?

Solution

First tax year (2010/11)
Actual basis
Basis period 1 February 2011 to 5 April 2011
2/15 × £30,000   £4,000

Second tax year (2011/12)
No period of account ending in 2nd tax year
Basis period 6 April 2011 to 5 April 2012
12/15 × £30,000   £24,000

Third tax year (2012/13)
Period of account ending in 3rd tax year more than 12 months
Basis period 1 May 2011 to 30 April 2012
12/15 × £30,000   £24,000

3 Overlap profits

Section overview

- The application of the opening year rules means that some taxable trading profits may be taxed twice.

- Such profits are called overlap profits.

3.1 Overlap profits

You may have noticed that the way the opening year rules apply means that some taxable trading profit is taxed in more than one tax year.

Choosing a period of account which ends on a date other than 5 April will result in this double counting and any trading profits taxed more than once are called **overlap profits**.

Overlap profits are carried forward to be relieved in the future, as we will see later in this chapter.

Worked example: Overlap profits

Maureen starts trading on 1 June 2011. She decides to make up accounts to 31 July.

For the 14 month period of account ended 31 July 2012, her taxable trading profit is £20,160.

Requirement

What amounts of taxable trading profits are taxed in the first two tax years of trading and what is the amount of overlap profits?

Solution

First tax year (2011/12)
Actual basis
Basis period 1 June 2011 to 5 April 2012
10/14 × £20,160   £14,400

Second tax year (2012/13)
Period of account in 2nd tax year exceeds 12 months
Basis period 1 August 2011 to 31 July 2012
12/14 × £20,160   £17,280

Overlap profits
Period of overlap 1 August 2011 to 5 April 2012
Overlap profits
8/14 × £20,160   £11,520

Interactive question 2: Opening years [Difficulty level: Exam standard]

Connie starts a trade on 1 January 2011 and has the following taxable trading profits:

6 months to 30 June 2011	£28,500
12 months to 30 June 2012	£48,000

Requirement

Using the standard format below, show the amounts of taxable trading profits taxed in the first three tax years of trading and the amount of overlap profits.

First tax year (20......./.......)

Basis period .... to ....

£ _____

Second tax year (20......./.......)

Basis period .... to ....

£ _____

Third tax year (20...../.....)

Basis period .... to ....

£ _____

Overlap profits
Period of overlap............. to .... and .... to ....
Overlap profits

£ _____

See the **Answer** at the end of this chapter.

4 Closing years

Section overview

- The final tax year is the tax year in which the business ceases to trade.

- The basis period for the final tax year is from the end of the basis period for the previous tax year to the date of cessation.

- Any overlap profits are deducted from taxable trading profits in the final tax year.

4.1 Final tax year

The final tax year for a business is the tax year in which the business ceases to trade, ie the tax year in which the date of cessation of trade falls.

The basis period for the final tax year is from the end of the basis period for the penultimate tax year to the date of cessation. Other rules apply if a business ceases within the first two tax years of trading, but these are not in the syllabus.

Worked example: Final tax year

Darren started trading on 1 May 2009. He chose to make up his accounts to 31 December each year. He had taxable trading profits of £10,000 for the year ended 31 December 2011.

Darren ceased trading on 30 November 2012. His final accounting period was the 11 months to 30 November 2012 and his taxable trading profits for that period were £6,000.

Requirement

What amounts of taxable trading profits are taxed in the final two tax years of trading?

Solution

Final tax year (2012/13)
End of previous basis period to cessation
Basis period 1 January 2012 to 30 November 2012
11 month p/e 30 November 2012   **£6,000**

Penultimate tax year (2011/12)
CYB
Basis period 1 January 2011 to 31 December 2011
y/e 31 December 2011   **£10,000**

4.2 Penultimate tax year

Usually, the current year basis will apply to the penultimate tax year (ie 12 month period of account ending in the penultimate tax year).

If the final period of account exceeds 12 months, there may be no period of account ending in the penultimate tax year. In this case, the basis period for the penultimate tax year will be the 12 months to the normal year-end date falling in that tax year.

4.3 Relief for overlap profits

Overlap profits arising in the opening years are deducted from the taxable trading profits in the final tax year.

 Interactive question 3: Opening and closing years   [Difficulty level: Exam standard]

Ian started trading on 1 August 2008. He chose to make up his accounts to 31 May each year.

Ian had the following taxable trading profits:

10 months to 31 May 2009	£24,000
y/e 31 May 2010	£31,000
y/e 31 May 2011	£44,000

Ian's business ceased on 30 April 2012. His taxable trading profits for the last eleven months of the business were £38,000.

Requirement

Using the standard format below, show the amounts of taxable trading profits taxed in all tax years.

First tax year (20...../........)
Basis period .... to ....

     £ _____

Second tax year (20...../........)
Basis period .... to ....

     £ _____

Third tax year (20...../......)
Basis period .... to ....

     £ _____

Overlap profits
Period of overlap .... to .... and .... to ....
Overlap profits

     £ _____

Penultimate tax year (20...../........)
Basis period .... to ....

     £ _____

Final tax year (20...../.....)
Basis period .... to ....
Less: overlap profits

     £ _____

See the **Answer** at the end of this chapter.

5 Partnerships

Section overview

- A partnership itself is not a taxable person.

- Each partner is liable to income tax on his share (and only his share) of the partnership's taxable trading profits.

- The current year basis applies to continuing partnerships.

- Opening and closing year rules apply to partners who join and leave the partnership but the continuing partners remain on the current year basis.

5.1 How partners are taxed

A partnership is a collection of one or more individuals carrying on a business with a view to profit. Usually, partnerships are based on unlimited liability of the partners. It is also possible to form a limited liability partnership (LLP). Both types of partnership are taxed in the same way.

The partnership itself is not a taxable person for income tax purposes. Instead, the partners will be liable to tax on their individual shares of the taxable trading profits of the partnership on the same basis as a sole trader. Therefore, for a continuing partnership, the basis of assessment for a tax year will be the current year basis. Opening and closing year rules also apply.

The partnership accounts will be produced in a similar way to those for a sole trader. As for a sole trader, adjustments will need to be made to the accounting profit and capital allowances deducted to produce a figure for taxable trading profits. In this section we will see how that figure is then divided between the partners to calculate the taxable trading profit taxable on each partner.

5.2 Allocation of partnership profits

The taxable trading profits of the partnership are allocated between the partners according to the profit-sharing agreement for the period of account.

The agreement may specify that one or more of the partners is entitled to a 'salary' (in fact, simply an allocation of profits) and/or interest on capital introduced into the partnership. These amounts should be allocated first and then the remaining amount of taxable trading profits should be allocated in accordance with the agreed profit-sharing ratio (PSR).

After allocation, assessments are calculated for the partners using the same rules as for sole traders.

Worked example: Partnership

Erin and Cassandra have been in partnership for several years. The taxable trading profit of the partnership for the year ending 31 March 2013 is £55,000.

The profit-sharing agreement for the partnership provides for Erin to be paid a salary of £10,000 a year and Cassandra to be paid a salary of £15,000 a year. Any remaining profits are divided between Erin and Cassandra in the ratio 2:1.

Requirement

What is the taxable trading profit for Erin and Cassandra for 2012/13?

Solution

	Total £	Erin £	Cassandra £
Salary	25,000	10,000	15,000
Balance 2:1	30,000	20,000	10,000
Totals	55,000	30,000	25,000

For the year ended 31 March 2013 Erin has taxable trading profits of £30,000 and Cassandra has taxable trading profits of £25,000. As the partnership is not new this will be taxed on each partner on a CYB in 2012/13.

You need to be particularly careful where there is a change in the profit-sharing agreement during the period of account. The best way of tackling such questions is to divide the period of account into the periods of the different profit sharing agreements. Make sure that you time-apportion any salaries and interest on capital as appropriate.

 Interactive question 4: Partnership profit allocation   [Difficulty level: Exam standard]

Calder, Scott and Tim have been in partnership for several years. Partnership accounts are made up to 31 May. The partnership had taxable trading profits of £136,000 for the year ended 31 May 2012.

Until 30 September 2011, the partnership had shared profits equally. From 1 October 2011 it was agreed that the partners should be paid a salary and the profit sharing ratio was amended as follows:

	Calder	Scott	Tim
Salary per year	£50,000	£40,000	£30,000
PSR	25%	35%	40%

Requirement

Using the standard format below, compute the amount of taxable trading profit for each partner in 2012/13.

	Total £	Calder £	Scott £	Tim £
First PSR period				
.... to				
PSR				
Second PSR period				
.... to				
Salaries				
PSR				
Totals				

See the **Answer** at the end of this chapter.

Summary and Self-test

Summary

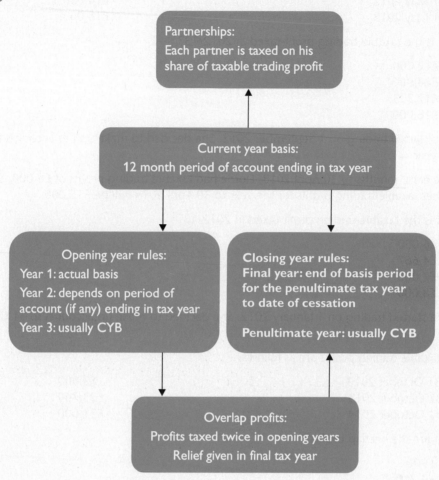

Partnerships:
Each partner is taxed on his
share of taxable trading profit

Current year basis:
12 month period of account ending in tax year

Opening year rules:
Year 1: actual basis
Year 2: depends on period of account (if any) ending in tax year
Year 3: usually CYB

Closing year rules:
Final year: end of basis period for the penultimate tax year to date of cessation

Penultimate year: usually CYB

Overlap profits:
Profits taxed twice in opening years
Relief given in final tax year

Answer the following questions.

1   Gordon has been trading for many years making up his accounts to 31 May each year. His taxable trading profits are as follows:

y/e 31 May 2011	£12,000
y/e 31 May 2012	£14,000
y/e 31 May 2013	£18,000

What is the taxable trading profit taxed in 2012/13?

A   £12,000
B   £14,000
C   £17,333
D   £18,000

2   Florrie started trading on 1 September 2012. She decided to make up her accounts to 30 April each year.

In the eight months to 30 April 2013, Florrie had taxable trading profits of £8,000. She estimates that her taxable trading profits for the year to 30 April 2014 will be £15,000.

What is the taxable trading profit taxed in 2012/13?

A   £6,000
B   £4,667
C   £7,000
D   £8,000

3   Ursula started trading on 1 January 2012. She decided to make up accounts to 31 October each year.

Her taxable trading profits are as follows:

p/e 31 October 2012	£3,000
y/e 31 October 2013	£23,760
y/e 31 October 2014	£31,000

What are the overlap profits?

A   £900
B   £4,710
C   £3,960
D   £4,860

4   Ross ceased trading on 31 March 2013. His taxable trading profits were:

y/e 31 December 2011	£6,800
y/e 31 December 2012	£5,600
p/e 31 March 2013	£4,500

Ross had £2,300 of overlap profits on commencement.

What is the taxable trading profit for 2012/13?

A   £10,100
B   £7,800
C   £6,400
D   £2,200

5   Anne and Jane have been in partnership for many years making up accounts to 30 November. The profit sharing agreement of the partnership is that Anne is entitled to an annual salary of £10,500 and Jane is entitled to an annual salary of £12,300. They are also entitled to interest at 5% on capital introduced to the partnership. Anne has capital of £52,500 and Jane has capital of £34,500. Any remaining profits are shared equally.

For the year ended 30 November 2012, the taxable trading profit of the partnership is £147,750.

What is the taxable trading profit of the partners for 2012/13?

A   Anne £60,300, Jane £60,300
B   Anne £73,425, Jane £74,325
C   Anne £73,875, Jane £73,875
D   Anne £87,000, Jane £87,900

Now go back to the Learning outcomes in the Introduction. If you are satisfied you have achieved these objectives, please tick them off.

Technical reference

Legislation

References relate to Income Tax (Trading and Other Income) Act 2005 (*ITTOIA 2005*) unless otherwise stated.

Current year basis	s.198
Opening years	ss.199-201
Overlap profits	ss.204-205
Closing years	ss.201-202
Partnerships	ss.846-856

HMRC manual

Business income manual (Found at http://www.hmrc.gov.uk/manuals/bimmanual/index.htm)

Computation of liability: The current year basis of assessment rules: General rule	BIM71010
Computation of liability: The current year basis of assessment rules: Basis of assessment in commencement years	BIM71015
Computation of liability: The current year basis of assessment rules: Overlap relief	BIM71075
Computation of liability: The current year basis of assessment rules: Basis of assessment on cessation	BIM71025
Partnerships: Computation & assessment: Profits and Losses Computed at Partnership Level	BIM72210
Partnerships: Computation & assessment: Allocation of Profits and Losses	BIM72240

This technical reference section is designed to assist you when you are working in the office. It should help you to know where to look for further information on the topics covered in this chapter. **You will not be examined on the contents of this section in your examination.**

Answers to Interactive questions

Answer to Interactive question 1

First tax year (2011/12)
Actual basis
Basis period 1 November 2011 to 5 April 2012
5/9 × £18,000 — £10,000

Second tax year (2012/13)
Period of account ending in second tax year less than 12 months
Basis period 1 November 2011 to 31 October 2012
9 months to 31 July 2012 — £18,000
1 August 2012 to 31 October 2012: 3/12 × £48,000 — £12,000
— £30,000

Answer to Interactive question 2

First tax year (2010/11)
Actual basis
Basis period 1 January 2011 to 5 April 2011
3/6 × £28,500 — £14,250

Second tax year (2011/12)
Period of account in second tax year less than 12 months
Basis period 1 January 2011 to 31 December 2011
6 months to 30 June 2011 — £28,500
1 July 2011 to 31 December 2011: 6/12 × £48,000 — £24,000
— £52,500

Third tax year (2012/13)
12 month period of account ending in third tax year
Basis period 1 July 2011 to 30 June 2012
y/e 30 June 2012 — £48,000

Overlap profits
Period of overlap 1 January 2011 to 5 April 2011 and 1 July 2011 to 31 December 2011
Overlap profits
3/6 × £28,500 — £14,250
6/12 × £48,000 — £24,000
— £38,250

Answer to Interactive question 3

First tax year (2008/09)
Actual basis
Basis period 1 August 2008 to 5 April 2009
8/10 × £24,000   £19,200

Second tax year (2009/10)
Period of account in second tax year less than 12 months
Basis period 1 August 2008 to 31 July 2009
10 months to 31 May 2009   £24,000
1 June 2009 to 31 July 2009: 2/12 × £31,000   £5,167
                                                                     £29,167

Third tax year (2010/11)
CYB
Basis period 1 June 2009 to 31 May 2010
y/e 31 May 2010   £31,000

Overlap profits
Period of overlap 1 August 2008 to 5 April 2009 and 1 June 2009 to 31 July 2009
Overlap profits
8/10 × £24,000   £19,200
2/12 × £31,000   £5,167
                                                                     £24,367

Penultimate tax year (2011/12)
CYB
Basis period 1 June 2010 to 31 May 2011
y/e 31 May 2011   £44,000

Final tax year (2012/13)
End of previous basis period to cessation
Basis period 1 June 2011 to 30 April 2012   £38,000
Less: overlap profits   £(24,367)
                                                                     £13,633

Answer to Interactive question 4

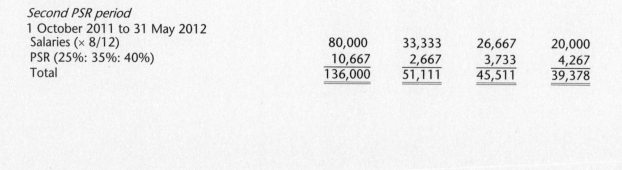

	Total £	Calder £	Scott £	Tim £
First PSR period				
1 June 2011 to 30 September 2011				
PSR (1:1:1)				
£136,000 × 4/12	45,333	15,111	15,111	15,111
Second PSR period				
1 October 2011 to 31 May 2012				
Salaries (× 8/12)	80,000	33,333	26,667	20,000
PSR (25%: 35%: 40%)	10,667	2,667	3,733	4,267
Total	136,000	51,111	45,511	39,378

1   B – £14,000

Current year basis applies to a continuing business. The taxable trading profit taxed in 2012/13 is that of the year ended 31 May 2012.

2   C – £7,000

The basis of assessment in the first tax year is the actual basis between commencement and the following 5 April.

7/8 × £8,000

Basis period 1 September 2012 to 5 April 2013   £7,000

3   D – £4,860

First tax year (2011/12)
Actual basis
Basis period 1 January 2012 to 5 April 2012

Second tax year (2012/13)
Period of account in second tax year less than 12 months
Basis period 1 January 2012 to 31 December 2012

Third tax year (2013/14)
Current year basis
Basis period 1 November 2012 to 31 October 2013

Overlap profits
Period of overlap 1 January 2012 to 5 April 2012 and 1 November 2012 to 31 December 2012
Overlap profits
3/10 × £3,000   £900
2/12 × £23,760   £3,960
                                                                                          £4,860

4   B – £7,800

Final tax year (2012/13)

Basis period 1 January 2012 to 31 March 2013
y/e 31 December 2012   £5,600
p/e 31 March 2013   £4,500
                                                                                £10,100
Less: overlap profits   £(2,300)
                                                                                          £7,800

5   B – Anne £73,425, Jane £74,325

	Total £	Anne £	Jane £
Salary	22,800	10,500	12,300
Interest (5% × £52,500/£34,500)	4,350	2,625	1,725
PSR 1:1	120,600	60,300	60,300
Totals	147,750	73,425	74,325

As the partnership is not new this will be taxed on each partner on a CYB in 2012/13.

CHAPTER 7

National insurance contributions

Introduction

Examination context

Topic List

Summary and Self-test

Technical reference

Answers to Interactive questions

Answers to Self-test

Learning outcomes

Tick off

- Identify the key features of the PAYE and national insurance system

- Calculate the total national insurance contributions payable by employees, employers and self-employed individuals

Specific syllabus references for this chapter are: 2b, 3j.

Syllabus links

It is important that you understand the calculations in this chapter as they are a vital element in considering the overall tax position of an individual and should not be overlooked.

When you tackle the Application paper later on in the Professional Stage, you will learn more about national insurance contributions, for example those paid by directors.

Examination context

In the examination candidates may be required to:

- Calculate national insurance contributions payable by employees and their employers
- Calculate national insurance contributions payable by sole traders and partners

For extra question practice on these topics go to the section of the Question Bank covering this chapter.

1 Classes and payment of national insurance contributions

> **Section overview**
>
> - National insurance contributions (NICs) are used to fund state benefits.
> - Class 1 contributions are paid by employees and employers.
> - Class 1A contributions are paid by employers.
> - Class 2 contributions and Class 4 contributions are paid by self-employed individuals.
> - NICs are administered by the National Insurance Contributions Office (NICO).

1.1 What are national insurance contributions?

National insurance contributions (NICs) are paid by self-employed individuals, employees and their employers. The contributions are used to bear part of the liability of the government to pay state benefits such as jobseekers allowance and state pensions.

The government has started a consultation process on the integration of the operation of income tax and national insurance contributions. The detail of the reforms is not expected until the Budget in 2013 and the reforms are unlikely to come into effect until 2017.

1.2 Classes of national insurance contributions

The classes of national insurance contributions with which you are concerned are:

Class 1   Paid by employees and their employers
Class 1A   Paid by employers
Class 2   Paid by self-employed individuals
Class 4   Paid by self-employed individuals

1.3 Payment of national insurance contributions

National insurance contributions are administered by the National Insurance Contributions Office (NICO) which is part of HM Revenue & Customs.

You have already seen that Class 1 contributions are collected under the PAYE system on a monthly basis.

Class 1A contributions are payable by 19 July (22 July if paid electronically) following the end of the tax year to which they relate.

Class 2 contributions are paid direct to NICO either by a monthly direct debit (four months in arrears) or twice yearly direct debit on 31 January in the tax year and 31 July following the tax year (in line with the self-assessment interim payment dates).

Class 4 contributions are collected together with income tax under the self assessment system, which is discussed later in this text.

2 Class 1 NICs

> **Section overview**
>
> - Class 1 primary contributions are paid by employees.
>
> - Class 1 secondary contributions are paid by employers.
>
> - Contributions are based on the employee's earnings period (usually weekly or monthly).
>
> - No contributions are due on earnings below the earnings threshold.
>
> - For primary contributions only, there is an upper earnings limit above which contributions are due at a lower rate.

2.1 Introduction

An employed individual is liable to Class 1 primary NICs. The employer is liable to Class 1 secondary NICs.

The amount of Class 1 NICs payable depends on the age of the employee, the level of the employee's earnings in the 'earnings period' and whether he is 'contracted out' of the State Second Pension (S2P).

All employees aged between 16 and state retirement age (currently 65 for men, 60 for women rising to 65 by November 2018) are liable to pay Class 1 primary NICs. Payments start on the employee's 16th birthday and cease on her 60th or his 65th birthday.

From December 2018 the state retirement age for both men and women will start to increase to reach 66 in October 2020.

Employers must pay Class 1 secondary NICs for all employees aged over 16. There is no upper age limit.

An employee's earnings for Class 1 NIC purposes include all earnings received in monetary form: salary, commission, bonus plus vouchers exchangeable for cash, goods or services. Earnings do not usually include any taxable benefits.

Most employees are paid at regular intervals (weekly or monthly). This period is the 'earnings period'.

Part of Class 1 NICs are used to fund the S2P. If the employee has contracted out of the S2P via membership of his employer's occupational pension scheme, Class 1 NICs are payable at a reduced rate. From 6 April 2012 contracting out is abolished for money-purchase schemes. It continues to be available for salary-related schemes. Additionally, from 6 April 2012 individuals can no longer contract out of S2P if they are members of a personal pension scheme. However, for the purposes of this exam, you should assume that employees are **not** contracted out of S2P.

2.2 Primary Class 1 contributions

The primary Class 1 NICs for 2012/13 for employees not contracted out of S2P are as follows:

Employee's earnings	Primary contributions payable
Not above primary earnings threshold (PT) (£146 per week or £634 per month)	Nil
Between PT and upper earnings limit (UEL) (£817 per week or £3,540 per month)	Earnings less PT × 12%
In excess of UEL	UEL less PT × 12% plus Earnings less UEL × 2%

Worked example: Class 1 primary contributions

Meg is employed by Green Ltd and is paid £424 weekly.

Munroe is also employed by Green Ltd and is paid £4,080 monthly.

Requirement

What are the weekly and monthly Class 1 primary contributions of Meg and Munroe respectively?

Solution

Meg
(£424 − £146) = £278 × 12%   £33

Munroe

	£
(£3,540− £634) = £2,906 × 12% =	349
(£4,080 − £3,540) = £540 × 2% =	11
Total	360

In the examination, you might be asked to work out the annual NICs payable by an employee. In this case, it is acceptable to use the annualised limits of £7,605 (PT) and £42,475 (UEL) if the employee is paid evenly throughout the tax year. If the employee receives an additional payment such as a bonus in one earnings period, it will be necessary to calculate the NICs in relation to weekly or monthly earnings periods instead.

Worked example: Annual Class 1 primary contributions

Raj and Debbie are employed by Magenta Ltd. They are each paid £2,300 a month. In addition, Raj is paid a bonus in January 2013 of £2,000.

Requirement

What are the Class 1 primary contributions payable by Raj and Debbie for 2012/13?

Solution

Raj
11 months

	£
(£2,300 − £634) = £1,666 × 12% = £200 × 11 months	2,200

1 month
(£3,540 − £634) = £2,906 × 12% =	349
(£4,300 − £3,540) = £760 × 2%	15
	2,564

Debbie
£2,300 × 12 = £27,600 − £7,605 = £19,995 × 12%   2,399

2.3 Secondary Class 1 contributions

The secondary Class 1 NICs for 2012/13 for employees not contracted out of S2P are as follows:

Employee's earnings	Secondary contributions payable
Not above secondary earnings threshold (ST) (£144 per week or £624 per month)	Nil
Above ST	Earnings less ST × 13.8%

Worked example: Class 1 secondary contributions

Meg is employed by Green Ltd and paid is £424 weekly.

Munroe is also employed by Green Ltd and paid is £4,080 monthly.

Requirement

Calculate the weekly and monthly secondary Class 1 contributions payable by Green Ltd in respect of Meg and Munroe respectively.

Solution

Meg
(£424 – £144) = £280 × 13.8%   £39

Munroe
(£4,080 – £624) = £3,456 × 13.8%   £477

Again, if you are required to compute the annual secondary NICs payable by an employer, you can use the annualised ST of £7,488. In this case, the payment of additional amounts, such as bonuses, will not affect the calculation since there is no upper earnings limit for secondary contributions.

Interactive question 1: Class 1 contributions   [Difficulty level: Exam standard]

Chloe is an employee of Cyan Ltd. She earns a salary of £26,196 which is paid monthly. In November 2012, she receives a bonus of £4,415.

Requirement

Using the standard format below, compute the Class 1 contributions payable in respect of Chloe's employment for 2012/13.

Class 1 Primary contributions
11 months

£

£ (............. – ....) = £............. × ....% = ... × 11 months

1 month
£ (............. – ....) = £............. × ....% =
£ (............. – ....) = £............. × ....% =

_____
=======

Class 1 Secondary contributions
11 months

£

£ (............. – ....) = £............. × ....% = ... × 11 months

1 month
£ (............. – ....) = £............. × ....% =

_____
=======

See **Answer** at the end of this chapter.

---

3 Class 1A NICs

Section overview

- Class 1A contributions are payable by employers on taxable benefits provided to employees.

3.1 Class 1A contributions

Employers are also liable to pay Class 1A contributions on taxable benefits provided to employees at the rate of 13.8%.

The value of the taxable benefits for NICs is generally the same as the taxable value for income tax. However, any benefits taxed as earnings under Class 1 are not also subject to Class 1A charge.

Worked example: Class 1A contributions

Beryl is employed by Z plc. During 2012/13, she received the following benefits:

	£
Medical insurance	810
Car benefit	3,500
Vouchers exchangeable for goods	750
Pension advice (available to all employees)	100

Beryl is a higher rate taxpayer.

Requirement

Calculate the Class 1A contributions payable by Z plc.

Solution

Class 1A

(£810 + £3,500) = £4,310 × 13.8%   £595

The vouchers exchangeable for goods are earnings and so will be subject to Class 1 NICs. Pension advice up to £150 is an exempt benefit.

4 Class 2 NICs

Section overview

- Class 2 contributions are paid by the self-employed at a fixed weekly rate.
- There is an exception where earnings are below the small earnings exception.

4.1 Flat rate contributions

A self-employed individual aged between 16 and state retirement age is required to pay flat rate weekly Class 2 contributions (£2.65 per week for 2012/13).

Payments start on the individual's 16th birthday and cease on her 60th or his 65th birthday.

4.2 Small earnings exception

No contributions are payable if the individual's earnings are below the small earnings exception (£5,595 for 2012/13).

Earnings for Class 2 purposes are the financial accounts net profit (not the taxable trading profit) earned over the tax year. If the individual does not produce accounts to 5 April, it will be necessary to time apportion the profits of the periods of account running through the tax year.

4.3 Registering to pay Class 2 NICs

A newly self-employed individual must register as self-employed as soon as possible, either via form CWFI or by telephone to HMRC.

5 Class 4 NICs

Section overview

- Class 4 contributions are based on tax adjusted earnings.
- No contributions are due on earnings below the annual lower profits limit.
- Contributions are due at a lower rate on earnings above the annual upper profits limit.

5.1 Earnings related contributions

In addition to the flat rate Class 2 liability, self-employed individuals may also be liable to pay Class 4 NICs based on their taxable trading profit.

An individual is liable to pay Class 4 contributions if aged 16 or over at the start of the tax year and ceases to be liable if his 65th (or her 60th) birthday has been reached by the start of the tax year.

In a partnership, each partner is responsible for paying Class 2 and 4 contributions based on his own share of the profits.

Class 4 NICs for 2012/13 are as follows:

Earnings	Class 4 contributions payable
Not above lower profits limit (£7,605)	Nil
Between lower profits limit and upper profits limit (£42,475)	Earnings less lower profits limit × 9%
In excess of upper profits limit	Upper profits limit less lower profits limit × 9% plus Earnings less upper profits limit × 2%

Worked example: Class 2 and 4 contributions

Andreas has been self-employed for many years. He makes up his accounts to 31 July each year. His recent results have been:

	Net accounting profit £	Taxable trading profit £
y/e 31 July 2012	7,800	8,150
y/e 31 July 2013	4,890	3,520

Requirement

What are the Class 2 and Class 4 NICs (if any) payable by Andreas in 2012/13?

Solution

Class 2 contributions
2012/13 tax year

	£
y/e 31 July 2012	
4/12 × £7,800	2,600
y/e 31 July 2013	
8/12 × £4,890	3,260
	5,860
Above small earnings exception	
52 × £2.65	138

Class 4 contributions
2012/13 tax year
y/e 31 July 2012
(£8,150 – £7,605) = £545 × 9%   49

 Interactive question 2: Class 2 and 4 contributions   [Difficulty level: Exam standard]

Nisar is self employed. He makes up accounts to 31 December each year. His taxable trading profit for the year ended 31 December 2012 is £45,000 and he estimates his taxable trading profit for the year to 31 December 2013 will exceed this figure.

Requirement

Using the standard format below, compute the Class 2 and Class 4 NICs payable by Nisar for 2012/13.

Class 2 contributions   £
.... × £ ....   ═══════

Class 4 contributions
(£............. – £.............) = £............. × ....%
(£............. – £.............) = £............. × ....%   ───────
                                                                                  ═══════

See **Answer** at the end of this chapter.

Summary

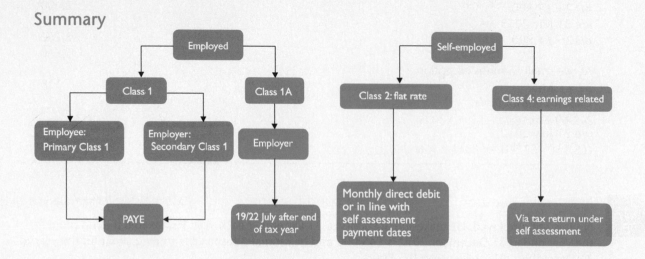

Self-test

Answer the following questions.

1   Caroline is paid an annual salary of £10,000, paid monthly, in 2012/13. In addition, she receives a bonus of £600 in December 2012 and her employer provides her with a video camera for which the taxable benefit is £300.

On what amounts are Class 1 secondary contributions payable by her employer?

A   £10,000
B   £10,300
C   £10,600
D   £10,900

2   Jeremy (who is not contracted out of S2P) has the following employment income for 2012/13:

Gross salary   £35,210
Taxable benefits   £5,000

What Class 1 secondary contributions are payable by his employer for 2012/13? Use an annualised basis.

A   £4,859
B   £3,826
C   £4,516
D   £3,313

3   Maureen is employed by Treen Ltd. In 2012/13, she was paid a monthly salary of £2,518. In September 2012 she was paid a bonus of £5,000.

What are the Class 1 primary contributions payable by Maureen for 2012/13?

A   £3,313
B   £2,915
C   £4,226
D   £3,822

4   James has been self-employed for many years. His taxable trading profits are as follows:

y/e 31 October 2012   £14,210
y/e 31 October 2013   £20,000

What are his Class 4 NICs for 2012/13?

A   £594
B   £855
C   £792
D   £1,279

5   Len is self-employed. He makes up his accounts to 31 March each year and for the year ended 31 March 2013, his taxable trading profit is £55,000.

What are the total NICs payable by Len for 2012/13?

A   £3,389
B   £3,527
C   £4,300
D   £4,430

6   Julie works for D Ltd earning £15,000 per year. She benefits from childcare vouchers provided by D Ltd of £55 per week for 50 weeks in the tax year. Julie has a company car on which there is a taxable benefit of £4,500 per year.

What Class 1A National Insurance contributions are D Ltd required to make?

Class 1A contributions £ [   ]

Your answer to this question must be to the nearest whole number.

Now go back to the Learning outcomes in the Introduction. If you are satisfied you have achieved these objectives, please tick them off.

Legislation

References relate to Social Security Contributions and Benefits Act 1992 (*SSCBA 1992*)

Class 1 contributions	ss.5 – 9
Class 1A contributions	s.10
Class 2 contributions	s.11
Class 4 contributions	ss.15 – 16

HMRC manual

National insurance manual (Found at http://www.hmrc.gov.uk/manuals/nimmanual/index.htm)

Class 1 Structural Overview: General	NIM01001
Class 1A Liability: Liability for Class 1A NICs	NIM13001
Class 2 Liability: Liability for Class 2 NICs	NIM20001
Class 4 NICs Liability: General	NIM24001

This technical reference section is designed to assist you when you are working in the office. It should help you to know where to look for further information on the topics covered in this chapter. **You will not be examined on the contents of this section in your examination.**

Answer to Interactive question 1

Class 1 Primary contributions
11 months

	£
(£2,183 – £602) = £1,581 × 12% = £190 × 11 months	2,090

1 month

(£3,540 – £602) = £2,938 × 12%	353
(£6,598 – £3,540) = £3,058 × 2%	61
	2,504

Class 1 Secondary contributions
11 months

	£
(£2,183 – £624) = £1,559 × 13.8% = £215 × 11 months	2,365

1 month

(£6,598 – £624) = £5,974 × 13.8%	824
	3,189

You could also have used the annualised method which would give:

(£30,611 – £7,488) = £23,123 × 13.8%	£3,191

The difference between the two figures is due to rounding.

Answer to Interactive question 2

Class 2 contributions

Clearly above small earnings exception

	£
52 × £2.65	138

Class 4 contributions

y/e 31 December 2010

(£42,475 – £7,605) = £34,870 × 9%	3,138
(£45,000 – £42,475) = £2,525 × 2%	51
	3,189

1   C – Class 1 secondary contributions on £10,600.

2   B – £3,826

Class 1 Secondary contributions
(£35,210 – £7,488) = £27,722 × 13.8%   3,826

3   B – £2,915

Class 1 Primary contributions
11 months

                                                                                   £
(£2,518 – £634) = £1,884 × 12% = £226 × 11 months   2,486

1 month
(£3,540 – £634) = £2,906 × 12%   349
(£7,518 – £3,540) = £3,978 × 2%   80
                                                                               2,915

4   A – £594

Class 4 contributions
y/e 31 October 2012
(£14,210 – £7,605) = £6,605 × 9%   594

5   B – £3,527 (£3,389 + £138)

Class 2 contributions
52 × £2.65   138

Class 4 contributions

y/e 31 March 2013

                                                                                   £
(£42,475 – £7,605) = £34,870 × 9%   3,138
(£55,000 – £42,475) = £12,525 × 2%   251
                                                                               3,389

6   The correct answer is £ ⎢ 621 ⎢

Class 1A is payable by D Ltd at 13.8% on the value of the car benefit of £4,500.

D Ltd would pay Class 1 secondary contributions on Julie's earnings. Childcare vouchers up to £55 per week are exempt as she is a basic rate taxpayer.

CHAPTER 8

Capital gains tax – individuals

Introduction

Examination context

Topic List

Summary and Self-test

Technical reference

Answers to Interactive questions

Answers to Self-test

Learning objectives

- Classify persons, assets and disposals as either chargeable or exempt for capital gains purposes

- Calculate the chargeable gains and losses on the disposal of assets

- Calculate total taxable gains for both individuals and companies and for individuals calculate the capital gains tax payable

Specific syllabus references for this chapter are: 4a, b, c.

Syllabus links

The topics in this chapter are basic knowledge that you will be expected to know very well when you study for the Application paper and at the Advanced Stage.

In the Application paper, you will learn more about capital gains, including the rules for more complicated disposals such as shares and leases, how to use capital losses and capital gains tax reliefs.

Examination context

In the examination candidates may be required to:

- Determine when a gain or loss arises
- Compute a gain or loss on disposal of a capital asset
- Calculate the capital gains tax payable for the tax year
- Calculate any gain or loss on disposal of a chattel

For extra question practice on these topics go to the section of the Question Bank covering this chapter.

1 Chargeable and exempt persons, assets and disposals

Section overview

- Individuals pay capital gains tax (CGT), companies pay corporation tax on their chargeable gains.
- Chargeable persons include individuals, partners and companies.
- Chargeable disposals include sales and gifts.
- Death is not an occasion of charge for CGT, but there is a tax-free uplift of the value of assets passed on death.
- Chargeable assets include tangible and intangible assets.
- Exempt assets include cars, some chattels and investments held in ISAs.

1.1 Introduction

A capital gain may arise on the disposal of a capital asset such as land, shares or a work of art. Usually, if the asset has increased in value since it was acquired, there will be a chargeable gain on its disposal. If the asset has fallen in value, there will be an allowable loss on its disposal.

In this chapter we will deal primarily with the rules on capital gains for individuals. Individuals pay capital gains tax (CGT) on their taxable gains. CGT applies to taxable gains in a tax year. For example, an individual will be liable to CGT in 2012/13 on gains arising between 6 April 2012 and 5 April 2013.

Similar rules apply to capital gains realised by companies and we will deal with the differences between the two sets of rules when you study corporation tax later in this text.

The first step in deciding whether there is a chargeable gain or allowable loss is to ascertain whether a **chargeable person** has made a **chargeable disposal** of a **chargeable asset**. We will deal with this question in the remainder of this section.

1.2 Chargeable persons

Chargeable persons include:

- Individuals
- Business partners, who are each treated as owning a share of partnership assets and taxed individually on the disposal of that share (details not in your syllabus)
- Companies, which pay corporation tax on their chargeable gains, not CGT

Some persons are specifically exempt from capital gains. These include registered charities and friendly societies, local authorities, registered pension schemes, investment trusts and approved scientific research associations.

1.3 Chargeable disposals

Chargeable disposals include:

- The sale of the whole or part of an asset
- The gift of the whole or part of an asset
- The loss or destruction of the whole or part of an asset

Exempt disposals include gifts to charities, art galleries, museums and similar institutions, provided that the asset is used for the purposes of the institution.

Death is not a disposal for capital gains tax purposes and so no CGT applies on death. However, the people entitled to receive the assets from the estate of the deceased person will acquire those assets at probate value (market value at the date of death). This is sometimes called the **tax-free uplift** on death.

The date of disposal is the date when the contract for sale is made. If the contract is conditional the date of disposal is the date when all conditions are satisfied. The date legal title passes, or physical possession is obtained, or the date payment is made, is irrelevant.

1.4 Chargeable and exempt assets

Chargeable assets are defined as all capital assets except those which are specifically exempt from CGT.

Chargeable assets include both tangible assets (such as land, furniture, works of art) and intangible assets (such as the goodwill of a business, shares, leases).

Exempt assets include:

- Legal tender (ie cash)

- Motor cars (including vintage and classic cars)

- Most wasting chattels

- Chattels which are not wasting chattels if acquisition cost and gross disposal consideration do not exceed £6,000

- Gilt-edged securities (such as Exchequer Stock or Treasury Stock)

- National Savings Certificates and premium bonds

- Shares and investments held in an Individual Savings Account (ISA)

2 Computing a gain or loss

Section overview

- A gain or loss is calculated by deducting allowable costs from disposal consideration.

- Disposal consideration is sale proceeds or market value.

- Allowable costs include costs of acquiring the asset and cost of enhancing its value.

Overview of computation of a chargeable gain or allowable loss:

	£
Disposal consideration	X
Less: Incidental costs of disposal	(X)
Net disposal consideration	X
Less: Allowable costs	(X)
Chargeable gain/Allowable loss	X/(X)

2.1 Disposal consideration

If the asset is sold in a commercial transaction, ie sold at arm's length, the disposal consideration is the gross sale proceeds.

If the asset is not sold at arm's length, for example the asset is gifted, the disposal consideration is the market value of the asset.

From the disposal value, incidental costs of disposal can be deducted to give the net disposal consideration.

Incidental costs of disposal include legal fees, estate agents' and auctioneers' fees and advertising costs.

2.2 Allowable costs for CGT purposes

In order to calculate a gain or loss, you need to deduct allowable costs from the net disposal consideration.

Allowable costs are:

- Acquisition cost of the asset: purchase price if bought, market value of asset if gifted, probate value if acquired on death

- Incidental costs of acquisition such as legal fees, surveyor's or valuer's fees, stamp duty land tax, stamp duty

- Enhancement expenditure: capital costs of additions and improvements to the asset reflected in the value of the asset at the date of disposal, such as extensions, planning permission and architects fees for extensions

Worked example: Allowable costs

Paul bought a holiday cottage in June 2000. The cottage cost £120,000 and he paid surveyor's fees of £1,500 and legal fees of £1,000 in connection with the acquisition.

In August 2001, Paul spent the following on improvements to the cottage:

£2,000 installing central heating

£500 on repairs to the roof

£1,200 redecoration

£5,000 on a sun room extension

In December 2005, during a storm, the sun room was destroyed and not replaced.

Paul sold the cottage at auction in July 2012. The gross sale proceeds were £180,000. Auctioneers' fees were £4,500 and he also paid legal fees of £1,200 on the sale.

Requirement

What is Paul's chargeable gain on sale?

Solution

	£	£
Gross sale proceeds	180,000	
Less: auctioneers' fees	(4,500)	
legal fees	(1,200)	
Net disposal consideration		174,300
Less: acquisition cost	120,000	
surveyor's fees	1,500	
legal fees	1,000	
enhancement expenditure (central heating)	2,000	(124,500)
Chargeable gain		49,800

Note that the repairs to the roof and the redecoration are not capital expenditure and so cannot qualify as enhancement expenditure. The cost of the sun room is not deductible as enhancement expenditure because it is not reflected in the value of the cottage at the time of disposal.

Mark bought a plot of land in May 1997 for £70,000. He incurred legal costs of £2,000 on the purchase and surveryor's fees of £1,400.

Mark sold the land in July 2012 for £76,000. He incurred advertising costs of £1,800 and legal costs of £2,600 on the sale.

Requirement

Using the standard format below, calculate Mark's chargeable gain/allowable loss on sale.

	£	£
Gross sale proceeds		
Less: incidental costs of sale		
		―――
Net disposal consideration		
Less: allowable costs		
	―――	
		(___)
Chargeable gain/Allowable loss		═══

See **Answer** at the end of this chapter.

3 Capital gains tax payable by individuals

Section overview

- Each individual is entitled to an annual exempt amount each tax year.
- CGT is chargeable separately from income tax, at 18% or 28%, depending on the individual's taxable income.

3.1 Annual exempt amount

Each individual is entitled to an annual exempt amount each tax year. For 2012/13 the annual exempt amount is £10,600.

The annual exempt amount is deducted from chargeable gains to produce gains liable to CGT, called **taxable gains.**

If the annual exempt amount is unused in a year it is wasted, and cannot be used in any other tax year.

3.2 Computing capital gains tax

Individuals are taxed on their taxable gains separately from their taxable income.

Taxable gains are taxed at the rate of 18% or 28% depending on the level of the individual's taxable income.

The rate of CGT is 28% if the individual is a higher or additional rate taxpayer. If the individual is a basic rate taxpayer then CGT is payable at 18% on an amount of taxable gains up to the amount of the individual's unused basic rate band and at 28% on the excess.

Worked example: CGT liability

Olly has taxable income in 2012/13 of £28,500. He makes taxable gains of £20,000 in the year. Olly's sister Alice has taxable income of £5,000 in 2012/13. She makes taxable gains of £17,000 in the year.

Requirement

Calculate Olly's and Alice's CGT liability for 2012/13.

Solution

	£
Olly	
(£34,370 – £28,500) £5,870 × 18%	1,057
(£20,000 – £5,870) £14,130 × 28%	3,956
CGT liability	5,013

Taxable gains are already net of the annual exempt amount.

Taxable income is net of the personal allowance. Olly has £5,870 of unused basic rate band remaining and this amount of the taxable gains are taxed at 18%. The remainder of the taxable gains of £14,130 are taxed at 28%.

	£
Alice	
£17,000 × 18%	3,060

Alice has £29,370 unused basic rate band so her taxable gains are all taxed at 18%

Interactive question 2: CGT liability   [Difficulty level: Exam standard]

Philippa made the following disposals during 2012/13:

- Vintage car (sold for £2,000, cost £9,500)
- Antique vase (sold for £45,000, cost £12,700)
- Cash (gift to her brother) £8,000
- Treasury stock (sold for £12,300, cost £8,250)

Philippa is a higher rate taxpayer.

Requirement

Using the standard format below, compute Philippa's taxable gains and capital gains tax liability for 2012/13.

	£
Net chargeable gains	
Less: annual exempt amount	( )
Taxable gains	
CGT liability:	

See **Answer** at the end of this chapter.

4 Chattels

Section overview

- Chattels are tangible moveable property.
- Wasting chattels are usually exempt from CGT.
- Non-wasting chattels are usually chargeable to CGT.
- Non-wasting chattels bought and sold for £6,000 or less are exempt.
- Marginal relief applies to gains on non-wasting chattels sold for more than £6,000.
- Losses are restricted on non-wasting chattels sold for less than £6,000.

4.1 What are chattels?

A chattel is an item of tangible moveable property, and specifically does not include goodwill, shares or leases.

A chattel is a **wasting chattel** if it has a predictable life at the date of disposal not exceeding 50 years. Examples include caravans, boats, and computers and animals. Plant and machinery are always treated as having a useful life of less than 50 years.

A **non-wasting chattel** is one with a predictable life at the date of disposal of more than 50 years. Examples include antiques, jewellery and works of art.

4.2 Wasting chattels

Wasting chattels are usually exempt from CGT so there will be no chargeable gain or allowable loss on disposal.

However, if the asset has been used solely in a business and the owner has, or could have, claimed capital allowances on the asset, it will be treated as a non-wasting chattel.

4.3 Non-wasting chattels

Non-wasting chattels are generally chargeable to CGT, subject to some special rules.

- If the asset is disposed of for gross disposal proceeds of £6,000 or less and acquired for £6,000 or less it is exempt.

- If the asset is disposed for gross disposal proceeds of more than £6,000 and the acquisition cost is £6,000 or less, there is marginal relief for the gain. The gain cannot exceed:

  5/3 × (Gross proceeds less £6,000)

Worked example: Chattels – gain

Martin bought a vase for £4,000 in July 2004. He sold it at auction for £7,000 in December 2012. The costs of sale amounted to £350.

Requirement

What is Martin's chargeable gain on sale?

Solution

	£	£
Gross proceeds	7,000	
Less: costs of sale	(350)	
Net disposal proceeds		6,650
Less: cost		(4,000)
Gain		2,650
Gain cannot exceed 5/3 × £(7,000 – 6,000)		1,667
Therefore chargeable gain on sale		1,667

If the chattel is sold for less than £6,000 and the disposal would result in a loss, the loss is restricted by assuming that the gross disposal proceeds were £6,000. This rule cannot turn a loss into a gain, only reduce the amount of the loss to nil.

Worked example: Chattels – loss

Lucinda bought an antique necklace in May 2004 for £8,000 and sold it at auction in July 2012 for £5,400. The costs of sale were £270.

Requirement

What is Lucinda's allowable loss?

Solution

	£	£
Gross proceeds (deemed)	6,000	
Less: costs of sale	(270)	
Net disposal proceeds		5,730
Less: cost		(8,000)
Allowable loss		(2,270)

Summary

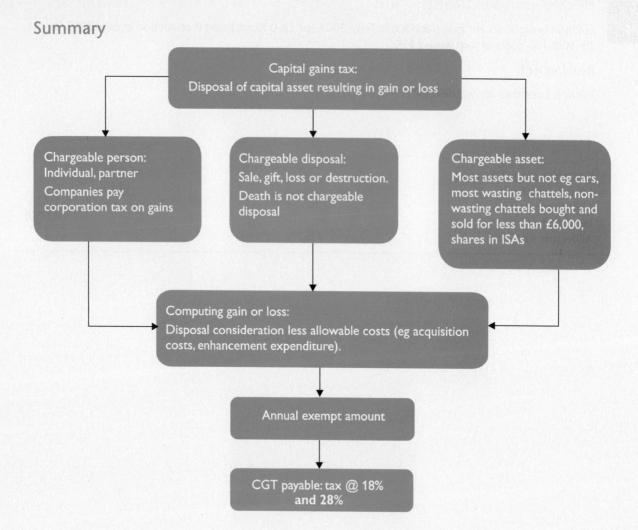

Capital gains tax:
Disposal of capital asset resulting in gain or loss

Chargeable person:
Individual, partner
Companies pay corporation tax on gains

Chargeable disposal:
Sale, gift, loss or destruction.
Death is not chargeable disposal

Chargeable asset:
Most assets but not eg cars, most wasting chattels, non-wasting chattels bought and sold for less than £6,000, shares in ISAs

Computing gain or loss:
Disposal consideration less allowable costs (eg acquisition costs, enhancement expenditure).

Annual exempt amount

CGT payable: tax @ 18% and 28%

Self-test

Answer the following questions.

1   Michael bought an asset in July 2001 for £10,000 and sold it for £25,500 in August 2012.
    Incidental costs of disposal amounted to £1,250. Michael made no other disposals in 2012/13.
    Michael had taxable income of £33,000 for 2012/13.

    What is Michael's capital gains tax liability for 2012/13?

    A   £885
    B   £1,235
    C   £3,853
    D   £1,022

2   Which **two** of the following are exempt assets for CGT?

    A   A vintage Bentley car
    B   A shop used by a sole trader in his business
    C   Painting worth £4,500 (cost £1,500)
    D   Shares in an unquoted trading company

3   George sold a holiday flat in October 2012. He had bought the flat in May 2000.

    Select **two** of the following costs which will be deductible in computing George's chargeable gain
    on sale.

    A   Cost of advertising on sale
    B   Minor repairs to guttering
    C   Installing completely new heating system
    D   Repainting walls

4   Norman inherited a painting from his aunt in July 2005. His aunt had bought the painting in 1996
    for £9,000. The market value of the painting at the date of her death was £15,000.

    Norman sold the painting for £40,000 in November 2012. He incurred auctioneers' costs of
    £2,000 on the sale.

    What is Norman's chargeable gain on the sale?

    A   £23,000
    B   £25,000
    C   £29,000
    D   £31,000

5   Which of the following statements is true?

    A   The gift of any asset is always an exempt disposal
    B   Goodwill is an exempt asset for individuals
    C   Shares are always exempt assets for individuals
    D   The gift of a painting to a charity is an exempt disposal

Now, go back to the Learning outcomes in the Introduction. If you are satisfied you have achieved these
objectives, please tick them off.

Technical reference

Legislation

References relate to Taxation of Chargeable Gains Act 1992 (*TCGA 1992*)

Chargeable persons	s.2
Assets and disposals	s.21
Computation of gains and losses	ss.15 – 17
Allowable deductions	ss.37 – 39
Annual exempt amount	s.3
Rates of tax	s.4
Chattels	s. 262

HMRC manual

Capital gains manual (Found at http://www.hmrc.gov.uk/manuals/cgmanual/index.htm)

Persons chargeable: general	CG10700
Chargeable assets: exemptions from capital gains charge	CG12600
Computation: introduction	CG14200
Chattels and wasting assets: introduction	CG76550

This technical reference section is designed to assist you when you are working in the office. It should help you to know where to look for further information on the topics covered in this chapter. **You will not be examined on the contents of this section in your examination.**

Answer to Interactive question 1

	£	£
Gross sale proceeds		76,000
Less: Incidental costs of sale:		
advertising costs		(1,800)
legal costs		(2,600)
		71,600
Net disposal consideration		
Less: allowable costs:		
acquisition cost	70,000	
legal costs	2,000	
surveyor's fees	1,400	
		(73,400)
Chargeable gain/Allowable loss		(1,800)

Answer to Interactive question 2

	£
Net chargeable gains (£45,000 – £12,700)	32,300
Less: annual exempt amount	(10,600)
Taxable gains	21,700
CGT liability: £21,700 × 28%	6,076

The vintage car, cash and Treasury stock are all exempt assets.

Philippa is a higher rate taxpayer therefore all her taxable gains are taxed at 28%.

1   A – £885

	£	£
Gross proceeds	25,500	
Less: costs of sale	(1,250)	
Net disposal proceeds		24,250
Less: cost		(10,000)
Chargeable gain		14,250
Less: annual exempt amount		(10,600)
Taxable gain		3,650
(£34,370 – £33,000) £1,370 @ 18%		247
(£3,650 – £1,370) £2,280 @ 28%		638
CGT liability		885

2   A and C.

A vintage Bentley car – all cars are exempt assets

Painting worth £4,500 (cost £1,500) – non-wasting chattel acquisition cost and disposal proceeds of £6,000 or less.

3   A and C.

Cost of advertising on sale

Installing completely new heating system

Repairs and redecoration are not capital in nature and are not enhancement expenditure.

4   A – £23,000

	£	£
Gross proceeds	40,000	
Less: auctioneers' fees	(2,000)	
Net disposal consideration		38,000
Less: acquisition cost (MV at date of death)		(15,000)
Chargeable gain		23,000

5   D – Gift of a painting to a charity is an exempt disposal

The gift of an asset is a chargeable disposal unless the gift is to a charity, art gallery, museum or similar institution or the gift is made on the death of an individual.

Goodwill is a chargeable asset for individuals.

Only shares held in an Individuals Savings Account (ISA) are exempt assets.

CHAPTER 9

Corporation tax

Introduction
Examination context
Topic List
Summary and Self-test
Technical reference
Answers to Interactive questions
Answers to Self-test

Learning outcomes

- Calculate total taxable gains for companies

- Identify chargeable accounting periods for a company

- Recognise the effect of having one or more associated companies on corporation tax payable

- Allocate given items of business expenditure as allowable or disallowable for tax purposes and calculate the adjusted trading profits after capital allowances on plant and machinery

- Calculate the taxable total profits and the corporation tax payable for a company resident in the UK which has no associated companies and an accounting period of 12 months or less

Specific syllabus references for this chapter are: 4c, 5a, b, c, d.

Syllabus links

The topics in this chapter form the basis of the charge to tax on companies. You will learn more details about how companies are taxed in the Application paper and at the Advanced stage, for example the use of trading losses and groups of companies.

Examination context

In the examination candidates may be required to:

- Identify the correct chargeable accounting periods of a company
- Calculate the taxable total profits for a company
- Calculate the corporation tax payable by a company
- Understand the impact of associated companies

For extra question practice on these topics go to the section of the Question Bank covering this chapter.

1 Charge to corporation tax

Section overview

- Companies are chargeable to corporation tax.
- A UK resident company is chargeable on its worldwide profits.
- A company is charged to tax for a chargeable accounting period which cannot exceed 12 months.

1.1 Who is chargeable to corporation tax?

Corporation tax is charged on the income and gains of a company. These are known as taxable total profits.

A UK company is formed by incorporation under the Companies Acts. A company is a legal person. It has a separate legal entity from its owners (shareholders) and its managers (directors).

1.2 Residence

A company is liable to corporation tax on its worldwide profits if it is resident in the United Kingdom.

A company is resident in the UK if either:

- It is incorporated in the UK; or
- It is incorporated outside the UK, but its central management and control are exercised in the UK

1.3 Chargeable accounting periods

A company is charged to corporation tax in respect of a **chargeable accounting period**.

The chargeable accounting period will usually be the same as the company's period of account (the period for which the company prepares its accounts).

A chargeable accounting period starts:

- When the company begins to trade or acquires a source of chargeable income
- When the previous accounting period ends and the company is still within the charge to corporation tax

A chargeable accounting period ends on the earliest of:

- The end of 12 months from the start of the accounting period; or
- The date the company begins or ceases to trade; or
- The date the period of account ends.

If a company has a period of account exceeding 12 months, there will be two chargeable accounting periods, each giving rise to a separate corporation tax computation.

The first chargeable accounting period of such a long period of account will be the first 12 months of the period. The second chargeable accounting period will be the remainder of the period of account.

Worked example: Long period of account

M Ltd has made up accounts to 31 December each year. For commercial reasons, it decides to prepare its next set of accounts for the period 1 January 2012 to 30 April 2013.

Requirement

What are the chargeable accounting periods for this long period of account?

Solution

First chargeable accounting period: 1 January 2012 to 31 December 2012

Second chargeable accounting period: 1 January 2013 to 30 April 2013

2 Taxable total profits

Section overview

- Trading profits after capital allowances is dealt with as trading income.

- Income from renting out property is dealt with as property income.

- Loan relationships include interest income and interest expense. Loan relationships may include trading credits and debits and non-trading credits and debits.

- Gains made by companies are chargeable to corporation tax, with indexation allowance available.

- Qualifying donations are deducted to arrive at taxable total profits.

2.1 Overview of corporation tax computation

Per chargeable accounting period

	£
Trading income	X
Property income	X
Non trading loan relationships (non trading interest)	X
Miscellaneous income	
Income not otherwise charged	X
Chargeable gains	X
Qualifying donations	(X)
Taxable total profits	X

2.2 Trading income

A company's trading profits are calculated in a similar way to the taxable trading profits of a sole trader or partnership.

The company will produce accounts for a period of account and these must be adjusted for tax purposes. Capital allowances are then deducted to produce a figure for trading income.

In general, the adjustment to profits calculation will follow the same rules as for a sole trader or partnership, including WDAs, the AIA and FYAs, but there are some differences.

- As a company is a legal entity separate from its shareholders and directors, there is no adjustment to profits needed for private expenses met by the company.

- For the same reason, there will be no adjustment for appropriation of profits (eg salary paid to a director).

- Interest paid by a company in respect of a trading loan relationship will be an allowable expense in the calculation of its trading income (see later in this section for more detail on loan relationships).

- Dividends paid by a company are not allowable as a trading expense in the calculation of its trading income.

- If the company has a long period of account, the tax-adjusted profits should be time apportioned into the relevant chargeable accounting periods at this stage.

- Capital allowances for companies are computed for chargeable accounting periods, not periods of account. This means that capital allowances for companies can never be computed for a period longer than 12 months.

- Capital allowance computations for companies never include private use adjustments.

- A 100% FYA is available for expenditure incurred by a company between 1 April 2012 and 31 March 2017 on new (not second-hand) plant and machinery for use in a designated enterprise zone.

Worked example: Capital allowances and long period of account

D Ltd makes up accounts for the 15-month period to 30 June 2012.

Its tax-adjusted profits for the period were £300,000.

The tax written down value of the main pool at 1 April 2011 was £24,000. D Ltd sold some plant in May 2012 for £3,000 (less than cost).

Requirement

What is the trading income for each chargeable accounting period?

Solution

Capital allowances

	Main pool	Allowances
	£	£
Chargeable accounting period		
1 April 11 to 31 March 12		
TWDV b/f	24,000	
WDA @ 20%	(4,800)	4,800
TWDV c/f	19,200	
Chargeable accounting period		
1 April 12 to 30 June 12		
Disposal	(3,000)	
	16,200	
WDA @ 18% × ³/₁₂	(729)	729
TWDV c/f	15,471	

	1.4.11 to 31.3.12	1.4.12 to 30.6.12
	£	£
Tax adjusted profits (12:3)	240,000	60,000
Less: capital allowances	(4,800)	(729)
Trading income	235,200	59,271

2.3 Property income

A company's rental income from property situated in the UK is taxed as property income. Rent received is dealt with on an accruals basis. This means that only rent relating to the chargeable accounting period is taken into account. The date of receipt is not relevant.

Worked example: Property income

H Ltd makes up its accounts to 31 July each year.

On 1 January 2012, H Ltd bought and immediately rented out a shop. The annual rental of £24,000 was payable on that date.

Requirement

What is the amount taxable as property income on H Ltd for the year ended 31 July 2012?

Solution

Rent accrued 1 January 2012 to 31 July 2012
£24,000 × 7/12   £14,000

Interest payable on a loan taken out by a company for the purpose of buying or improving let property is not an allowable expense for property income. Instead it is dealt with under the loan relationship rules (see later in this section). No further knowledge of the property income calculation is required at this level.

2.4 Dividends received

A company rarely pays tax on dividends received from other companies. They are therefore ignored in computing taxable total profits. For the purposes of the exam, assume all dividends received by a company are exempt.

However, grossed-up dividends received from other companies are taken into account in determining the rate of tax that a company pays on its taxable profits. This is dealt with in the next section of this chapter.

2.5 Loan relationships – interest

Interest payable and receivable, such as investment interest, is allowable and taxable respectively as a profit or loss on non-trading loan relationships (see later in this section).

This income is received gross.

2.6 Chargeable gains

Chargeable gains are included in the computation of taxable total profits.

Overview of computation of a chargeable gain for a company

	£
Disposal consideration	X
Less: Incidental costs of disposal	(X)
Net disposal consideration	X
Less: Allowable costs	(X)
Unindexed gain	X
Less: Indexation allowance	(X)
Chargeable gain	X

Gains are initially computed in the same way as for individuals (see earlier in this text), however, for companies, 'indexation allowance' is also available in arriving at the chargeable gain. Indexation allowance is designed to ensure that the inflationary element of gains is not subject to tax.

Each item of acquisition cost is indexed from the date when the expenditure was incurred to the date of the disposal. Costs incurred in the same month can be added together.

The indexation factor is calculated as follows:

$$\frac{RD - RI}{RI}$$

where RD is the Retail Prices Index (RPI) for the month of disposal and RI is the RPI for the month in which the expenditure was incurred. In this examination relevant RPIs will be provided. If RD is less than RI (ie the RPI falls) then the indexation factor is nil.

The indexation factor is rounded to three decimal places. It is then applied to the item of allowable cost as appropriate to produce the indexation allowance for that item.

Worked example: Indexed gain

Lilliput Ltd bought an asset on 3 March 1990 (RPI 121.4) for £19,560. In addition, there were legal expenses of £150 on the purchase.

The company sold the asset on 15 September 2012 (RPI 247.9) for £42,300, and paid legal costs of £450 on sale.

Requirement

What is Lilliput Ltd's chargeable gain on sale?

Solution

	£	£
Gross proceeds	42,300	
Less: legal fees	(450)	
Net disposal consideration		41,850
Less: acquisition cost	19,560	
legal fees	150	(19,710)
Unindexed gain		22,140
Less: indexation allowance		

$$\frac{247.9 - 121.4}{121.4} = 1.042 \times £19,710 \qquad \qquad (20,538)$$

Chargeable gain		1,602

Interactive question 1: Company chargeable gain   [Difficulty level: Exam standard]

Swift Ltd bought a warehouse in July 2000 (RPI 170.5) for £120,000, including incidental costs of acquisition. It added an extension in August 2001 (RPI 174.0) at a cost of £45,000.

Swift Ltd sold the warehouse in November 2012 (RPI 248.5) for net disposal proceeds of £265,000.

Requirement

Using the standard format below, compute the chargeable gain of Swift Ltd.

	£	£
Net disposal consideration		
Less: acquisition cost		
enhancement expenditure	....	(..........)
Unindexed gain		
Less: indexation allowance		
on acquisition cost		

$$\frac{.......... - ....}{..........} = ... \times £.......... \qquad (..........)$$

       on enhancement expenditure

$$\frac{.......... - ....}{..........} = ... \times £.......... \qquad (..........)$$

Chargeable gain		

See **Answer** at the end of this chapter.

The indexation allowance cannot create or increase an unindexed loss.

Worked example: Restriction of indexation allowance

Munodi plc bought a plot of land in May 1997 (RPI 156.9) for £70,000, incurring legal costs of £2,000 on the purchase and surveyors' fees of £1,400.

Munodi plc sold the land in July 2012 (RPI 244.7) for £80,000. The company incurred advertising costs of £1,800 and legal costs of £2,600 on the sale.

Requirements

(a) What is Munodi plc's chargeable gain or allowable loss on the sale?
(b) What would the chargeable gain or allowable loss be if the gross sale proceeds were £76,000?

Solution

	(a)		(b)	
	£	£	£	£
Gross proceeds	80,000		76,000	
Less: incidental cost of disposal (£1,800 + £2,600)	(4,400)		(4,400)	
Net disposal consideration		75,600		71,600
Less: acquisition cost	70,000		70,000	
Cost of acquisition (£2,000 + £1,400)	3,400		3,400	
		(73,400)		(73,400)
Unindexed gain/Allowable loss		2,200		(1,800)
Less: indexation allowance				

$$\frac{244.7 - 156.9}{156.9} = 0.560 \times £73,400 = £41,104$$
(restricted)

	(a)		(b)	
		(2,200)		–
Chargeable gain/allowable loss		Nil		(1,800)

(a) There is no chargeable gain nor allowable loss on the disposal as indexation cannot create a loss.

(b) The allowable loss is £1,800. Indexation cannot increase an allowable loss.

Companies are not entitled to an annual exempt amount.

Exempt assets for companies are as for individuals (see earlier in this text), with the addition of goodwill created or acquired on or after 1 April 2002. The examination will not require knowledge of the treatment of goodwill created or acquired by companies before 1 April 2002.

2.7 Miscellaneous income – income not otherwise charged

Miscellaneous income received by a company is taxable as income not otherwise charged. Such income is received gross.

2.8 Qualifying donations

A company may make a charitable donation. The conditions for a donation to qualify for tax relief are the same as for individuals.

The method of tax relief for a company differs from that used for individuals.

A company makes qualifying donations gross. The amount **paid** in the chargeable accounting period is deducted from the company's total income and gains. This is called a qualifying donation.

2.9 Taxable total profits

A company's total income and gains less qualifying donations is its taxable total profits.

Worked example: Taxable total profits

X Ltd makes up its accounts for the 12 month period to 31 December 2012.

It has the following results:

Tax-adjusted trading profits before capital allowances	£120,000
Capital allowances	£10,000
Rental income after expenses	£5,000
Interest received from bank	£1,000
Chargeable gain	£2,000
Qualifying donation paid	£3,000

Requirement

What are the taxable total profits of X Ltd?

Solution

	£
Tax-adjusted trading profits before capital allowances	120,000
Less: capital allowances	(10,000)
Trading income	110,000
Property income	5,000
Non-trading loan relationship (bank interest is received gross by companies)	1,000
Chargeable gains	2,000
	118,000
Less: Qualifying donations	(3,000)
Taxable total profits	115,000

2.10 Loan relationships

A company has a **loan relationship** if it loans money as a creditor or is loaned money as a debtor.

In practical terms, a loan relationship includes bank and building society accounts, bank overdrafts, government gilt-edged securities and loans to and from other companies which are often in the form of debentures. It does not include trade debts.

All profits and losses on loans (whether the company is a lender or borrower) are treated as income. Interest payments are taxed or relieved on an accruals basis.

If the company has been lent money for trade purposes there is a trading loan relationship.

Trading loan relationships

	Gross interest payable	Gross interest receivable
Treatment for corporation tax	Allowable trading expense to set against trading income	Trading receipt treated as trading income
Basis of assessment	Accruals basis	Accruals basis
Main examples	Bank overdraft interest Interest on loans to buy plant and machinery Interest on loans to buy premises for use in the trade	Rare – a company will not usually lend money for trade purposes

If the company has been lent money or lends money for a non-trade purpose, there is a non-trading loan relationship.

Non-trading loan relationships

	Gross interest payable	Gross interest receivable
Treatment for corporation tax	Non-trading loan relationship 'debit'	Non-trading loan relationship 'credit'
Basis of assessment	Accruals basis	Accruals basis
Main examples	Interest on loans to: • purchase/improve a let property • acquire shares in another company • interest on overdue corporation tax • write off of a non-trading loan such as a loan to a former employee	Interest on • bank and building society accounts • gilt-edged securities • debentures and other loan stock • repayments of overpaid corporation tax (repayment interest)

The **credits** (income) and **debits** (expenses) on loan relationships are combined. If there is a net profit, this amount is taxable as a non-trading loan relationship.

If there is a net deficit, there will be no amount taxable under loan relationships. The deficit can be relieved in a number of ways, but these are beyond the syllabus of this exam.

Worked example: Non-trading loan relationships

K Ltd makes up its accounts to 31 December each year.

In the year to 31 December 2012, K Ltd had the following accrued income received and interest paid:

Building society interest receivable	£5,000
Bank interest receivable	£2,000
Repayment interest on overpaid corporation tax	£50
Payable on loan taken out to acquire let property	£3,250

Requirement

What is the amount taxable as a non-trading loan relationship?

Solution

	£
Building society interest	5,000
Bank interest	2,000
Repayment interest on overpaid tax	50
	7,050
Less: Interest on loan taken out to acquire let property	(3,250)
Non-trading loan relationship	3,800

3 Computation of corporation tax

Section overview

- The rate of corporation tax depends on the augmented profits of the company.
- The main rate applies if the company has augmented profits above the upper limit.
- The small profits rate applies if the company has augmented profits below the lower limit.
- Marginal relief applies for companies between the limits.
- The limits for the rates are scaled down in short accounting periods.
- The limits are divided between associated companies.

3.1 Augmented profits

In the last section, we looked at the computation of taxable total profits.

You also need to work out the augmented profits of a company as this will govern what rate of corporation tax applies.

Definitions

Augmented profits: taxable total profits plus franked investment income

Franked investment income (FII): exempt dividends and tax credits received from UK and overseas companies, other than those received from companies which are 51% subsidiaries of the receiving company. The net dividend received needs to be grossed up by 100/90 to arrive at FII.

3.2 Main rate of corporation tax

Rates of corporation tax are fixed for Financial Years (FYs). FY 2012 runs from 1 April 2012 to 31 March 2013.

If the chargeable accounting period falls wholly within FY 2012, the main rate of tax applies if a company has augmented profits exceeding £1,500,000. The main rate of tax applied to taxable total profits is 24%. The level of augmented profits also affects payment dates (see later in this study manual).

Worked example: Main rate of corporation tax

T Ltd makes up its accounts to 31 March each year. In the year to 31 March 2013, the company has taxable total profits of £1,300,000 and receives exempt dividends from unrelated UK companies of £189,000.

Requirement

What is the corporation tax liability of T Ltd?

Solution

	£
Taxable total profits	1,300,000
Add: £189,000 × 100/90	210,000
Augmented profits	1,510,000
Main rate applies	
£1,300,000 × 24%	312,000

Note that the rate of tax is applied to taxable total profits, not to augmented profits.

3.3 Small profits rate of corporation tax

If the company's chargeable accounting period falls wholly within FY 2012, the small profits rate of tax applies if the company has augmented profits of £300,000 or less. The small profits rate of tax is 20%. (See also 'associated companies' later in this section.)

3.4 Marginal relief

If the company's chargeable accounting period falls wholly within FY 2012, marginal relief applies if a company has augmented profits of over £300,000 but not exceeding £1,500,000.

First, compute corporation tax at the main rate on taxable total profits and then deduct:

$$(U - A) \times N/A \times 1/100$$

where   U = upper limit (£1,500,000)
A = augmented profits
N = taxable total profits
And 1/100 is the standard fraction for FY2012

Worked example: Marginal relief

Z Ltd makes up its accounts to 31 March each year. In the year to 31 March 2013, the company has taxable total profits of £500,000 and receives exempt dividends of £9,000.

Requirement

What is the corporation tax liability of Z Ltd?

Solution

	£
Taxable total profits	500,000
Add: £9,000 × 100/90	10,000
Augmented profits	510,000

Marginal relief applies

	£
£500,000 × 24%	120,000
Less: (£1,500,000 – £510,000) × $\frac{500,000}{510,000}$ × $\frac{1}{80}$	(9,706)
Corporation tax liability	110,294

3.5 Short chargeable accounting periods

The limits for augmented profits relate to a 12-month chargeable accounting period.

If the chargeable accounting period is less than 12 months, the limits must be scaled down.

Interactive question 2: Short accounting period [Difficulty level: Exam standard]

R Ltd makes up its accounts for the nine-month period to 31 December 2012. The company has taxable total profits of £200,000 and receives exempt dividends from unrelated UK companies of £27,000.

Requirement

Using the standard format below, compute the corporation tax liability of R Ltd.

	£
Taxable total profits	
Add: £................... × 100/90	
Augmented profits	_____

Limits for marginal relief for nine-month period:
Upper limit (£................... × ....) = ...
Lower limit (£................... × ....) = ...
.... applies

	£
£................... × ....%	
Less: (£................... – ....) × .... ×	(_____)
Corporation tax liability	_____

See **Answer** at the end of this chapter.

3.6 Chargeable accounting period in more than one financial year

A chargeable accounting period may fall within more than one financial year. For example, a 12-month chargeable accounting period ending 31 December 2012 has 3 months to 31 March 2012, falling within FY 2011 and 9 months to 31 December 2012, falling within FY 2012.

If the rates and limits for corporation tax are the same in both financial years, tax can be computed on the 12-month chargeable accounting period as if it fell within one financial year.

If the rate or limits for corporation tax are different in the financial years, taxable total profits and augmented profits are time apportioned between the financial years. The limits for marginal relief will also need to be scaled down appropriately.

In FY2011 the main rate of corporation tax was 26% and the standard fraction was 3/200. The small profits rate of corporation tax was however the same as it is in FY2012 at 20%.

Worked example: Financial year straddle

K Ltd makes up its accounts to 31 December each year. In the year to 31 December 2012, the company has taxable total profits of £1,450,000 and receives franked investment income of £100,000.

Requirement

What is the corporation tax liability of K Ltd?

Solution

	y/e 31.12.12 £
Taxable total profits	1,450,000
FII	100,000
Augmented profits	1,550,000
	Main rate

	FY2011 3/12 £	FY2012 9/12 £
Taxable total profits	362,500	1,087,500
FII	25,000	75,000
Augmented profits	387,500	1,162,500
Corporation tax limits:		
Upper limit £1,500,000 × 3/12:/9/12	375,000	1,125,000
Lower limit £300,000 × 3/12/:9/12	75,000	225,000
	£	£
FY2011: taxable total profits × 26% = £362,500 × 26%	94,250	
FY2012: taxable total profits × 24% = £1,087,500 × 24%		261,000
Total corporation tax liability		£355,250

Note: Once it is determined that K Ltd pays tax at the main rate the corporation tax liability could be calculated as follows.

	£
FY2011: 3/12 × £1,450,000 × 26%	94,250
FY2012: 9/12 × £1,450,000 × 24%	261,000
Total corporation tax liability	355,250

Worked example: Financial year straddle with marginal relief

G Ltd makes up its accounts to 30 September each year. In the year to 30 September 2012, the company has taxable total profits of £650,000 and receives franked investment income of £50,000.

Requirement

What is the corporation tax liability of G Ltd?

Solution

	y/e 30.09.12 £
Taxable total profits	650,000
FII	50,000
Augmented profits	700,000
	Marginal relief applies

	FY2011 6/12 £	FY2012 6/12 £
Taxable total profits	325,000	325,000
FII	25,000	25,000
Augmented profits	350,000	350,000
Corporation tax limits:		
Upper limit £1,500,000 × 6/12	750,000	750,000
Lower limit £300,000 × 6/12	150,000	150,000

	£	£
FY2011: taxable total profits × 26% = £325,000 × 26%	84,500	
FY2012: taxable total profits × 24% = £325,000 × 24%		78,000
Less marginal relief		

FY2011: $(£750,000 - £350,000) \times \dfrac{325,000}{350,000} \times \dfrac{3}{200}$ (5,571)

FY2012: $(£750,000 - £350,000) \times \dfrac{325,000}{350,000} \times \dfrac{1}{80}$ (3,714)

	78,929	74,286
Total corporation tax liability		£153,215

3.7 Associated companies

The small profits rate limits apply to a company and its associates.

A company is associated with another company if:

- One company is under the control of the other; or
- Both are under common control of a third party (individual, partnership or another company).

Control means over 50% of the issued share capital or voting power or distributable profits or assets if the company ceases to exist.

Associated companies include non-UK resident companies.

Companies which are associated for only part of the chargeable accounting period are deemed to have been associated for the whole of the chargeable accounting period.

Dormant companies (companies which are not carrying on a trade or business) are ignored.

Worked example: Associated companies

T Ltd owns the following shareholdings during the 12-month accounting period ending 31 March 2013:

A Ltd (UK) 60%
B Ltd (UK) 100% (dormant)
C Ltd (UK) 70% (sold shares 30 September 2012)
D Inc (US) 80%
E Ltd (UK) 75% (acquired shares 1 December 2012)
F Ltd (UK) 30%

Requirement

How many companies are associated with T Ltd?

Solution

A Ltd, C Ltd, D Inc, and E Ltd as T Ltd has over 50% of the shares of each company. All four companies are treated as associated with T Ltd for the whole of the chargeable accounting period. There are five associated companies in total ie remember to include the parent company.

B Ltd is not associated because it is dormant.

F Ltd is not associated because T Ltd owns 50% or less of the shares of the company.

Sub-subsidiaries, ie where one company controls another, which in turn controls another, are also included as associated companies.

Worked example: Sub-subsidiaries

X Ltd owns 51% of Y Ltd which in turn owns 51% of Z Ltd during the year ended 31 December 2012.

Requirement

How many associated companies are there for the year ended 31 December 2012?

Solution

```
            X Ltd
              |
              | 51%
              |
            Y Ltd
              |
              | 51%
              |
            Z Ltd
```

X Ltd controls Y Ltd, and Y Ltd controls Z Ltd. Therefore X Ltd effectively controls Z Ltd through its shareholding in Y Ltd.

X Ltd, Y Ltd and Z Ltd are all treated as associated companies, so there are three associated companies.

Where a company is associated with one or more companies, the small profits rate limits are divided equally between the associated companies.

Worked example: Effect of associated companies

Mr Smith owns 100% of C Ltd and 100% of D Ltd.

C Ltd makes up its accounts to 31 March 2013. The company has taxable total profits of £740,000 and receives exempt dividends from unrelated UK companies of £18,000.

Requirement

What rate of tax will be payable by C Ltd?

Solution

	£
Taxable total profits	740,000
Add: £18,000 × 100/90	20,000
Augmented profits	760,000

Mr Smith controls both C Ltd and D Ltd so there are two associated companies.

Limits for marginal relief for 2 associated companies:

Upper limit £1,500,000 ÷ 2 = £750,000
Lower limit £300,000 ÷ 2 = £150,000

Main rate of corporation tax (24%) applies.

You will not be expected to compute the corporation tax liability of a company with associated companies.

Summary

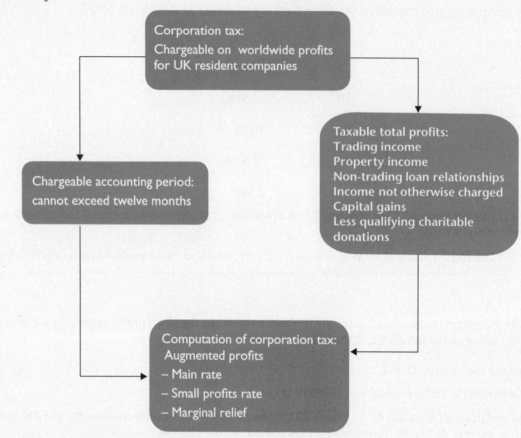

Corporation tax:
Chargeable on worldwide profits
for UK resident companies

Chargeable accounting period:
cannot exceed twelve months

Taxable total profits:
Trading income
Property income
Non-trading loan relationships
Income not otherwise charged
Capital gains
Less qualifying charitable
donations

Computation of corporation tax:
Augmented profits
– Main rate
– Small profits rate
– Marginal relief

Self-test

Answer the following questions.

1 G Ltd has a ten-month period of account from 1 April 2012 to 31 January 2013. The company bought a car (with CO_2 emissions of 153g/km) on 4 August 2012 for £20,000. The car is used 30% privately by one of the directors.

What are the maximum capital allowances that G Ltd can claim?

A £2,100
B £2,520
C £3,000
D £3,600

2 P Ltd started trading on 1 December 2011 and made up its first set of accounts to 31 March 2013.

P Ltd's chargeable accounting periods will be:

A 4 months to 31 March 2012, 12 months to 31 March 2013
B 4 months to 5 April 2012, 12 months to 31 March 2013
C 12 months to 30 November 2012, 4 months to 31 March 2013
D 16 months to 31 March 2013

3 Which **two** of the following are non-trading loan relationship debits of a company under the loan relationship rules?

A Interest payable on loan to purchase property to let
B Bank overdraft interest
C Interest on loan to purchase machinery
D Interest on overdue corporation tax

4 R Ltd has produced the following results for the year ended 31 March 2013.

Trading income	£490,000
Chargeable gains	£60,000
Interest accrued on gilts	£90,000
Qualifying donation paid	£50,000

What is the amount of corporation tax payable by R Ltd?

A £141,600
B £132,500
C £118,000
D £145,000

5 R Ltd had the following shareholdings during the year ended 31 March 2013:

S Ltd 40%
T Ltd 60% (acquired 1 October 2012)
U Ltd 75% (disposed 30 September 2012)
V Ltd 90%

Which companies are associated for the purposes of determining the limits for corporation tax rates?

A R Ltd and V Ltd only
B R Ltd, V Ltd and S Ltd
C R Ltd, V Ltd, U Ltd and T Ltd
D All of them

6 W Ltd sold a building in June 2012 (RPI 245.2) for £200,000, which had cost £145,000 in February 1994 (RPI 142.1).

The indexation allowance relating to the building is £...........................

7 J Ltd makes up its accounts to 31 December each year. In the year to 31 December 2012, the company has taxable total profits of £1,310,000 and receives exempt dividend income from unrelated companies of £270,000.

What is the amount of corporation tax payable by J Ltd?

Now go back to the Learning outcomes in the Introduction. If you are satisfied you have achieved these objectives, please tick them off.

C
H
A
P
T
E
R

9

Corporation tax   155

Technical reference

HMRC manual

Company Taxation manual (Found at http://www.hmrc.gov.uk/manuals/ctmanual/index.htm)

This technical reference section is designed to assist you when you are working in the office. It should help you to know where to look for further information on the topics covered in this chapter. **You will not be examined on the contents of this section in your examination.**

Answer to Interactive question 1

	£	£
Net disposal consideration (November 2012)		265,000
Less: acquisition cost (July 2000)	120,000	
enhancement expenditure (August 2001)	45,000	(165,000)
Unindexed gain		100,000
Less: indexation allowance		
on acquisition cost		

$$\frac{248.5-170.5}{170.5} = 0.457 \times £120,000 \qquad\qquad (54,840)$$

on enhancement expenditure

$$\frac{248.5-174.0}{174.0} = 0.428 \times £45,000 \qquad\qquad (19,260)$$

Chargeable gain	25,900

Answer to Interactive question 2

	£
Taxable total profits	200,000
Add: £27,000 × 100/90	30,000
Augmented profits	230,000

Limits for marginal relief for nine-month period:

Upper limit (£1,500,000 × 9/12) = £1,125,000
Lower limit (£300,000 × 9/12) = £225,000

Marginal relief applies

	£
£200,000 × 24%	48,000

$$\text{Less:} \ (£1,125,000 - 230,000) \times \frac{200,000}{230,000} \times \frac{1}{100}$$

	(7,783)
Corporation tax liability	40,217

1 C – £3,000

£20,000 × 18% × 10/12 = £3,000

There is no private use reduction for companies. A taxable benefit will arise for the director.

2 C – 12 months to 30 November 2012, 4 months to 31 March 2013

A chargeable accounting period cannot be more than 12 months long. A long period of account is always split into a first chargeable accounting period of 12 months and then a second chargeable period of the remainder of the period of account.

3 A and D – interest payable on loan to purchase property to let and interest on overdue corporation tax.

Bank overdraft interest and interest on a loan to purchase machinery are dealt with as trading loan relationships and deductible from trading income.

4 B – £132,500

	£
Trading income	490,000
Chargeable gains	60,000
Loan relationships	90,000
	640,000
Less: Qualifying donation	(50,000)
Taxable total profits	590,000

Marginal relief applies

	£
£590,000 × 24%	141,600
Less: (£1,500,000 – £590,000) × $\frac{1}{80}$	(9,100)
Corporation tax payable	132,500

5 C – R Ltd, V Ltd, U Ltd and T Ltd

S Ltd is not an associated company because R Ltd does not control over 50% of the shares.

U Ltd and T Ltd are treated as associated for the whole of the accounting period.

6 £105,270

$$\frac{245.2 - 142.1}{142.1} = 0.726 \text{ (to 3 dp)} \times £145,000 = £105,270$$

7

	y/e 31 December 2012
	£
Taxable total profits	1,310,000
FII (£270,000 × 100/90)	300,000
Augmented profits	1,610,000

Main rate applies

FY 2011 (3/12)/FY 2012 (9/12)

	£
Corporation tax:	
FY2011: 3/12 × £1,310,000 × 26%	85,150
FY2012: 9/12 × £1,310,000 × 24%	235,800
Corporation tax liability	320,950

CHAPTER 10

Value added tax

Introduction

Examination context

Topic List

    1   The principles of value added tax (VAT)

    2   Classification of supplies

    3   Registration and deregistration

    4   Output VAT

    5   Input VAT

Summary and Self-test

Technical reference

Answer to Interactive question

Answers to Self-test

Learning outcomes

- Classify supplies in straightforward situations as exempt, zero rated, standard rated, subject to a reduced rate of 5% or outside the scope of VAT

- Recognise the implications of supplies being classified as standard rated, zero rated or exempt

- Identify when a business could or should register or deregister for VAT and state the time limits

- Determine the tax point for a supply of goods or services

- State the principles of VAT payable or repayable on the supply of goods or services by a taxable person

Specific syllabus references for this chapter are: 6a, b, c, d, e.

Syllabus links

The topics in this chapter and the following chapter form the basis of your understanding of value added tax.

At Application level you will deal with further aspects of VAT such as groups and overseas transactions.

Examination context

In the examination candidates may be required to:

- Determine when a transaction is within the scope of VAT, and the impact of it being a taxable or exempt supply

- Identify when VAT registration/deregistration are required/desirable

- Calculate the VAT applying to a supply, starting at either the VAT inclusive or exclusive figure

- Determine the tax point of a supply

- Deal with additional aspects of input tax and output tax such as bad debts, discounts etc

For extra question practice on these topics go to the section of the Question Bank covering this chapter.

Candidates have historically been weak at VAT questions. This is probably because there are a large number of small issues to learn rather than one main pro forma to contend with. It is essential that candidates take time to understand and become competent at VAT at an early stage.

1 The principles of value added tax (VAT)

Section overview

- VAT is payable by the final consumer of goods and services.

- VAT is collected at each stage of the distribution chain.

- VAT is charged on a taxable supply by a taxable person in the course of a business carried on by him.

1.1 How VAT works

Value added tax (VAT) is a tax payable on the consumption of goods and services by the final consumer.

However, instead of all the tax being collected at the final point of consumption, VAT is collected as value is added to the goods or services.

As the goods or services go through the production and distribution process, each VAT registered business charges VAT on the value of the goods or services it supplies. This is called **output VAT**.

Each VAT registered business receives credit for any VAT that it has paid. This is called **input VAT**.

The business sets off input VAT against output VAT. Usually this results in a net excess of output VAT which the business pays over to HMRC.

The total tax is ultimately borne by the final consumer of the goods or services at the end of the distribution chain.

Worked example: Operation of VAT

Gerald makes car components which attract VAT of 20%. He sells them to William, a car component wholesaler, for £80 plus VAT of £16 (20% of £80).

William holds the car components in stock until he sells them to Fiona, who runs a car dealership, for £120 plus VAT of £24 (20% of £120).

Fiona sells the components to Richard, a private customer, for £160 plus VAT of £32 (20% of £160).

Requirement

How does VAT operate in this distribution chain?

Solution

	Gerald	William	Fiona
	£	£	£
Output tax	16	24	32
Less: input tax	(nil)	(16)	(24)
Net excess	16	8	8

The total amount payable to HMRC is (£16 + £8 + £8) = £32

Richard is unable to reclaim any VAT as he is a private customer and not VAT registered and therefore suffers the total VAT charge of £32. Gerald, William and Fiona do no suffer any net VAT; they merely collect and pay the VAT to HMRC.

We will look at the administration of VAT later in this text.

1.2 Scope of VAT

VAT is charged on the **taxable supply** of goods and services in the United Kingdom (UK) by a **taxable person** in the course of a business carried on by him.

Definition

Taxable supply: any supply of goods or services made in the UK other than an exempt supply or a supply outside the scope of VAT.

We will look at this definition in more detail when we consider the classification of supplies later in this chapter.

Definition

Taxable person: a person making taxable supplies who is, or who is required to be, registered for VAT. Person includes a sole trader, a partnership (not the individual partners) and a company.

A taxable person is required to charge output VAT on any taxable supplies made, and may also recover input VAT on supplies paid for. A person who is not a taxable person cannot charge output VAT on supplies or recover input VAT.

We look at the conditions to register for VAT later in this chapter.

2 Classification of supplies

Section overview

- Supplies may be outside the scope of VAT, exempt or taxable.
- A supply of goods arises when ownership of goods passes from one person to another.
- A supply of services arises when there is a supply for consideration which is not a supply of goods.
- Exempt supplies do not have output VAT charged on them.
- Taxable supplies may be at zero rate, reduced rate or standard rate.
- Taxable supplies have output VAT charged on them.

2.1 Supplies of goods and services

A supply of goods or services may fall into one of three categories:

- Outside the scope of VAT
- Exempt supplies
- Taxable supplies

We will look at each type of supply in turn in the rest of this section.

First, however, we need to consider the meaning of a **supply** upon which VAT should be accounted for.

A supply of goods takes place when ownership of the goods passes from one person to another.

Examples of supplies of goods include:

- Sales of goods for consideration

- Gifts of business assets except samples or where total gifts made to the same person do not exceed £50 in any 12-month period. Unlimited samples can be given to the same person without the need to account for output tax.

- Goods permanently taken out of a business for private use by the owner or an employee

- Sales of goods on hire purchase

A supply of services is any supply for a consideration which is not a supply of goods. Consideration is any form of payment in money or in kind. Therefore a gift of services is not a taxable supply. Examples of supplies include:

- Sales of services for consideration

- Hiring of goods to a customer

- Goods owned by a business temporarily taken for private use by the owner or an employee

- Private use, by the owner or an employee, of business services supplied to the business

- Private use of fuel for motoring by the owner or an employee (but not the private use of a business motor car itself)

2.2 Supplies outside the scope of VAT

Supplies outside the scope of VAT do not have any effect for VAT.

Examples include the payment of wages and dividends.

An awareness that these supplies are outside the scope of VAT will be required in the examination.

2.3 Exempt supplies

An exempt supply is one on which output VAT cannot be charged. In general, input VAT cannot be recovered by a trader making exempt supplies.

Examples include some supplies of land, insurance and postal services.

If a person only makes exempt supplies, VAT registration is not allowed. The person cannot be a taxable person, but is treated as the final consumer of the goods or services.

In the examination you will not be expected to identify that a specific supply is exempt.

2.4 Taxable supplies

Taxable supplies fall into one of three categories:

- Zero rated (0%)
- Reduced rate (5%)
- Standard rated (20%)

A taxable supply is one on which output VAT is chargeable and input VAT can be recovered. Note the difference between exempt supplies (no input VAT recoverable) and zero rated supplies (input VAT can be recovered).

Examples of zero rated supplies include human and animal food, books and newspapers and drugs and medicines on prescription or provided by private hospitals.

Examples of reduced rate supplies include domestic fuel and children's car seats.

Any taxable supply not classified as zero rated or reduced rate is a standard rated supply.

In the examination you will not be expected to classify specific taxable supplies into each category.

3 Registration and deregistration

Section overview

- Compulsory registration is required if a person's taxable turnover exceeds the registration threshold.

- Voluntary registration may be applied for if a person is making taxable supplies below the registration threshold.

- There is an exemption from registration if a person is making only or mostly zero rated supplies.

- Deregistration applies if taxable supplies cease or fall below the deregistration threshold.

3.1 Compulsory registration

A person making taxable supplies is required to register for VAT if the total value of taxable supplies (**taxable turnover**) exceeds the statutory threshold. Taxable supplies include zero rated, reduced rate and standard rated supplies. It does not include supplies of capital assets of the business.

A person's registration covers all of his business activities as it is the person who is registered, not his business. From October 2012 it will be compulsory to register for VAT online.

The statutory threshold from 1 April 2012 is £77,000.

There are two situations where compulsory registration is required.

Under the **historic test**, a person must register for VAT if, at the end of any month, the taxable turnover in the prior period exceeds the threshold. The prior period is the previous 12 months or the period from the commencement of the business, whichever is the shorter.

If a person is liable to register under the historic test, he must notify HMRC within thirty days of the end of the month in which the threshold was exceeded (the **relevant month**).

Registration then takes effect from the first day after the end of the month following the relevant month.

Registration is not required if the taxable turnover during the next twelve months will not exceed the deregistration threshold (see later in this section).

If a taxpayer fails to notify HMRC of the liability to register on time, a penalty is payable (see chapter 12).

Worked example: Historic test for registration

Caroline started trading on 1 July 2012. Her monthly turnover (excluding VAT) is:

	£
Standard rated supplies	7,000
Zero rated supplies	750
Exempt supplies	500
	8,250

On 1 February 2013, Caroline sold a machine used in her business for £2,500 (excluding VAT).

Requirement

On what date is the VAT registration threshold first exceeded by Caroline, by what date will she need to notify HMRC and what is the date from which she will be registered?

Solution

Exempt supplies and supply of a capital asset of the business are not taken into account.

The taxable monthly supplies are therefore:

	£
Standard rated supplies	7,000
Zero rated supplies	750
	7,750

The threshold will therefore be exceeded after 10 months (£7,750 × 10 = £77,500) which is 30 April 2013.

Caroline must notify HMRC by 30 May 2013.

She will be registered from 1 June 2013.

The other test is the **future prospects** test.

Under the future prospects test, the person must register for VAT if, at any time, there are reasonable grounds for believing that the taxable turnover in the next 30 days alone will exceed the threshold.

If a person is liable to register under the future prospects test, he must notify HMRC by the end of the 30-day period in which the threshold is expected to be exceeded.

Registration takes effect from the beginning of the 30-day period.

For both the historic and the future prospects tests, a person failing to apply for registration is still liable to account for output VAT on taxable turnover from the compulsory registration date, as if registration had taken place at the correct time. This taxable turnover is treated as being the VAT-inclusive amount (see later in this chapter).

3.2 Voluntary registration

A person making taxable supplies below the registration threshold may apply for voluntary registration. HMRC will register that person for VAT from a mutually agreed date.

The main advantage of voluntary registration is the ability to recover input VAT.

3.3 Exemption from registration

Where a person is making only zero rated supplies, he may request exemption from registration.

HMRC may also allow exemption from registration if only a small proportion of supplies are standard rated and the person would normally have a net recovery of input VAT.

3.4 Deregistration

Deregistration may be compulsory or voluntary.

Deregistration is **compulsory** if a person ceases to make taxable supplies and has no intention of making taxable supplies. The person must notify HMRC within 30 days. Deregistration will take effect on the date taxable supplies ceased.

A person is eligible for **voluntary** deregistration if his estimated taxable turnover for the next twelve months will not exceed the statutory deregistration threshold.

From 1 April 2012, the deregistration threshold is £75,000.

Voluntary deregistration takes effect from the date on which the request is made or from an agreed later date.

From October 2012 it will be compulsory to deregister from VAT online.

On deregistration, a VAT charge is made on a deemed supply of trading stock and capital assets on which input VAT has been recovered. Output tax is then paid on the deemed supply. If the amount of output VAT is £1,000 or less, it does not have to be paid.

4 Output VAT

Section overview

- VAT is charged on the value of the taxable supply.
- The time of supply is called the tax point.
- The basic tax point is when goods are removed or made available or when services are completed.
- The actual tax point may be before or after the basic tax point.
- Any discount, even if not taken up, is taken into account when valuing the supply.
- Fuel for private motoring by the owner or an employee is charged at a scale rate.
- Bad debt relief is given for debts more than six months old.

4.1 Charge to VAT

VAT charged on taxable supplies is based on the VAT exclusive value of the supply. For standard rated items, the rate of VAT is 20%. If the VAT inclusive price is given, the VAT component of the consideration is:

$$\frac{20}{120} \text{ or } \frac{1}{6}$$

This is called the **VAT fraction**.

Worked example: Charge to VAT – standard rated supplies

J Ltd makes standard rated supplies. It makes the following standard rated supplies:

VAT-exclusive supplies	£395
VAT-inclusive supplies	£3,450

Requirement

What is the VAT charged?

Solution

VAT on VAT-exclusive supplies	
£395 × 20%	£79
VAT on VAT-inclusive supplies	
£3,450 × 1/6	£575

For reduced rate supplies VAT is charged at 5% on the VAT exclusive value of the supply.

If the VAT-inclusive price is given for reduced rate supplies, the VAT component of the consideration is 5/105.

Worked example: Charge to VAT – reduced rate supplies

H Ltd makes reduced rated supplies. It makes the following supplies:

VAT-exclusive supplies	£500
VAT-inclusive supplies	£1,260

Requirement

What is the VAT charged?

Solution

VAT on VAT-exclusive supplies	
£500 × 5%	£25
VAT on VAT-inclusive supplies	
£1,260 × 5/105	£60

If VAT is not charged on a taxable supply in error then it is the responsibility of the trader who made the supply to pay the outstanding VAT over to HMRC. The amount received by the trader on the sale is treated as being inclusive of VAT.

4.2 Time of supply (tax point)

VAT becomes due on a supply of goods or services at the time of supply. This is called the **tax point**. Normally VAT must be accounted for on the VAT return for the period in which the tax point occurs.

The basic tax point is the date on which goods are removed or made available to the customer or the date on which services are completed.

However, the actual tax point may occur before or after the basic tax point as follows:

- Payment received before the basic tax point: actual tax point is the date of payment

- Invoice issued before the basic tax point: actual tax point is the date of invoice

- Invoice issued within 14 days after basic tax point: actual tax point is the date of invoice (can be extended by agreement with HMRC, eg for month-end invoicing)

The actual tax point cannot be later than the date on which payment is actually received.

If a deposit is paid, there will be separate tax points for the deposit and the balancing payment.

Goods supplied on a sale or return basis (ie if the customer does not sell the goods, they may be returned to the supplier) are treated as having a basic tax point which is the earlier of the adoption of the goods by the customer or twelve months after the date of despatch.

The basic tax point may be overridden by an actual tax point as described above.

Interactive question 1: Tax point
[Difficulty level: Exam standard]

What is the tax point for each of these supplies of goods? Give brief reasons for your answer.

Question	Fill in your answer
Goods removed 10 May, invoice issued 26 May, payment received 1 June	
Goods removed 28 May, invoice issued 26 May, payment received 1 June	
Goods removed 16 May, invoice issued 26 May, payment received 1 June	
Goods removed 20 May, invoice issued 26 May, payment received 18 May	
Goods removed 8 May, invoice issued 26 May, deposit received 1 May, balance received 1 June	

See **Answer** at end of this chapter.

4.3 Value of supply

Usually the value of the supply is the amount charged by the supplier, exclusive of any VAT.

Where the supply is a gift of business assets, the value of the supply is the VAT exclusive amount that would be payable by the person making the supply at that time to purchase goods identical to the goods concerned (ie replacement cost).

Non-business use of business assets is valued at the full cost of provision to the taxable person.

Supplies offered at a discount (eg for prompt payment or trade discount) are valued net of the maximum discount. This rule applies even if the discount is not taken up.

Worked example: Sale with discount

B Ltd makes a standard rated taxable supply of goods. It issues an invoice for £1,000 (exclusive of VAT) to V Ltd on 30 June 2012.

A 3% discount is offered for payment within 30 days of the invoice date.

Requirement

What is the value of the supply and how much output VAT is charged, assuming that V Ltd pays the invoice after 35 days?

Solution

	£
Value before discount	1,000
Less: discount (3% × £1,000)	(30)
Value of supply	970
VAT charged (£970 × 20%)	£194

Note that it is irrelevant that the discount is not taken up.

Fuel provided for private motoring by the owner or an employee is charged at a scale rate. The **fuel scale charge** is based solely on the CO_2 rating of a car. There are no adjustments for fuel type. Fuel scale charges will be provided in the exam when fuel for private motoring is tested.

Worked example: Fuel scale charge

Jethro is employed by A Ltd. He is provided with a car with CO_2 emissions of 175g/km and petrol for business and private use.

The VAT inclusive quarterly scale rate for a car with CO_2 emissions between 171g/km and 175 g/km is £416.

Requirement

What is the output VAT due for the quarter to 31 March 2013?

Solution

£416 × 1/6   £69

4.4 Bad debts

Output VAT is accounted for according to the tax point and therefore output VAT may be payable before payment of an invoice has been received from the customer.

Where an invoice has not been paid for more than six months after the due date of payment and the debt has been written off in the supplier's accounts, bad debt relief is available.

Bad debt claims must be made within four years of the time the debt became eligible for relief. The supplier must have a copy of the VAT invoice and records to show that the output VAT has been paid. The VAT is reclaimed in the supplier's VAT return together with input tax on purchases.

5 Input VAT

Section overview

- Most input VAT can be recovered by a taxable person who is VAT registered.

- VAT is not recoverable on motor cars (unless used exclusively for business purposes) or business entertaining.

- Pre-registration input VAT may be recoverable.

5.1 Recoverable VAT

Normally, a taxable person making wholly taxable supplies (zero rated, reduced rate or standard rated) can recover input VAT on purchases and expenses relating to the taxable supply of goods.

The goods or services must actually be supplied for a taxable person to be able to recover the input tax.

The input VAT recoverable must be supported by a VAT invoice.

The goods or services must be used for a business purpose. Where goods are bought partly for business use, the taxable person may either:

- Deduct all the input tax and account for the output tax in respect of private use; or
- Deduct only the business proportion of input tax.

Where services are bought partly for private use, only the second method can be used.

Input VAT is also recoverable on fuel supplied for private use where the VAT scale charge for output tax applies.

Input tax on assets purchased for the use of employees (as opposed to directors or sole traders or partners) which have an element of private use is allowable in full. Such benefits are a legitimate business expense and are provided for the purposes of the business – mainly to reward or motivate staff. The VAT incurred on their provision is consequently all input tax and no apportionment is necessary to reflect the private use. Examples include the cost of purchasing a mobile telephone (but not the cost of usage), or a computer but not cars which have special rules regarding private usage (see below).

5.2 Irrecoverable VAT

Input VAT is not usually recoverable in respect of:

- Motor cars (including optional extras acquired with the car) unless the car is used exclusively for business purposes;

- Goods or services used for the purposes of business entertaining which is not allowable when computing taxable trading profits. Input VAT *is* however usually recoverable in respect of staff entertainment as well as entertainment of foreign customers (but not other foreign business contacts);

- Non-business items;

- Items for which no VAT receipt is held.

5.3 Pre-registration VAT

Input VAT can be recovered on goods supplied in the four years before registration. The goods must have been supplied to the taxable person for business purposes and must still be on hand at the time of registration. They must not have been supplied onwards or consumed.

Input VAT can be recovered on services supplied in the six months before registration. The services must have been supplied to the taxable person for business purposes.

Summary and Self-test

Summary

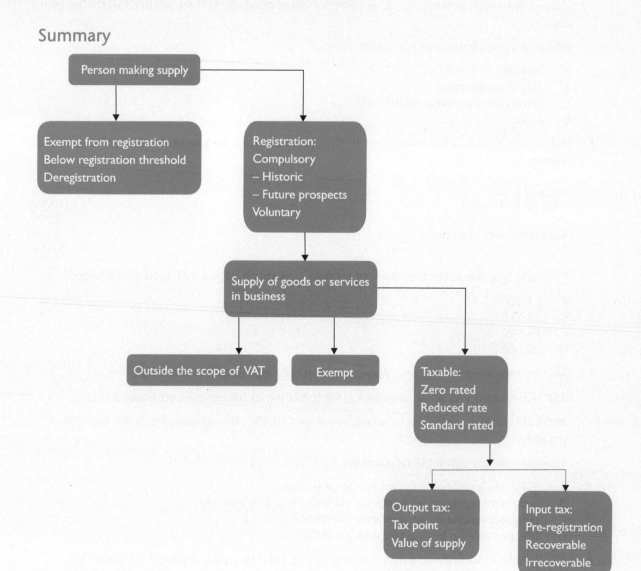

Self-test

Answer the following questions.

1   Gita, who is registered for VAT, runs a business selling beauty products. She gives one sample worth £10 to each potential customer. She also takes goods from stock worth £150 for her own use.

Which of these transactions is a taxable supply?

A   Neither
B   Gift of sample only
C   Goods for own consumption only
D   Both

2   Joel intends to issue a VAT invoice on 30 November 2012 for the sale of standard rated goods as follows:

	£
Value of goods	10,000
Less trade discount	(1,000)
	9,000
Less settlement discount	(450)
	8,550

Assuming only the settlement discount is taken, how much output VAT should be charged?

A   £1,800
B   £1,710
C   £1,910
D   £2,000

3   ABC Ltd registered for VAT on 1 August 2012. It only makes standard rated supplies.

ABC Ltd incurred VAT on accountancy services relating to the business on 1 May 2012.

ABC Ltd bought a car for use by an employee for £10,000. The employee uses the car 40% privately.

To what extent is input VAT recoverable?

A   Fully recoverable on both accountancy and car
B   Fully recoverable on accountancy, partially recoverable on car
C   Fully recoverable on accountancy, irrecoverable on car
D   Irrecoverable on both accountancy and car

4   On 30 April, Jones ordered a new machine. On 16 May, he paid a deposit of £10,000. The machine was despatched to Jones on 31 May. On 13 June, an invoice was issued to Jones for the balance due of £45,000. This was paid on 20 June.

What is the tax point for the £10,000 deposit?

A   30 April
B   16 May
C   31 May
D   13 June

5   Julie should have registered for VAT on 1 March 2013.

On 5 March 2013, she supplied services to Wilma for £1,000 without charging VAT. Wilma is also registered for VAT and makes standard rate supplies.

How much output VAT is payable on this supply and who should pay it?

A   £167 payable by Julie
B   £167 payable by Wilma
C   £200 payable by Julie
D   £200 payable by Wilma

Now go back to the Learning outcomes in the Introduction. If you are satisfied you have achieved these objectives, please tick them off.

Technical reference

Legislation

References relate to Value Added Tax Act 1994 (*VATA 1994*) unless otherwise stated

Scope of VAT on taxable supplies	s.4
Taxable persons	s.3
Exempt supplies	s.31
Standard rate	s.2
Reduced rate	s.29A
Zero rate	s.30
Registration	Sch 1
Input and output tax	s.24
Time of supply	s.6
Value of supply	s.19
Fuel for private use	ss.56-57
Bad debts	s.36
Input tax disallowance on cars	SI 1992/3222 art 7
Pre-registration input tax	SI 1995/2518 reg 111

To find out more practical information about VAT, access the relevant section of the HMRC website through the main home page (http://www.hmrc.gov.uk/).

A series of guides is available online at http://www.hmrc.gov.uk/vat/index.htm?_nfpb=true&_pageLabel. For example, Introduction to VAT is a summary of the most common VAT issues and a good place to start finding out how it affects you and your business.

There is also a VAT telephone helpline: +44 (0)845 010 9000 (+44 2920 501 261 from abroad)

This technical reference section is designed to assist you when you are working in the office. It should help you to know where to look for further information on the topics covered in this chapter. **You will not be examined on the contents of this section in your examination.**

Answer to Interactive question

Answer to Interactive question 1

Question	Fill in your answer
Goods removed 10 May, invoice issued 26 May, payment received 1 June	10 May (basic tax point)
Goods removed 28 May, invoice issued 26 May, payment received 1 June	26 May (actual tax point, invoice before basic tax point)
Goods removed 16 May, invoice issued 26 May, payment received 1 June	26 May (actual tax point, invoice within 14 days after basic tax point)
Goods removed 20 May, invoice issued 26 May, payment received 18 May	18 May (actual tax point, payment before basic tax point)
Goods removed 8 May, invoice issued 26 May, deposit received 1 May, balance received 1 June	Deposit: 1 May (actual tax point, payment before basic tax point) Balance: 8 May (basic tax point)

1   C – goods taken for own use are a taxable supply

      Gifts of trade samples are not taxable supplies.

2   B – £1,710

      Value of supply is after discounts, even if not taken up.

      £8,550 × 20%   <u>£1,710</u>

3   C – fully recoverable on accountancy, irrecoverable on car

      The VAT on accountancy services is pre-registration VAT incurred for business purposes within six months of registration.

      VAT on motor cars is not recoverable unless the car is used exclusively for business purposes.

4   B – 16 May

      There is a separate tax point for the deposit. The actual tax point is the date of payment since this is before the basic tax point (date of despatch of goods).

5   A – £167 payable by Julie

      VAT inclusive supply

      £1,000 × 1/6   <u>£167</u>

      Although Julie failed to apply for registration on time, she is still liable to account to HMRC for output VAT on her taxable supplies from the compulsory registration date.

CHAPTER 11

Value added tax: further aspects

Introduction

Examination context

Topic List

Introduction

Learning outcomes

Tick off

- Identify the records which companies and individuals must retain for tax purposes
- Determine, in straightforward cases, due dates for businesses' VAT returns and payments
- Calculate the monthly, quarterly and annual VAT payable or repayable by a business
- State the alternative schemes for payment of VAT by businesses

Specific syllabus references for this chapter are: 2a, d, 6e, f.

Syllabus links

The topics in this chapter and the previous chapter form the basis of your understanding of value added tax.

Many of the administrative aspects of VAT are not tested in the Taxation paper, so you may expect to find them in the Principles of Taxation paper. At Application level you will deal with further aspects of VAT such as groups and overseas transactions.

Examination context

In the examination candidates may be required to:

- Calculate the VAT payable or reclaimable for a period
- Identify the schemes available to small businesses and apply the rules of the schemes

For extra question practice on these topics go to the section of the Question Bank covering this chapter.

1 Accounting for VAT

Section overview

- VAT is normally accounted for in three-monthly VAT periods.
- The VAT return and VAT payable are due by the end of the month following the end of the VAT period.
- Substantial traders must make payments on account of VAT for each quarter.

1.1 VAT periods

The period covered by a VAT return is called a **VAT period** or **tax period**. Normally the VAT period is a three-month period ending on a date specified in the certificate of registration.

HMRC will allow taxable persons to have a one month VAT period where input tax regularly exceeds output tax ie where the taxable person is in a net VAT repayment position.

Small businesses may submit an annual VAT return (see later in this chapter).

1.2 VAT return

From 1 April 2012, all VAT registered businesses must submit their VAT returns (Form VAT100) online and pay any VAT due in respect of those returns electronically.

The VAT return must show the amount of VAT payable or recoverable and be submitted to HMRC not later than seven calendar days after the last day of the month following the end of the return period. This is also usually the due date for any VAT payment. If payment is made by direct debit, it is automatically collected a further 3 working days after the due date. Cheque payments are only accepted when made at a bank via an HMRC paying-in slip.

Businesses that file annual returns or make payments on account have special due dates for their returns and payments (see later in this chapter).

Worked example: VAT due

F Ltd is a manufacturing company. For the quarter to 30 September 2012, the following information is given (all figures excluding VAT):

	£	£
Sales (standard rated)		134,285
Sales (zero rated)		12,500
		146,785
Purchases	37,750	
Wages	23,000	
Bad debt written off	1,500	
UK customer entertaining	750	
Staff entertaining	14,464	(77,464)
Profit		69,321

All purchases and entertaining expenses are standard rated. The bad debt, in respect of a standard rated supply, was written off in August 2012. The payment for the original sale was due on 31 January 2012.

Requirement

What is the VAT payable for the quarter and when is it due for payment?

Solution

Output tax

	£
Standard rate supplies (£134,285 × 20%)	26,857

Input tax

	£	
Purchases	37,750	
Bad debt	1,500	
Staff entertaining	14,464	
	53,714 × 20%	(10,743)
VAT payable (due electronically by 7.11.12 as after 1 April 2012)		16,114

Bad debt relief is available because the debt is more than six months old from the due date of payment.

Wages are outside the scope of VAT.

Input tax on UK customer entertaining is irrecoverable.

Worked example: Tax point and accounting for VAT

Jason has the following standard rated sales during the quarter ended 30 June 2012:

Order 1

Goods dispatched on 2 March 2012. Invoice issued on 25 March 2012 for £1,200 plus VAT. Payment was received on 12 June 2012.

Order 2

Goods dispatched on 28 March 2012. Invoice issued on 10 April 2012 for £680 plus VAT. Payment was received on 7 July 2012.

Requirement

What is the VAT payable for the quarter ended 30 June 2012 and when is it due for payment?

Solution

Tax point is the basic tax point for order 1, and the invoice date for order 2 (as it is within 14 days of basic tax point and before payment received).

The quarter ended 30 June 2012 only includes the VAT charged on order 2 as the quarter runs from 1 April 2012 to 30 June 2012. The VAT payable electronically on 7 August 2012 is £136.

Order 1

Tax point is 2 March 2012
VAT @ 20% of £1,200   £240

Order 2

Tax point is 10 April 2012
VAT @ 20% of £680   £136

Interactive question 1: VAT due

[Difficulty level: Exam standard]

Dev is registered for VAT. His VAT period ends on 31 March 2013.

During this period Dev made zero rated supplies of £46,000 and standard rated supplies of £59,070. These are VAT-exclusive figures.

Dev made standard rated purchases, not including motor expenses, of £40,285 (inclusive of VAT) during the period.

Dev is provided with private fuel for his car which has CO_2 emissions of 215g/km. The VAT inclusive quarterly scale rate is £550. The total motor expenses for the quarter, including the cost of private fuel, were £1,204 (inclusive of VAT).

Requirement

Using the standard format below, compute the VAT due for the quarter.

Output tax

£

_____

Input tax   £

_____

_____ × (_____)

VAT payable

See **Answer** at the end of this chapter.

1.3 Payments on account

Substantial traders are taxable persons with an annual VAT liability in excess of £2m. A substantial trader must make **payments on account** of VAT for each quarter. This must be done electronically.

Returns are due at the end of each month with payments, which must be made electronically, due at the end of the second and third months of the quarter. There is no seven day extension. The amount of each payment is 1/24 of the total VAT liability for the previous year.

The final payment is due at the end of the month following the end of the quarter, again with no seven day extension.

2 Small business reliefs

Section overview

- The annual accounting scheme allows a business to submit one VAT return a year.
- The cash accounting scheme allows a business to account for VAT on a cash basis.
- Under the flat rate scheme, output VAT is based on a fixed percentage of VAT inclusive turnover but there is no recovery of input VAT.

2.1 Annual accounting scheme

The annual accounting scheme is helpful to small businesses as it cuts down on the administrative burden of VAT by allowing the business to submit one VAT return every 12 months. The VAT return is due within two months of the end of the year.

A business may join the annual accounting scheme if the value of taxable supplies (excluding VAT and supplies of capital items) in the following year is not expected to exceed £1.35m.

Businesses already in the scheme may continue to use it until the value of taxable supplies in the previous 12 months exceeds £1.6m.

The annual accounting scheme requires the trader to make payments on account either as:

- Nine interim payments at monthly intervals throughout the year, or
- Three quarterly interim payments throughout the year.

The trader then must either pay any outstanding VAT or receive a refund if he has overpaid VAT, at the end of the year. In total the trader will therefore either make ten payments or four.

If the trader has opted to make nine equal monthly payments, each payment must be electronic and will be 10% of the total VAT liability for the previous year, or 10% of the estimated VAT liability for the current year if the trader has been registered for VAT for less than 12 months. The first payment is due at the end of the fourth month, with no seven day extension.

If the trader has opted to make three quarterly instalments, each payment must be electronic and will be 25% of the previous year's VAT liability, or 25% of the estimated VAT liability for the current year if the trader has been registered for VAT for less than 12 months. The payments are due by the end of months 4, 7 and 10 of the annual accounting year.

In the examination, you will always be given the VAT liability for the previous year or HMRC's estimate of the VAT liability for the current year where a trader has been registered for VAT for less than 12 months.

Any balancing payment is due when the VAT return is made, ie within two months of the end of the year. There is no seven day extension for either the return or the balancing payment, although, if paid by online VAT direct debit, HMRC will collect it three working days after the due date for the return.

Worked example: Annual accounting scheme

W Ltd joined the annual accounting scheme two years ago. On 1 June 2012, HMRC estimated W Ltd's total VAT liability for the year to 31 May 2013 would be £12,800.

The actual VAT liability was £16,250.

Requirement

What are the payments on account and balancing payment and when are they due?

Solution

Payments on account
1/10 × £12,800   £1,280

Due by 30 September 2012 and then at the end of each month until 31 May 2013

Balancing payment
(£16,250 – [£1,280 × 9])   £4,730

Due by 31 July 2013

The main advantages of the annual accounting scheme are therefore:

- The reduction in the number of VAT returns required
- One additional month to complete the annual return and make the balancing payment

The annual accounting scheme can be used in conjunction with either the cash accounting scheme or the flat rate scheme.

2.2 Cash accounting scheme

The cash accounting scheme allows businesses to account for VAT on the basis of cash paid and received, rather than on invoices received and issued.

Small businesses may join the cash accounting scheme if the value of taxable supplies (excluding VAT and supplies of capital items) in the following year is not expected to exceed £1.35m. The business must have submitted all its VAT returns to date and paid all outstanding VAT. It must not have been convicted of a VAT offence or penalty in the previous twelve months.

Businesses already in the cash accounting scheme may continue to use it until the value of taxable supplies in the previous twelve months exceeds £1.6m.

The main advantages of the scheme are:

- Output VAT does not have to be accounted for until payment is received
- Automatic bad debt relief since no output VAT is payable if payment is not received

However, note that input VAT cannot be recovered until the business has actually paid the supplier for purchases.

2.3 Flat rate scheme

The flat rate scheme allows businesses to calculate net VAT due by applying a flat rate percentage to their VAT inclusive turnover rather than accounting for VAT on individual sales and purchases.

The flat rate percentage is set by the type of business carried on. It ranges from 4% (food retailers) to 14.5% (building or construction services where labour only is supplied). There is a 1% reduction during the first year of VAT registration. For examination purposes, always use the percentage given in the question.

The business will issue tax invoices using the normal rules, eg standard rate, zero rate. It does not have to keep records of the input VAT on individual purchases.

The VAT payable to HMRC at the end of the VAT period is the flat rate percentage multiplied by the VAT inclusive turnover for the period. There is no deduction for input VAT. The VAT inclusive turnover includes taxable supplies, exempt supplies and supplies of capital assets.

Worked example: Flat rate scheme

Leon uses the flat rate scheme for his business. He has been registered for VAT for five years, making standard rated supplies. The flat rate percentage is 9 %.

In the quarter to 30 June 2012, Leon had the following transactions:

	£
Sales	25,200
Purchases	7,100
Expenses	2,500

All figures exclude VAT.

Requirement

What is the VAT due for the quarter?

Solution

VAT inclusive turnover

$£25,200 \times \dfrac{120}{100}$ (or $\dfrac{6}{5}$) £30,240

VAT due £30,240 × 9 % £2,722

A business may join the flat rate scheme if the value of its annual taxable supplies (excluding VAT) does not exceed £150,000.

The main advantages of the scheme are:

- Reduction in the burden of administration of preparing the VAT return as no records of input VAT need be kept

- Frequently less VAT payable to HMRC than under the normal rules

If a business has total annual income (inclusive of VAT) in excess of £230,000 it must leave the flat rate scheme. This condition includes exempt income.

3 VAT records and accounts

Section overview

- VAT records must be kept to support output VAT charged and the claim for recoverable input VAT.

- Records must be kept for at least six years.

- A VAT invoice must contain details such as the tax point, VAT registration number and details of the supply.

3.1 Records

HMRC requires a taxable person to keep 'adequate' records and accounts of all transactions to support both output VAT charged and the claim for recoverable input VAT.

The main records to be kept should include:

- Order and delivery notes
- Purchase invoices, copy sales invoices and credit notes
- Purchase and sales day books
- Records of daily takings (eg till rolls)
- Cash book
- Bank statements and paying-in slips
- Annual accounts (P&L account and Balance Sheet)

3.2 VAT invoices

The VAT invoice is the key record to support a claim to recover input VAT and must therefore be issued when a taxable person makes a taxable supply to another taxable person.

If the supply is to a customer who is not a taxable person, it is not necessary to issue a VAT invoice, but in practice VAT invoices are usually issued to all customers.

A VAT invoice must contain a number of details such as the tax point date, VAT registration number, a description of the goods or services and the total VAT chargeable.

A less detailed invoice can be issued if the consideration does not exceed £250.

Summary and Self-test

Summary

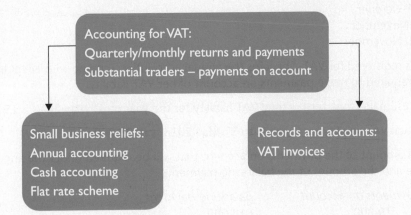

Self-test

Answer the following questions.

1   O Ltd's VAT accounting periods are in line with its accounting year which ends on 30 September.

By what date must O Ltd submit its final VAT return for its accounting year?

A   30 October
B   31 October
C   7 November
D   10 November

2   Tertia is registered for VAT. She joins the annual accounting scheme with effect from 1 June 2012 and is required to make payments on account of her VAT liability.

HMRC estimates that Tertia's total VAT liability for the year to 31 May 2013 is £90,000.

The actual VAT liability for the year to 31 May 2013 is £108,000.

What is amount of the payments on account that will be required under the annual accounting scheme and the amount of the balancing payment?

	Payments on account	Balancing payment
A	9 × £10,000	£18,000
B	9 × £9,000	£27,000
C	9 × £12,000	nil
D	9 × £10,800	£10,800

3   Which of the following statements about the cash accounting scheme is **not** true?

A   VAT is accounted for on the basis of amounts received for supplies and amounts paid for purchases

B   The scheme gives automatic bad debt relief

C   The scheme allows deferral of payment for VAT where an extended time for payment is given to customers

D   The scheme is compulsory for taxable persons who have taxable supplies not exceeding £1.35m in the following twelve months

4   Linda is registered for VAT and has opted to account for VAT under the flat rate scheme. The VAT rate applicable to her business is 5%.

Which **two** of the following statements are true?

A   Linda must calculate net VAT due by applying 5% to the value of her turnover (excluding VAT)

B   Linda does not have to keep records of her input VAT

C   Linda must calculate net VAT due by applying 5% to her VAT inclusive turnover

D   Linda will issue tax invoices to her customers showing the value of the supply plus VAT at 5%

Now go back to the Learning outcomes in the Introduction. If you are satisfied you have achieved these objectives, please tick them off.

Technical reference

Legislation

References relate to Statutory Instrument 1995/2518 (*SI 1995/2518*) unless otherwise stated

VAT returns	para 25
Payment of VAT	para 40
Substantial traders – payments on account	SI 1993/2001
Annual accounting scheme	paras 49-55
Cash accounting scheme	paras 56-65
Flat rate scheme	paras 55A-V
Records	para 31
Invoices	paras A13-16

To find out more practical information about VAT, access the relevant section of the HMRC website through the main home page (http://www.hmrc.gov.uk/).

A series of guides is available online at
http://www.hmrc.gov.uk/vat/index.htm?_nfpb=true&_pageLabel.

Information about the range of special schemes and options to simplify VAT for small businesses is available at http://www.hmrc.gov.uk/vat/start/schemes/basics.htm.

There is also a VAT telephone helpline: 0845 010 9000 (+44 2920 501 261 from abroad)

> This technical reference section is designed to assist you when you are working in the office. It should help you to know where to look for further information on the topics covered in this chapter. **You will not be examined on the contents of this section in your examination.**

Answer to Interactive question 1

Output tax

	£
Standard rated supplies £59,070 × 20%	11,814
Fuel scale charge £550 × 1/6	92
	11,906

Input tax

	£	
Purchases	40,285	
Motor expenses	1,204	
	41,489 × 1/6	(6,915)
VAT payable		4,991

1   C – 7 November

Businesses must file VAT returns (and pay their VAT liability) electronically from 1 April 2012. The deadline for both filing and payment is seven days after the end of the month following the return period. O Ltd must file its VAT return by 7 November.

2   B – Payments on account 9 × £9,000 and balancing payment of £27,000.

Payments on account are nine equal monthly payments which are 1/10 of the total VAT liability for the year as estimated by HMRC.

3   D – the cash accounting scheme is not compulsory.

All the other statements are true. B and C are advantages of the cash accounting scheme that you should recognise.

4   B and C are true

Note that D is not true. Linda will issue tax invoices using the normal rules, eg standard rated, zero rated.

CHAPTER 12

Administration of tax

Introduction

Examination context

Topic List

Summary and Self-test

Technical reference

Answers to Interactive questions

Answers to Self-test

Learning outcomes

- Identify the records which companies and individuals must retain for tax purposes and state the periods for which the records must be retained ☐

- Identify the key features of the self assessment system for both companies and individuals ☐

- Determine, in straightforward cases, due dates for:

    - Companies', sole traders', partners' and individuals' tax returns, tax payments and payments on account; and ☐

    - Employers' PAYE and national insurance returns and payments

- Identify and calculate the interest and penalties due for:

    - Late submissions of and/or incorrect returns; and ☐

    - Late and/or incorrect payments of tax

- Identify the periods within which HM Revenue & Customs can enquire into a taxpayer's returns or other information and tax liabilities and recognise the taxpayer's right of appeal and the process for dealing with disputes ☐

Specific syllabus references for this chapter are: 2a, c, d, e, f.

Syllabus links

The topics in this chapter are important background knowledge which you will require for the Application paper and at the Advanced Stage.

Examination context

In the examination candidates may be required to:

- Determine due dates for employers' PAYE and national insurance returns and payments, including penalties for non compliance

- Determine when a tax return is required and its submission date, including the penalties for non compliance

- Identify the administrative issues affecting individuals and companies

- Determine the payment dates and amounts of payments to be made by both individuals and by companies of all sizes

- Identify and calculate the penalties and interest payable by individuals and companies for non compliance

- Recognise when penalties for VAT are due and determine the amount of the penalties

For extra question practice on these topics go to the section of the Question Bank covering this chapter.

1 Penalties for errors

Section overview

- A common penalty regime applies to the making of errors in tax returns.

- Penalties are based on the Potential Lost Revenue (PLR) arising as a result of the error.

- Maximum penalties range from 30% to 100% of the PLR dependent on whether the error is careless or deliberate.

- Penalties can be reduced if the taxpayer discloses the error to HMRC or if there is reasonable excuse. They can also be suspended in certain circumstances.

- Appeals can be made against the penalties levied.

1.1 Common penalty regime

A common penalty regime relates to situations where a taxpayer has made an error/inaccuracy in a tax return. The regime covers income tax, national insurance contributions, corporation tax and value added tax. Penalties are based on the Potential Lost Revenue (PLR) and range from 30% to 100% of the PLR. Penalties may be reduced or suspended.

1.2 Circumstances in which a penalty may be charged

A penalty is charged where a taxpayer makes an inaccurate return and the inaccuracy can be classified as:

- Careless – ie the taxpayer has not taken reasonable care in completing the return; or

- Deliberate but not concealed – ie the taxpayer has deliberately made an inaccurate return but has not positively done anything to conceal the inaccuracy; or

- Deliberate and concealed – ie the taxpayer has deliberately made an inaccurate return and has positively done something to conceal the inaccuracy such as produced false invoices or bank statements.

In order for a penalty to be charged, the inaccurate return must result in:

- An understatement of the taxpayer's tax liability; or
- A false or increased loss for the taxpayer; or
- A false or increased repayment of tax to the taxpayer.

If a return contains more than one error, a penalty can be charged for each error.

The rules also extend to errors in claims for allowances and reliefs, and in accounts submitted in relation to a tax liability.

Penalties for errors also apply where HMRC has issued an estimate of a person's liability where:

- A return has been issued to that person and it has not been returned, or
- The taxpayer was required to deliver a return to HMRC but has not delivered it.

The taxpayer will be charged a penalty where:

- The assessment understates the taxpayer's liability to income tax, capital gains tax, corporation tax or VAT, and

- The taxpayer fails to take reasonable steps within 30 days of the date of the assessment to tell HMRC that there is an under-assessment.

Examples

Careless inaccuracy

- Keeping inaccurate books and records that are incomplete in some respects
- Omitting occasional items of income or gains
- Failing to check the return is consistent with the underlying records
- Making arithmetical errors that are too large or too many to be simply isolated mistakes

Deliberate inaccuracies

- Systematically paying wages without operating PAYE
- Not keeping books and records at all
- Including personal expenditure in business expenditure
- Omitting significant amounts of income in relation to overall liability from a return

Deliberate and concealed inaccuracies

- Creating false invoices
- Backdating or post-dating invoices
- Altering invoices or other documents
- Destroying books, records and documents in order that they are not available
- Creating fictitious minutes of meetings or minutes of fictitious meetings

1.3 Amount of the penalty

The amount of the penalty is based on the Potential Lost Revenue (PLR) to HMRC as a result of the error. For example, if there is an understatement of tax, this understatement is the PLR.

The maximum amount of the penalty depends on the type of error/ inaccuracy.

There is no penalty if a person can demonstrate he took reasonable care to ensure his tax was right, but despite this, submits an incorrect return. Otherwise:

Type of error	Maximum penalty payable
Careless	30% of PLR
Deliberate but not concealed	70% of PLR
Deliberate and concealed	100% of PLR

Worked example: Penalties

Ruth is a sole trader. She files her tax return for 2012/13 on 19 January 2014. The return shows her trading income to be £49,000. In fact, due to an arithmetical error this was incorrectly stated. Her trading income should have been £57,000.

Requirement

State the maximum penalty that HMRC could charge Ruth for her error.

Solution

The Potential Lost Revenue as a result of Ruth's error is:
£(57,000 – 49,000) = £8,000 × [40% (income tax) + 2% (NICs)]   £3,360

Ruth's error is careless so the maximum penalty is:
£3,360 × 30%   £1,008

1.4 Failure to send a return

The penalty payable where tax has been under-assessed because the taxpayer has failed to send a return is 30% of Potential Lost Revenue.

1.5 Reduction of penalties

A penalty may be reduced if the taxpayer tells HMRC about the error/ inaccuracy. The reduction depends on the circumstances of the disclosure and the help that the taxpayer gives to HMRC in relation to that disclosure.

An unprompted disclosure is one made at a time when there is no reason to believe that HMRC has discovered or is about to discover the error. Otherwise, the disclosure is a prompted disclosure.

The minimum penalties that can be imposed are as follows:

Type of error	Disclosure	
	Unprompted	Prompted
Careless	0% of PLR	15% of PLR
Deliberate but not concealed	20% of PLR	35% of PLR
Deliberate and concealed	30% of PLR	50% of PLR

Unprompted disclosure where a careless mistake has been made can reduce the penalty to nil.

1.6 Quality of disclosure

The reductions that are given by HMRC depend on the quality of the disclosure. To calculate the reduction HMRC will consider three elements of disclosure and to what degree the taxpayer:

* Tells HMRC about the error, making full disclosure and explaining how the error was made
* Helps HMRC to work out what extra tax is due
* Allows access to business and other records and other relevant documents to check the figures

 Worked example: Reduction of a penalty

Graham is a sole trader. He files his tax return for 2012/13 on 31 January 2014. The return shows trading income of £65,000. HMRC initiates a review into Graham's return and discovers interest received from a previously undisclosed bank account. Graham's initial explanation is that the account holds monies that he has inherited. He later discloses that the account holds £12,000 of undisclosed property income relating to 2012/13.

Requirement

State the maximum and minimum penalties that Graham could be charged by HMRC for his error.

Solution

The Potential Lost Revenue as a result of Graham's error is:
£12,000 × 40%   £4,800

Graham's error is deliberate but not concealed so the maximum penalty for the error is:
£4,800 × 70%   £3,360

Graham has made a prompted disclosure so the minimum penalty for the error is:
£4,800 × 35%   £1,680

1.7 Reasonable care

Where a taxpayer has taken reasonable care in completing a return and has taken reasonable steps to disclose any errors, no penalty applies.

'Reasonable care' varies according to the person, their circumstances and their abilities.

HMRC expects taxpayers to make and keep sufficient records to provide a complete and accurate return and to check the position when they do not understand something.

If taxpayers do not promptly tell HMRC when they discover an error, HMRC will treat the errors as careless inaccuracies even where the taxpayer took reasonable care.

Where the taxpayer uses an agent such as an accountant to complete a return, it remains the taxpayer's responsibility to make sure that the return is correct.

1.8 Issue of penalty

If a person is liable to a penalty, HMRC sends him a penalty assessment. This states what he owes and that the penalty must be paid within 30 days.

The taxpayer must pay any:

- Tax that is due
- Penalties that are due
- Interest that is due on late tax and penalties

1.9 Suspension of penalties

A penalty may be suspended by HMRC to allow the taxpayer to take action to ensure that the error/inaccuracy does not occur again (eg where the error has arisen from failure to keep proper records).

HMRC will impose conditions which the taxpayer has to satisfy eg establishing proper record keeping systems.

The penalty will be cancelled if the conditions imposed by HMRC are complied with by the taxpayer within a period of up to two years. Otherwise, if the conditions are not met, the penalty must be paid.

The penalty cannot be suspended if it results from a deliberate error/inaccuracy.

1.10 Appeals

Appeals can be made against:

- The imposition of a penalty
- The amount of a penalty
- A decision not to suspend a penalty
- The conditions set by HMRC in relation to the suspension of a penalty

Appeals are made to an independent tribunal, which will usually be the First-tier Tribunal of the Tax Chamber.

It is also possible to opt for an internal review by an independent HMRC officer. This is potentially a quick and inexpensive way to resolve a dispute.

2 Penalties for failure to notify

Section overview

- A common 'failure to notify' penalty applies to failures on or after 1 April 2010.

- Maximum penalties are based upon Potential Lost Revenue but can be reduced under certain circumstances.

- Penalties may be mitigated if there is reasonable excuse.

2.1 Introduction

Where a duty to notify chargeability or liability to register occurs on or after 1 April 2010, a unified set of rules applies if the failure results in a loss of tax.

The rules apply to failure by either the taxpayer or his tax adviser, unless the taxpayer can show that he took all reasonable steps to avoid the failure.

Penalties can also be collected (in part or in full) from an officer (eg director) of a company if a 'deliberate action' is attributable to him.

The taxes affected are:

- Income tax
- National insurance contributions
- Income tax and NIC collected via PAYE
- Capital gains tax
- Corporation tax
- VAT

2.2 Amount of penalty

Penalties are behaviour related, increasing for more serious failures, and are based on the Potential Lost Revenue.

The 'Potential Lost Revenue' is the amount of tax outstanding at the end of the tax year (income tax and CGT) or accounting period (corporation tax). For VAT purposes it is the amount outstanding on the acquisition to which the failure relates.

Reductions are available for disclosure, with higher reductions if the disclosure is unprompted.

The minimum and maximum penalties are as follows:

Behaviour	Maximum penalty	Minimum penalty with unprompted disclosure		Minimum penalty with prompted disclosure	
Deliberate and concealed	100%	30%		50%	
Deliberate but not concealed	70%	20%		35%	
		>12m	<12m	>12m	<12m
Any other case	30%	10%	Nil	20%	10%

The minimum penalties shown above presume that the maximum reductions for disclosure apply. In practice, however, the reductions given are up to the HMRC officer involved and could result in a higher penalty being payable.

Note that there is no zero penalty for reasonable care (unlike for penalties for errors on returns), although the penalty may be reduced to 0% if the failure is rectified within 12 months through unprompted disclosure.

The penalties may also be reduced at HMRC's discretion in 'special circumstances'. 'Special circumstances' are expected to be very rare.

2.3 Reasonable excuse

Where the taxpayer's failure is not classed as deliberate, there is no penalty if he can show he has a 'reasonable excuse'.

Reasonable excuse does not include having insufficient money to pay the penalty.

2.4 Appeals

Taxpayers have a right of appeal against penalty decisions to the First-tier Tribunal, which may confirm, substitute or cancel the penalty.

3 Record keeping

Section overview

- A common framework exists for record keeping for IT, CGT, CT, VAT and PAYE.
- There are time limits for the retention of records and penalties may be levied for failure to do so.
- Large companies must appoint a senior accounting officer who is responsible for maintaining adequate tax accounting arrangements. Failure to do so can result in penalties.

3.1 Introduction

There is a common framework for record keeping for income tax, capital gains tax, corporation tax, VAT and PAYE.

One set of high level rules applies across the above taxes, but the detailed rules for each tax remain unchanged.

3.2 General provisions

Taxpayers must keep 'information' (rather than 'records') to show that they have prepared a complete and correct tax return. The information must also be able to be provided in a legible form on request. Records can be kept in electronic format.

HMRC can specify a shorter time limit for keeping records where the records are bulky and the information they contain can be provided in another way.

HMRC can inspect 'in-year' records, ie *before* a return is submitted, if it believes it is reasonably required to check a tax position.

3.3 Which records must be kept?

For income tax, capital gains tax, corporation tax and VAT the requirement is for taxable persons to keep 'adequate' business and accounting records.

'Adequate' means keeping records to be sure that the right profit, loss, tax declaration or claim is made.

For PAYE, employers are required to keep specified records.

3.4 Time limits for keeping records

The time limits for keeping records are:

(a) Corporation tax — 6 years from end of accounting period

(b) Income and capital gains tax — 5th anniversary of 31 January following end of tax year if the taxpayer is in business

— 1st anniversary of 31 January following the end of the tax year if the taxpayer is not in business

(c) VAT — 6 years

HMRC has the flexibility to shorten the periods for which records need to be retained.

3.5 Record keeping penalties

The maximum (mitigable) penalty for each failure to keep and retain records is £3,000 per tax year/accounting period.

3.6 Time limits for taxpayer claims

The general time limit for taxpayers making claims, which applies in the absence of any specific time limit, is four years from the end of the tax year or accounting period.

3.7 Duties of senior accounting officers

Senior accounting officers of 'qualifying' companies must take reasonable steps to establish and maintain appropriate tax accounting arrangements.

A qualifying company has, at the end of its previous financial year:

(a)   Turnover of more than £200 million, and/ or
(b)   A balance sheet total of more than £2 billion

Qualifying companies must notify HMRC of the name of their senior accounting officer (SAO). The SAO must certify annually that the company's accounting systems are adequate for the purposes of accurate tax reporting or specify the nature of any inadequacies.

The SAO may be liable to a £5,000 penalty, in each of the following cases, for his failure to:

(a)   Establish and maintain appropriate tax accounting arrangements.

(b)   Provide an annual certificate to HMRC or provide a certificate that contains a careless or deliberate inaccuracy.

HMRC may impose a £5,000 penalty on the company for failure to notify the name of the SAO.

4   Penalties for late filing of returns

Section overview

*   There is a common penalty regime for the late filing of tax returns.

*   These penalties apply to returns for periods of at least six months and combine a mixture of fixed and tax geared penalties.

4.1 Introduction

There is a common penalty regime for the late filing of tax returns. It applies to all the main taxes including income tax, capital gains tax and corporation tax.

4.2 Amount of penalty

The penalties for late filing of a return are as follows:

*   Immediate £100 fixed penalty, regardless of whether the tax has been paid (note that the £100 still applies even if the tax due is £0)

*   Daily fixed penalties of up to £10 per day if the return is more than three months late (for up to 90 days, so a maximum of £900)

*   Where the delay is greater than six months but less than twelve months a tax geared penalty of 5% of the tax due (for income tax purposes this means the tax payable for the year after the deduction of tax deducted at source)

*   Where the delay is greater than twelve months the following tax geared penalties apply:

    –   100% of tax due where withholding of information is deliberate and concealed
    –   70% of tax due where withholding of information is deliberate but not concealed
    –   5% of tax due in other cases

The tax geared penalties are all subject to a minimum of £300.

Where the return is more than 12 months late and the withholding of information **was deliberate** the penalty can be reduced for disclosure, with higher reductions if the disclosure is unprompted, as follows:

Behaviour	Maximum penalty	Minimum penalty with prompted disclosure	Minimum penalty with unprompted disclosure
Deliberate and concealed	100%	50%	30%
Deliberate but not concealed	70%	35%	20%

4.3 Returns covered by the penalty regime

These late filing penalties apply to the following documents:

- Income tax – personal tax return, partnership tax return, employer's PAYE annual return
- Capital gains tax – personal tax return
- Corporation tax – company tax return

These are all annual returns. There are separate penalty provisions for taxes where there are more frequent return obligations ie for periods of less than six months (see later in this chapter).

5 Pay As You Earn (PAYE)

Section overview

- There are a number of PAYE forms used to provide information to ensure that tax is deducted correctly.
- Non compliance with PAYE requirements will lead to penalties.

5.1 PAYE forms

The PAYE system has many forms which are used to provide information to enable tax to be calculated correctly. The most important forms are listed below:

Name	Function	Important dates
P9D	End of year form recording details of benefits provided to employees in excluded employment	Send to HMRC and copy to employee by 6 July following end of tax year
P11D	End of year form recording details of benefits provided to employees not in excluded employment	Send to HMRC and copy to employee by 6 July following end of tax year
P60	End of year form recording details of gross pay, tax deducted and NICs for both employer and employee	Supply to each employee by 31 May following end of tax year
P14	Same details as P60	Send to HMRC by 19 May following end of tax year
P35	End of year summary of tax and NICs deducted for all employees	Send to HMRC by 19 May following end of tax year
P45	Particulars of employee leaving: 4 part document recording tax code, gross pay to date, tax and NICs deducted	One part sent to HMRC when employee leaves, other three parts given to employee (one kept by employee, one by his new employer and the third sent by new employer to HMRC)

From 6 April 2011 all employers must submit their end of year P14 and P35 forms, and P45 leaver forms electronically. Other PAYE forms may be submitted either on paper or electronically. The introduction of

the Real Time Information (RTI) PAYE reporting system will eventually remove the need for employers to send these forms to HMRC (see Chapter 3).

Employers with at least 250 employees must also pay income tax/Class 1 national insurance contributions electronically. They receive an extension of three days to make their payment, therefore payments are due by 22nd rather than 19th of a month.

5.2 PAYE forms: penalties

Penalties may be charged for both incorrect PAYE returns and for PAYE returns filed late.

Forms	Initial delay	Continuing delay	Delay exceeds 12 months
P14 and P35,		£100 monthly per 50 employees	Penalty not exceeding 100% of the income tax and NICs payable for the year of assessment but not paid by 19 April (22 April for electronic payment) following the end of the year of assessment
P9D and P11D	£300 per return	£60 per day	

5.3 PAYE payments: penalties

There is also a penalty for late payment of in-year deductions collected via PAYE (ie income tax and NIC apart from Class 1A and Class 1B). The penalty applies to all employers, irrespective of the number of employees.

The penalty depends on the number of defaults in any 12 month period.

Number of late payments	Percentage of tax unpaid
1st	Nil (as long as payment is less than 6 months late)
2nd to 4th	1%
5th to 7th	2%
8th to 10th	3%
11th and more	4%

The percentage penalty is applied to the total amount that is late in the tax year, but ignoring the first late payment in the year. Where a penalty has been imposed and the tax remains unpaid at 6 or 12 months the penalty is 5% of tax unpaid, even if there is only one late payment in the year.

The total penalty for the year to date is calculated each time the penalty is imposed and any amounts already imposed are deducted from the total due.

Worked example: PAYE in-year late payment penalty

Genevieve is an employer with a regular monthly liability under PAYE of £12,000 but pays that amount one week late on eight occasions in the year.

Requirement

State the total penalty payable by Genevieve for the late payment of her PAYE liability.

Solution

As there are eight failures in the year, the penalty percentage is 3% of the total amount of the late payments, excluding the first. Therefore the total penalty will be calculated as 3% of £84,000 (being 7 × £12,000), so £2,520.

Genevieve may have paid more than one penalty during the year, however her total penalty will be £2,520.

Late payment penalties can be suspended where the taxpayer agrees a time to pay arrangement, unless he abuses the arrangement.

6 Income tax and capital gains tax – returns and payment

Section overview

- Not all taxpayers have to submit a tax return.

- A taxpayer may be issued with a full tax return or a short tax return.

- Partnerships are required to submit a tax return.

- Income tax not deducted at source and Class 4 NICs are payable in a maximum of three instalments.

- Capital gains tax is payable in one lump sum.

- Underpayments of less than £2,000 may be collected through the PAYE system.

6.1 Issue of tax return

Under the self assessment system, an individual may be required to submit a tax return giving details of his taxable income and gains for a tax year.

Some taxpayers do not have to submit a tax return, for example if tax has been deducted at source under PAYE and from savings income.

In April each tax year, HMRC issues tax returns and/or notices to file to taxpayers who are likely to need to file a return such as sole traders and higher rate / additional rate taxpayers.

If a tax return or notice to file is not automatically issued, the individual must notify HMRC by 5 October following the end of the tax year unless:

- There is no capital gains tax liability; and

- No higher rate or additional rate tax is due; and

- Either all of the income is covered by the personal allowance, or all of the tax due has been deducted at source, eg under PAYE.

If notification of self employment has already been given to HMRC for NIC purposes (see Chapter 7) it is not necessary to make a separate request for the issue of a tax return.

If a taxpayer fails to notify HMRC, a penalty will be payable (see earlier in this chapter).

6.2 Full tax return

A full tax return (SA100) consists of a summary form, supplementary pages dealing with different types of income and gains, and a tax calculation section.

The individual must complete the summary form and such supplementary pages as are relevant. He must also report whether he has a student loan.

Completion of the tax calculation section is optional. If the taxpayer does complete the tax calculation, this is called a **self assessment**.

Alternatively, the taxpayer may ask HMRC to calculate the tax liability. This is still treated as a self assessment by the taxpayer, not an official assessment by HMRC. As a result, the self assessment may be amended by the taxpayer (see later in this chapter).

The due date for submission of the tax return is determined according to whether a return is submitted on paper or online. The due date for submission of an electronic return online is the later of 31 January following the end of the tax year or three months after the return was issued. The due date for submission of a paper return is the later of 31 October following the end of the tax year or three months after the return was issued.

If the taxpayer wishes HMRC to calculate his tax liability for him, then the filing deadline for a paper return is slightly different and is the later of 31 October following the tax year end and two months after the notice to make a return is issued.

There are penalties for late submission (see earlier in this chapter).

 Worked example: Submitting a tax return

Winifred was issued with a full tax return for 2012/13.

Requirement

By what date should Winifred submit her tax return to HMRC if:

(a) The return was issued on 10 April 2013 and Winifred wishes HMRC to compute her tax liability and submit a paper return

(b) The return was issued on 12 December 2013, Winifred wishes to compute her own tax liability and submit an electronic return online

(c) The return was issued on 14 October 2013, Winifred wishes to compute her own tax liability and submit a paper return

Solution

(a) Later of 31 October 2013 and 10 June 2013, ie 31 October 2013
(b) Later of 31 January 2014 and 12 March 2014, ie 12 March 2014
(c) Later of 31 October 2013 and 14 January 2014, ie 14 January 2014

If a taxpayer is sent a return by HMRC it must be submitted to HMRC by the due date even if there is no income to declare.

6.3 Short tax return

HMRC aims to send taxpayers a short tax return if they are employees (not directors), sole traders with a turnover of less than £77,000 (the VAT registration limit) or pensioners.

The short tax return asks only for information likely to be relevant to these individuals and the form does not contain a tax calculation section. Therefore HMRC will automatically compute the tax liability.

The short tax return should be submitted by 31 October following the end of the tax year if possible, to enable HMRC to compute the tax liability. The latest submission date is 31 October or three months after the issue of the tax return. The short tax return is not available online.

It is the responsibility of the taxpayer to check whether his circumstances are still covered by the short tax return and to request a full tax return if necessary.

6.4 Partnership tax returns

Although a partnership is not itself liable to tax on the income and gains of the partners, it is important for partnership income and gains to be reported to HMRC so that these can be checked against the partners' individual returns.

A partnership therefore submits a tax return to HMRC in the same way as individuals. The partnership tax return (SA800) must be submitted by the later of 31 January following the end of the tax year or three months after the return was issued where an electronic return is submitted online. If a paper return is submitted, the filing date is the later of 31 October following the end of the tax year or three months after the return was issued.

6.5 Right to amend tax returns

HMRC has the right to correct a taxpayer's tax return for obvious errors such as errors of principle and arithmetic errors. Such corrections must be made within nine months of the date the return is actually filed. HMRC's powers to correct a return extend to correct 'anything else in the return that the officer has reason to believe is incorrect in the light of information available to the officer'.

The taxpayer has the right to amend a tax return for any reason within 12 months of the normal due submission date (not the actual submission date). For amendment purposes, the due submission date is the later of 31 January following the end of the tax year or three months after the return was issued, regardless of whether it was submitted on paper or electronically.

In addition, a taxpayer may make a claim for 'overpayment relief' for errors in the tax return where tax would be overcharged as a result. Such a claim must be made within four years of the end of the tax year to which the tax return relates.

Interactive question 1: Important dates

[Difficulty level: Exam standard]

State the latest relevant date for the following questions.

Question	Fill in your answer
Normal due date for tax return for 2012/13 issued 20 November 2013, taxpayer to submit an electronic return online	
Notify HMRC of need to issue tax return for 2012/13	
Overpayment relief claim relating to 2012/13	
Keep business records for 2012/13	
Normal due date for tax return for 2012/13 issued 31 May 2013, HMRC to calculate tax and paper return to be submitted	
Keep personal records for 2012/13	
Amend tax return for 2012/13 submitted 30 November 2013	

See **Answer** at the end of this chapter.

6.6 Payment dates

Income tax (which has not been deducted at source) and Class 4 NICs are paid as follows:

- First payment on account by 31 January in the tax year
- Second payment on account by 31 July following the end of the tax year
- Balancing payment by 31 January following the end of the tax year

6.7 Payments on account

Each payment on account is half of the income tax and Class 4 NICs paid under self assessment for the previous year.

Worked example: Payment on account

Josiah is a sole trader who paid tax as follows in 2011/12:

Total income tax liability	£18,400
Tax deducted at source on savings income	£6,400
Class 4 NICs	£3,800

Requirement

What are his payments on account for 2012/13 and when are they due?

Solution

	£
Total income tax liability 2011/12	18,400
Less: deducted at source	(6,400)
Income tax payable under self-assessment	12,000
Class 4 NICs	3,800
	15,800
Payments on account	
31 January 2013 £15,800 × ½	7,900
31 July 2013 £15,800 × ½	7,900

For the tax year 2012/13 payments on account are not required where the amount of the tax paid under self assessment in the previous year was less than:

- £1,000; or
- 20% of the total tax liability (income tax and Class 4)

6.8 Balancing payments

A balancing payment or repayment is due by 31 January following the end of the tax year. The balancing payment comprises any unpaid income tax and Class 4 NICs, together with capital gains tax payable for the year.

Worked example: Balancing payments

The following information relates to Irene for 2012/13:

Total income tax liability	£20,000
Tax deducted under PAYE and at source	£12,500

Payments on account:

31 January 2013	£3,000
31 July 2013	£3,000
Capital gains tax liability 2012/13	£5,000

Requirement

What are the amounts payable by Irene by 31 January 2014?

Solution

Amounts payable on 31 January 2014:

	£
Total income tax liability	20,000
Less: tax deducted under PAYE and at source	(12,500)
	7,500
Less: payments on account 2 × £3,000	(6,000)
Balancing payment for 2012/13	1,500
CGT 2012/13	5,000
First payment on account for 2013/14 £7,500 × ½	3,750

Where the taxpayer is an employee and has underpaid tax of less than £3,000, the underpayment can usually be collected by adjusting his PAYE code for the following tax year, unless the taxpayer requests otherwise. For the underpayment to be collected via PAYE the return must be filed on paper by 31 October following the tax year end or online by 30 December following the tax year end.

6.9 Paying tax on extra income

An employee may also have non-employment income such as investment income and rental income. The employee can choose how to pay tax on this extra income.

Where extra income is not more than £10,000 in any year, the additional tax may be paid via PAYE rather than by self assessment. However, if a taxpayer earns more than £10,000 of extra income in any year then he will have to complete a tax return and pay the tax via self assessment.

7 Income tax and capital gains tax – penalties and interest

Section overview

- Penalties are used to enforce the self assessment system, for example for late submission of tax returns and for late payment of tax.

- Interest is payable by the taxpayer on late paid tax and penalties. Interest is payable by HMRC on overpaid tax.

7.1 Penalties

The self assessment system is enforced through a system of penalties, some of which were considered earlier in this chapter, including those for late filing of returns.

7.2 Penalties for late payment of tax

The penalties for late payment of income tax or capital gains tax are:

- 5% of tax unpaid 30 days after the payment due date
- Further 5% penalty where tax remains unpaid six months after the payment due date
- Further 5% penalty where the tax remains unpaid 12 months after the payment due date.

This gives a maximum penalty of 15% of the unpaid tax.

A penalty may be charged on late payment of:

- Balancing payments under self assessment
- Additional tax payment arising from amendments to a self assessment
- Tax payable under a discovery assessment (see later in this chapter)

Note that penalties do not apply to payments on account.

Late payment penalties can be suspended where the taxpayer agrees a time to pay arrangement, unless he abuses the arrangement.

Worked example: Penalty for late payment of tax

Arslan gives you the following information about his payments of tax relating to 2011/12:

First payment on account of £2,000 paid in full on 31 March 2012

Second payment on account of £2,000 paid in full on 31 July 2012

Balancing payment of £3,000 paid in full on 16 March 2013

Requirement

Calculate any penalties due.

Solution

First payment on account due 31 January 2012, paid 31 March 2012, but no penalties on payments on account.

Second payment on account paid on due date 31 July 2012.

Balancing payment due 31 January 2013, paid 16 March 2013. Initial penalty of 5% of tax due of £150 (5% × £3,000). No further penalty due as the tax was paid within six months of the due date.

Interactive question 2: Penalties   [Difficulty level: Exam standard]

State the maximum penalties for the following events.

Question	Fill in your answer
Notified HMRC of new source of income for 2012/13 on 5 December 2013, paid all £4,000 of tax due on 25 January 2014	
Tax return for 2012/13 issued May 2013, submitted return electronically on 30 March 2014	
Balancing payment of tax of £2,000 for 2012/13 paid 30 April 2014	
Destroyed supporting records for 2012/13 on 1 May 2014	
Tax return for 2012/13 issued June 2013, submitted electronically on 15 February 2015, tax liability £1,000	
Balancing payment of tax of £3,000 for 2012/13 paid 30 September 2014	

See **Answer** at the end of this chapter.

7.3 Late payment interest

A taxpayer is liable to interest on late payment of income tax, capital gains tax, national insurance and penalties.

Interest on payments on account, balancing payments and penalties runs from the due date of payment to the day before the payment is made.

Interest on additional tax payments due to amendments to a self assessment and tax payable under a discovery assessment runs from the *annual* submission date to the day before the payment is made.

Worked example: Interest on late paid tax

Arslan gives you the following information about his payments of tax relating to 2011/12:

First payment on account of £2,000 paid in full on 31 March 2012
Second payment on account of £2,000 paid in full on 31 July 2012
Balancing payment of £3,000 paid in full on 16 March 2013

Requirement

Calculate the interest due (interest rate on overdue tax is 3%), working to the nearest day and pound. Assume that any penalties are paid on time.

Solution

First payment on account due 31 January 2012, paid 31 March 2012, 59 days late (1.2.12 – 30.3.12). Interest = 59/366 × £2,000 × 3% = £10

Second payment on account paid on due date 31 July 2012, so no interest due.

Balancing payment due 31 January 2013, paid 16 March 2013, 43 days late (1.2.13 – 15.3.13). Interest 43/365 × £3,000 × 3% = £11

7.4 Repayment interest

Repayment interest is payable by HMRC on overpaid payments on account, balancing payments and penalties.

Repayment interest runs from the later of the date that the tax was paid to HMRC and the due date for payment of the tax, to the day before the repayment is made. Repayment interest is exempt from income tax.

8 Corporation tax – returns and payment

Section overview

- If a company has taxable total profits it must notify HMRC of its chargeability to corporation tax.

- HMRC will issue a company with a tax return shortly after the end of its period of account.

- The tax return includes a tax computation and the company must also submit accounts and supporting calculations.

- Small and medium sized companies pay corporation tax in one lump sum.

- Large companies are required to pay corporation tax in four equal instalments.

8.1 Issue of tax return

Companies have an obligation to notify HMRC when their first chargeable accounting period begins. The company must give written notice to HMRC within three months of the start of the first chargeable accounting period. The notice must state when the first chargeable accounting period began.

If a company fails to notify HMRC, a penalty may be payable (see Section 9.1).

Most companies prepare their accounts to the same date each year. HMRC normally issues a notice requiring a company to submit a corporation tax return within a few weeks of the end of each period of account.

Where a notice and/or return is not issued, a company is required to notify HMRC where it has taxable total profits for a chargeable accounting period. Notification of chargeability must be made within twelve months of the end of the chargeable accounting period. If notification is not given, a penalty may be payable (see Section 2).

8.2 Full tax return

A full corporation tax return (CT600) consists of an eight-page summary form and tax calculation, together with a number of supplementary forms.

The company is required to complete the summary form and tax calculation and such supplementary forms as are relevant. Note that there is **no** option for HMRC to calculate the tax liability of the company.

The company must also submit accounts for the period covered by the return and computations showing how entries on the return have been calculated from the figures in the accounts.

The tax return and supporting information must normally be submitted within twelve months of the end of the period of account.

8.3 Short tax return

The short corporation tax return (CT600 Short) is a four-page form. Most companies which do not have to make payments on account and which have straightforward tax affairs can use the short return, provided the form has boxes for all the entries it needs to make.

Use of the short return does not affect the filing deadline or the requirement for the company to calculate its own tax liability.

8.4 Online filing

From 1 April 2011 all companies must submit their tax returns online and pay their tax liabilities electronically for any accounting period ending after 31 March 2010.

Additionally, tax computations and the accounts that form part of the Company Tax Return, must be submitted in Inline eXtensible Business Reporting Language (iXBRL) format. iXBRL is an IT standard designed specifically for business financial reporting.

8.5 Right to amend tax returns

HMRC has the right to amend a company's tax return so as to correct obvious errors or omissions in the return such as errors of principle and arithmetic errors. HMRC's powers to correct a return extend to correct 'anything else in the return that the officer has reason to believe is incorrect in the light of information available to the officer'.

HMRC corrections must be made within nine months of the date the return is actually filed.

The company has the right to amend its tax return for any reason within twelve months of the normal due submission date (not the actual submission date).

In addition, the company may make a claim for 'overpayment' relief for errors in the tax return where tax would be overcharged as a result. Such a claim must be made within four years of the end of the chargeable accounting period.

8.6 Payment – large companies

A large company is one which pays corporation tax at the main rate.

However, a company is not treated as large if:

- It has a tax liability of less than £10,000 (scaled down for short accounting periods); or

- It was not a large company in the preceding 12 months and it has augmented profits of £10 million or less in this chargeable accounting period

The small profits upper limit and the £10 million de minimis limit are scaled down for short accounting periods and for associated companies, but based on the number of associated companies at the end of the previous accounting period.

A large company must pay corporation tax in four equal instalments based on the company's estimated liability for the accounting period. In practice, since the total liability cannot be known until the end of the accounting period, the company will make revised estimates of how much each instalment should be as the accounting period progresses.

The instalments are due on the 14th day of the 7th, 10th, 13th and 16th months after the start of a 12-month accounting period.

Worked example: Payment by instalments

T Ltd pays corporation tax at the main rate and makes up accounts to 31 December each year.

Requirement

When will T Ltd be required to pay instalments of corporation tax for the year ended 31 December 2012?

Solution

Chargeable accounting period starts 1 January 2012.

Instalments due 14 July 2012, 14 October 2012, 14 January 2013 and 14 April 2013

8.7 Payment – other companies

The due date for corporation tax payable by companies not treated as large is nine months and one day after the end of the chargeable accounting period.

Worked example: Payment of corporation tax

Q Ltd does not pay corporation tax at the main rate and has a chargeable accounting period ending on 30 April 2012.

Requirement

What is the due date for payment of corporation tax?

Solution

1 February 2013

9 Corporation tax – penalties and interest

Section overview

- Penalties are payable, for example on late submission of tax returns and late payment of tax.
- Interest is payable by a company on late paid tax and penalties.
- Interest is payable by HMRC on overpaid tax.

9.1 Penalties

A fixed penalty is charged where a company fails to notify commencement of the first chargeable accounting period. Failure to notify commencement within three months can lead to a maximum penalty of £300.

Penalties are also charged if a company submits a late return. Tax-geared penalties may also apply to returns submitted late. These penalties have been considered earlier in this chapter.

9.2 Penalties for late payment of tax

The penalties for late payment of corporation tax are as follows:

- 5% of tax unpaid at the filing date
- Further 5% penalty where tax remains unpaid three months after the filing date
- Further 5% penalty where the tax remains unpaid nine months after the filing date

Worked example: Penalties

K plc makes up accounts to 30 June each year.

For the year to 30 June 2012, K plc submits its tax return and pays its corporation tax on 1 February 2014.

The corporation tax liability of K plc for the year to 30 June 2012 is £50,000. K plc does not pay corporation tax at the main rate and has made no payments of corporation tax in respect of this year.

Requirement

What is the maximum penalty payable by K plc?

Solution

Tax return should have been submitted by 30 June 2013. The return was therefore seven months late.

Maximum penalty for late filing of the return is:

£100 plus £900 (£10 per day × 90 days) plus (5% × £50,000)   £3,500

The tax liability was due to be paid on 1 April 2013. The tax was paid 10 months late.

Maximum penalty for late payment of tax is:

(10% × £50,000)   £5,000

There is a 5% penalty at the filing date and a further 5% penalty three months after the filing date. The tax had been paid by nine months after the filling date.

Interactive question 3: Penalties   [Difficulty level: Exam standard]

State the maximum penalties for the following events, briefly stating the reason for your answer.

Question	Fill in your answer
Notified HMRC on 10 January 2014 of chargeability for accounting period ended 30 November 2012. This is not the company's first chargeable accounting period. Corporation tax liability £7,500 paid on same date	
Tax return for accounting period ended 31 July 2012 submitted 30 November 2013	
Destroyed records on 10 August 2016 for accounting period ended 31 December 2012	
Tax return for accounting period ended 31 October 2012 submitted 30 November 2014, corporation tax due of £10,000 paid 30 September 2014	

See **Answer** at the end of this chapter.

9.3   Interest on late paid corporation tax

Interest is payable on late paid corporation tax. Interest runs from the date the tax should have been paid to the day before the tax is actually paid.

Worked example: Interest on late paid tax

H Ltd does not pay corporation tax at the main rate and makes up accounts to 30 September each year.

For the year to 30 September 2011, H Ltd had a corporation tax liability of £50,000. It paid this on 14 September 2012.

Requirement

What is the interest payable by H Ltd? Assume an interest rate of 3% on late paid corporation tax.

Solution

Corporation tax due 1 July 2012, paid 14 September 2012, so 74 days late.

Interest 74/365 × £50,000 × 3%   £304

Interest charged on late paid corporation tax is an allowable non-trading loan relationships expense.

9.4 Interest on overpaid corporation tax (repayment interest)

Repayment interest is payable by HMRC on overpaid corporation tax. Repayment interest runs from the later of the date the tax was originally paid and the date the tax was due to be paid.

Repayment interest is taxable as a non-trading loan relationships profit.

10 Value added tax – penalties and interest

Section overview

- There are penalties for late registration; late returns and late payments of VAT; failure to file returns online and incorrect returns.

- Interest may be payable on late paid VAT and overpayments of VAT.

10.1 Late registration penalty

A taxable person who fails to register for VAT by the appropriate date may be liable to a late registration penalty (see Section 2 of this chapter).

10.2 Penalty for late filing of VAT returns

The penalty regime for the late filing of returns (see section 4 of this Chapter) also applies to VAT but as returns are typically filed at intervals of less than one year, a separate set of rules apply.

The rules apply to a 'penalty period'. Once a penalty period has started, each subsequent late return in that period causes the penalty period to be extended to the day after the anniversary of the most recent default.

Penalties for further late returns within a penalty period gradually increase as the number of late returns increases.

Although the penalty regime is being implemented over a number of years only the new late filing penalties explained here are examinable.

The penalties are as follows:

	Monthly Returns	Quarterly Returns
Initial penalty	£100	£100
Further late returns within penalty period (expires 12 months after the most recent late return)	1st to 5th late return: £100 6th and subsequent late return: £200	1st late return: £200 2nd late return: £300 3rd or subsequent late return: £400

If a return is still outstanding after six months a further penalty applies of 5% of the tax due.

If a return is still outstanding after 12 months a further penalty applies:

- 100% of tax due where withholding of information is deliberate and concealed
- 70% of tax due where withholding of information is deliberate but not concealed
- 5% of tax due in other cases

The tax geared penalties are all subject to a minimum of £300 and can be reduced for disclosure, with higher reductions if the disclosure is unprompted (see earlier in this chapter).

Worked example: Late filing of VAT returns

Gate Ltd has submitted its recent VAT returns as follows:

VAT quarter end	Date submitted
30.4.12	10.6.12
31.7.12	29.8.12
31.10.12	30.11.12
31.1.13	16.3.13

The company is not currently in a penalty period.

Requirement

What penalties will be payable by Gate Ltd for the late filing of its VAT returns?

Solution

The VAT return for the quarter ended 30 April 2012 was due by 7 June 2012. This is the first failure so will start a penalty period for the company for twelve months until 7 June 2013. It will also result in a fixed penalty of £100.

The VAT return for the quarters ended 31 July 2012 and 31 October 2012 were submitted on time so there is no penalty and no change to the penalty period.

The VAT return for the quarter ended 31 January 2013 was due on 7 March 2013 and was therefore submitted late. A penalty of £200 will be charged and the penalty period will be extended to 7 March 2014.

If the taxpayer can satisfy HMRC that there is 'reasonable excuse' for the late filing of the return, no penalty is payable nor does the failure count for the purpose of starting a penalty period to run.

10.3 Penalty for failing to file VAT return online

This section is new.

Penalties apply where a return is submitted on paper which should have been submitted online.

The amount of the penalty depends on the trader's VAT-exclusive turnover in the 12 months up to and including those on the paper return which triggers the penalty.

Annual VAT exclusive turnover	Penalty
£100,000 and under	£100
£100,001 to £5,600,000	£200
£5,600,001 to £22,800,000	£300
Above £22,800,000	£400

10.4 Penalty for late payment of VAT

The new penalty regime for the late payment of tax also applies to VAT. However as liabilities are more frequent, because the return period is usually less than six months, a system based on penalty periods applies in a similar way to the penalties for late returns (above).

The first late payment of VAT does not attract a penalty but it starts a twelve month 'penalty period' that runs from the payment due date.

If a further late payment of VAT occurs within the penalty period, a penalty is charged, based on the amount of tax paid late. The penalty period is also extended for a further twelve months.

The penalties are as follows:

	Monthly Returns	Quarterly returns
Penalty for default within penalty period	1st, 2nd or 3rd default: 1%	1st default: 2%
	4th, 5th or 6th default: 2%	2nd default: 3%
	7th, 8th or 9th default: 3%	3rd or subsequent default: 4%
	10th or subsequent default:4%	
After 6 months	5% of tax still unpaid	
After 12 months	5% of tax still unpaid	

Late payment penalties can be suspended where the taxpayer agrees a time to pay arrangement, unless he abuses the arrangement.

Worked example: Late payment of VAT

Gate Ltd has paid the VAT due from its recent quarterly returns as follows:

VAT quarter end	VAT due £	Date VAT paid
30.4.12	30,000	14.6.12
31.7.12	26,000	29.8.12
31.10.12	28,500	21.12.12
31.1.13	31,200	21.9.13

The company is not currently in a penalty period.

Requirement

What penalties will be payable by Gate Ltd for the late the late payment of VAT?

Solution

The VAT payment for the quarter ended 30 April 2012 was due by 7 June 2012. This is the first default and will initiate a penalty period for the company for twelve months until 7 June 2013. There is no penalty charged for the first default.

The VAT for the quarter ended 31 July was paid on time so there is no penalty and no change to the penalty period.

The VAT due for the quarter ended 31 October 2012 was due on 7 December 2012 and was therefore paid late. As this is the first default within the penalty period the penalty charged is 2% of the tax due of £28,500, which is £570. The penalty period is extended to 7 December 2013.

The VAT due for the quarter ended 31 January 2013 was due on 7 March 2013. The VAT was paid late. The penalty for a second default within a penalty period is 3% of the tax due of £31,200. There will be a penalty of £936 and an extension to the penalty period to 7 March 2014. In addition as the VAT due is not paid until 21 September 2013 it is over six months late. A further penalty will be payable as this is a prolonged failure. The penalty will be 5% of the VAT due, which is £1,560.

10.5 VAT errors

The common penalty regime for making errors in tax returns discussed in section 1 of this chapter also applies to value added tax.

An error made on a VAT return can be corrected on the next return provided it was not deliberate and does not exceed the greater of:

- £10,000 (net under-declaration minus over-declaration); or
- 1% × net VAT turnover for return period (maximum £50,000)

Alternatively, a small careless (not deliberate) error may be corrected on form VAT652. A tax payer may choose to both correct a small careless error on the VAT return and also submit form VAT652.

'Large' errors or deliberate small errors should be notified to HMRC on form VAT652.

In both cases a penalty for error may be imposed. Correction of an error on a later return is not, of, itself an unprompted disclosure of the error and fuller disclosure is required for the penalty to be reduced.

However if the inaccuracy in the return was neither careless nor deliberate when the return was made and the net value of the inaccuracy was below the de minimis limit and the error was corrected in a later VAT return HMRC will deem reasonable steps to have been taken to inform it of the inaccuracy and no penalty will be due.

In addition, as discussed in section 2 of this chapter, a penalty may not be due if the trader can show there is reasonable excuse for the failure.

10.6 Interest on unpaid VAT

A taxable person may be charged interest where:

- HMRC raises an assessment for output VAT under declared or input VAT over claimed; or

- The taxpayer voluntarily discloses an error and the net value of errors exceeds the 'error reporting threshold' (see above).

Interest runs from the date the VAT should have been paid until the date of payment.

10.7 Interest on overpaid VAT

A taxable person may receive repayment interest only where there has been an error by HMRC leading to overpayment of output VAT or an under claim of input VAT.

Interest runs from the later of the date of payment to HMRC and the due date for payment, to the date of repayment.

11 Compliance checks and appeals

Section overview

- HMRC may conduct a compliance check into a tax return and can make determinations or discovery assessments.

- Appeals may be made by the taxpayer, for example against discovery assessments. HMRC may raise an assessment of VAT where a return is not submitted, or is incomplete or incorrect.

11.1 Compliance checks

HMRC has the power to conduct a compliance check into an individual's or company's tax return.

Some returns are selected for a compliance check at random, others for a particular reason, for example, if HMRC believes that there has been an underpayment of tax due to the taxpayer's failure to comply with tax legislation.

There are two main types of compliance checks:

- pre-return checks and

- enquiries into returns, claims or elections which have already been submitted.

In addition, HMRC may conduct a check after a return has become final (or where no return has been submitted) where it believes that an assessment or determination may need to be issued under the discovery provisions (see further below).

Examples of when a pre-return check may be carried out in practice include:

- to assist with clearances or ruling requests

- where a previous check has identified poor record-keeping

- to check that computer systems will produce the information needed to support a return

- to find out about planning or avoidance schemes, and

- where fraud is suspected
- where a person regularly discloses an error after the submission of a VAT return.

Notice must be given by HMRC of the intention to conduct an enquiry by:

- The first anniversary of the actual submission date; or
- If the return is filed after the due submission date, the quarter day following the first anniversary of the actual submission date. The quarter days are 31 January, 30 April, 31 July and 31 October.

HMRC has only one opportunity to open a formal enquiry and a tax return cannot be subject to a formal enquiry more than once.

11.2 HMRC determinations

If a return is not received by the filing date HMRC may make a determination (to the best of its information and belief) of the tax due. This may include a determination of any amounts added or deducted in the computation of the tax payable, or any amount from which those figures are derived. The determination must be made within three years of the statutory filing date.

The determination is treated as if it were a self assessment. This enables HMRC to enforce payment of tax demanded, to charge interest and to levy tax geared penalties. A determination may be displaced by a self-assessment.

11.3 Discovery assessments

A determination may only be raised if no return has been submitted, and, once a return has been filed, there are strict deadlines for opening a compliance check into a return. Although this normally gives the taxpayer certainty that its tax liabilities are agreed, HMRC has the power via a discovery assessment to collect extra tax where it discovers a loss of tax.

HMRC can make a discovery assessment after the usual time for a compliance check if it is discovered that full disclosure has not been made by the taxpayer.

If the reason for the discovery assessment is that the taxpayer has made an incomplete disclosure resulting in a loss of tax the time limits for a discovery assessment are:

Reason for loss of tax	Income tax and CGT	Corporation tax	VAT
Not due to careless or deliberate behaviour	4 years	4 years	4 years
Due to 'careless' behaviour	6 years	6 years	6 years
Due to 'deliberate' behaviour	20 years	20 years	20 years

The time limits run from the end of the accounting period (corporation tax), tax year (income tax and CGT) or prescribed accounting period (VAT).

11.4 Appeals

A taxpayer may make an appeal against:

- A request by HMRC to submit documents, supporting records etc in the course of a compliance check
- Amendments made to a self assessment as the result of a compliance check
- HMRC's right to raise a discovery assessment
- A discovery assessment
- A VAT assessment
- Imposition of a penalty

The appeal must be made in writing within 30 days of the relevant event and must specify the grounds for the appeal.

The taxpayer may also apply to postpone payment of all or part of the tax whilst waiting for the appeal decision. This only applies in the case of appeal against a discovery assessment or tax payable as a result of a compliance check.

Most appeals are settled by agreement between the taxpayer and HMRC. Appeals which are not settled are heard by the Tax Chamber of the First-tier Tribunal. Appeals can be made in writing within 56 days to the Upper Tribunal on a point of law, with the First-tier or Upper Tribunals' permission.

As VAT is a European Union tax, these cases may be referred by the UK courts to the European Court of Justice for a ruling on a point of law.

12 HMRC powers

This section is new.

Section overview

- HMRC may use its statutory powers to request information and documents from taxpayers and even third parties via a written information notice.

- HMRC can issue an inspection notice and enter the premises of a taxpayer whose liability is being checked.

12.1 Information and inspection powers

HMRC has one set of information and inspection powers covering income tax, capital gains tax, corporation tax, VAT and PAYE to ensure taxpayers comply with their obligations, pay the right amount of tax at the right time and claim the correct reliefs and allowances.

These powers allow HMRC to make compliance checks by:

- Asking taxpayers and third parties for information and documents
- Visiting business premises to inspect the premises, assets and records.

12.2 Information powers

12.2.1 General provisions

HMRC usually informally requests information and documents from taxpayers in connection with their tax affairs. If, however, a taxpayer does not co-operate fully HMRC can use its statutory powers to request information and documents from taxpayers and even third parties via a written 'information notice'.

12.2.2 Taxpayer notices

HMRC can only issue a taxpayer notice if the information and documents requested are 'reasonably required' for the purpose of checking the taxpayer's tax position.

A taxpayer notice may be issued either with or without the approval of the First-tier Tribunal. An authorised HMRC officer must agree before the request is referred to the First-tier Tribunal.

HMRC can request both statutory records and supplementary information, such as appointment diaries, notes of board meetings, correspondence and contracts.

12.2.3 Third party notices

An information notice issued to a third party must be issued with the agreement of the taxpayer or the approval of the First-tier Tribunal, unless the information relates only to the taxpayer's statutory VAT records.

The taxpayer to whom the notice relates must receive a summary of the reasons for the third party notice unless the Tribunal believes it would prejudice the assessment or collection of tax.

Tax advisers and auditors cannot be asked to provide information connected with their functions. For example, a tax adviser does not have to provide access to his working papers used in the preparation of the taxpayer's return.

In addition, HMRC cannot ask a tax adviser to provide communications between himself and either the taxpayer or his other advisers.

12.2.4 Unknown-identity notices

In addition to the above HMRC also has the power, to require any person to provide information or documents which are required to check the tax position of a person(s) for whom HMRC does not hold full identity details where HMRC believes there is a serious loss of tax.

From 1 April 2012 this power has been extended to require any person to provide basic identity information ie name, last known address and date of birth without HMRC having to have grounds to suspect there is a serious loss of tax.

12.2.5 Data-holder notices

HMRC may issue a data-holder notice to certain data-holders (for example, employers and banks) requiring them to provide 'relevant data', which may be general data or data relating to particular persons or matters. It may include personal data such as names and addresses of individuals.

HMRC may use this power for general effective risk assessment and also to target non-compliant taxpayers. Where this power overlaps with the general information powers detailed above, those general powers take priority.

12.2.6 Right of appeal

The recipient of an information notice has a right of appeal against that notice, unless:

- The First-tier Tribunal has approved the issue of the notice, or
- The information or documents relate to the taxpayer's statutory records.

12.3 Inspection powers

An authorised HMRC officer can enter the business premises of a taxpayer whose liability is being checked and inspect the premises, and the business assets and business documents that are on the premises. The power does not extend to any part of the premises used solely as a dwelling. If an information notice has been issued, the documents required in that notice can be inspected at the same time. The inspection must be reasonably required for the purposes of checking the taxpayer's tax position.

HMRC will usually agree a time for the inspection with the taxpayer. However, an inspection can be carried out at 'any reasonable time' if either:

(a)   The taxpayer receives at least seven days' written notice, or
(b)   The inspection is carried out by, or with the approval of, an authorised HMRC officer.

There is no right of appeal against an inspection notice.

13 Business Payment Support Service

A Business Payment Support Service (BPSS) is in place to assist businesses which are unable, or anticipate they will be unable, to meet income tax, national insurance, corporation tax, VAT or other payments owed to HMRC.

The service reviews the circumstances of the business and may arrange temporary options such as for payments to be made over a longer period. Additional late payment penalties will not be charged on payments included in the arrangement, provided the tax payer makes payments in line with the arrangement. However interest will continue to be payable as applicable.

Where a business is making a trading loss in the current tax year, the BPSS will take into account the anticipated loss when rescheduling dates for tax payments.

Summary

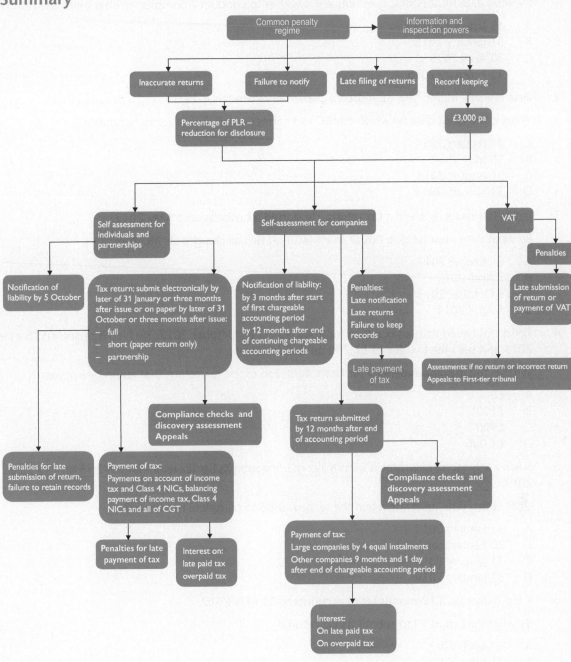

Self-test

Answer the following questions.

1   Jane submitted her 2012/13 tax return electronically on 13 January 2014. The return had been issued to her in May 2013.

     By what date must HMRC give notice if it wishes to conduct a compliance check into the return?

     A   13 January 2015
     B   31 January 2015
     C   30 April 2015
     D   13 February 2015

2   Zeta is a sole trader. She submitted a paper tax return for 2012/13 on 15 August 2013.

     What is the latest date by which HMRC can correct an obvious error in her return?

     A   31 January 2014
     B   15 May 2014
     C   31 August 2014
     D   31 January 2015

3   James has never received a tax return. He started a business on 5 May 2012.

     By what date must he give notice to HMRC that he has chargeable income?

     A   5 October 2012
     B   5 April 2013
     C   5 October 2013
     D   5 April 2014

4   Todd was issued with a tax return for 2011/12 on 20 October 2012. He filed it online on 15 March 2013 and paid the tax due of £1,700 on the same date.

     What is the maximum penalty for late submission of the tax return that could be imposed?

     A   £0
     B   £100
     C   £900
     D   £1,000

5   Susan's only source of income is savings income. She submits her tax return for 2012/13 on 1 October 2013.

     Until which date must she retain the records used to complete her return?

     A   31 January 2014
     B   30 September 2014
     C   31 January 2015
     D   31 January 2019

6   Y Ltd makes up a 12-month set of accounts to 31 May 2012.

     By what date must Y Ltd submit its tax return?

     A   1 March 2013
     B   31 May 2013
     C   31 January 2014
     D   31 May 2014

7   L Ltd makes up a 12 month set of accounts to 30 June 2012. It pays corporation tax at the main rate.

     When must L Ltd make its second instalment payment on account of corporation tax?

     A   14 October 2012
     B   14 July 2012
     C   14 April 2012
     D   14 January 2012

8   P Ltd makes up a 12-month set of accounts to 28 February 2013.

Until which date must P Ltd retain its records relating to this accounting period?

A   28 February 2013
B   28 February 2015
C   28 February 2018
D   28 February 2019

9   U Ltd prepares accounts to 30 September each year. U Ltd has never paid tax at the main rate. It has paid tax and filed returns as set out below:

y/e	CT due	Tax return submitted	CT paid
30.09.12	£70,000	14.05.14	21.06.14

What is the maximum penalty payable by U Ltd for the year ended 30 September 2012 for the late filing of its return?

A   £100
B   £1,000
C   £4,500

What is the maximum penalty payable by U Ltd for the year ended 30 September 2012 for the late payment of its tax?

D   £3,500
E   £7,000
F   £10,500

10   S Ltd makes up its accounts to 30 November each year. It has no associated companies.

It has had the following taxable total profits in its first three years of trading:

y/e 30.11.11   £800,000
y/e 30.11.12   £1,650,000
y/e 30.11.13   £2,100,000

How will S Ltd pay its corporation tax for the years to 30 November 2012 and 30 November 2013?

	y/e 30.11.12	y/e 30.11.13
A	One payment by 1 September 2013	One payment by 1 September 2014
B	One payment by 1 September 2013	By instalments
C	One payment by 30 November 2013	By instalments
D	By instalments	By instalments

11   John files his tax return for 2012/13 on 31 January 2014. This shows property income of £54,000. John has purposely overstated the property expenses by £7,000 by creating false invoices for the additional expenses. HMRC initiates a review into John's return and in reply John then makes a disclosure of the error.

State the minimum penalty that could be charged by HMRC for his error.

A   £2,800
B   £1,960
C   £1,400
D   £980

12   Amelia has submitted an inaccurate return to HMRC. The error is deliberate and concealed.

What is the maximum penalty HMRC could levy on Amelia?

A   100% of potential lost revenue
B   70% of potential lost revenue
C   30% of potential lost revenue

Amelia makes an unprompted disclosure of the error to HMRC.

What is the minimum penalty HMRC could levy on Amelia?

D   20% of potential lost revenue
E   30% of potential lost revenue
F   50% of potential lost revenue

13 Employers are required to file PAYE forms P14, P35 and P45 for 2012/13 electronically if they have

    A   At least 250 employees
    B   At least 50 employees
    C   Any number of employees

Employers are required to pay their PAYE and Class 1 national insurance contributions electronically if they have

    D   At least 250 employees
    E   At least 50 employees
    F   Any number of employees

Now, go back to the Learning outcomes in the Introduction. If you are satisfied you have achieved these objectives, please tick them off.

Legislation

Penalties for incorrect returns	Sch 24 FA 2007
HMRC's powers	Sch 36 FA 2008
Records	Sch 37 FA 2008
Penalties for failure to notify	Sch 41 FA 2008
Duties of senior accounting officers	Sch 46 FA 2009
Penalties for late filing or late payment	Schs 55 & 56 FA 2009

Income tax and Capital gains tax – References relating to Taxes Management Act 1970 (*TMA 1970*) unless otherwise stated

Notification of liability to income tax and CGT	s.7
Personal return	s.8
Partnership return	s.12AA
HMRC corrections	s.9ZB
Taxpayer amendments	s.9ZA
Notice of enquiry	s.9A
Discovery assessments	s.29
Appeals	ss.48-54
Payments on account	s.59A
Balancing payment	s.59B
Penalty for failure to make return	s.93
Interest on overdue tax	s.86
Overpayment relief claim	Sch 1AB

Corporation tax – References relate to Finance Act 1998 (*FA 1998*) Schedule 18 unless otherwise stated

Notification of liability within three months of the start of the first chargeable accounting period	FA 2004 s.55
Tax return	para 3
HMRC corrections	para 16
Company amendments	para 15
Overpayment relief claim	paras 51-51G
Notice of enquiry	para 24
Discovery assessments	para 41
Payment of tax	FA 1998 s.30
Interest on late paid tax	FA 1998 s.33
Interest on overpaid tax	FA 1998 s.34

VAT – References relate to Value Added Tax Act 1994 (*VATA 1994*) unless otherwise stated

Assessments	s.73
Appeals	SI 1986/590
Late registration penalty	s.67
Interest on late paid tax	s.74
Repayment interest	s.79

HMRC manuals

Income Tax Self Assessment: The Legal Framework (Found at
http://www.hmrc.gov.uk/manuals/salfmanual/Index.htm)

Payment of Tax: Payments on Account	SALF303
Payment of Tax: Balancing Payments	SALF304
Payment of Tax: Automatic Interest and Late Payment Penalties: Interest Charged on Late Payments of Tax	SALF305
Payment of Tax: Automatic Interest and Late Payment Penalties: Late Payment Penalties on Unpaid Income Tax and Capital Gains Tax	SALF308A
Enquiring into Tax Returns: Outline	SALF402

For corporation tax there is the company taxation manual. This can be found at
http://www.hmrc.gov.uk/manuals/ctmanual/index.htm

To find out more practical information about VAT, access the relevant section of the HMRC website
through the main home page (http://www.hmrc.gov.uk/).

A series of guides is available online at
http://www.hmrc.gov.uk/vat/index.htm?_nfpb=true&_pageLabel.

Information about the range of special schemes and options to simplify VAT for small businesses is
available at http://www.hmrc.gov.uk/vat/start/schemes/index.htm.

There is also a VAT telephone helpline: 0845 010 9000

> This technical reference section is designed to assist you when you are working in the office. It should
> help you to know where to look for further information on the topics covered in this chapter. **You will
> not be examined on the contents of this section in your examination.**

Answers to Interactive questions

Answer to Interactive question 1

Question	Fill in your answer
Normal due date for tax return for 2012/13 issued 20 November 2013, taxpayer to submit an electronic return online	Later of 31 January 2014 and 20 February 2014, ie 20 February 2014
Notify HMRC of need to issue tax return for 2012/13	5 October 2013
Overpayment relief claim relating to 2012/13	5 April 2017
Keep business records for 2012/13	31 January 2019
Normal due date for tax return for 2012/13 issued 31 May 2013, HMRC to calculate tax and paper return to be submitted	Later of 31 October 2013 and 31 July 2013, ie 31 October 2013
Keep personal records for 2012/13	31 January 2015
Amend tax return for 2012/13 submitted 30 November 2013	31 January 2015

Answer to Interactive question 2

Question	Fill in your answer
Notified HMRC of new source of income for 2012/13 on 5 December 2013, paid all £4,000 of tax due on 25 January 2014	Maximum £1,200 penalty (for failure to notify – 30% × potential lost revenue). This may be reduced to nil for unprompted disclosure and payment in full within 12 months.
Tax return for 2012/13 issued May 2013, submitted return electronically 30 March 2014	Due date was 31 October 2013, less than six months late. Initial penalty of £100 and daily penalty of £10 from 1 February 2014 up to 29 March.
Balancing payment of tax of £2,000 for 2012/13 paid 30 April 2014	£2,000 × 5% = £100 – due date was 31 January 2014, less than six months late
Destroyed supporting records for 2012/13 on 1 May 2014	£3,000
Tax return for 2012/13 issued June 2013, submitted electronically on 15 September 2014, tax liability £1,000.	Due date was 31 January 2014, over 6 months late. Initial penalty of £100, daily penalty of £10 for 90 days (£900), 5% of tax due but subject to minimum of £300 once six months late.
Balancing payment of tax of £3,000 for 2012/13 paid 30 September 2014	£3,000 × 10% = £300 – due date was 31 January 2014, over six months late

Question	Fill in your answer
Notified HMRC on 10 January 2014 of chargeability for accounting period ended 30 November 2012. This is not the company's first chargeable accounting period. Corporation tax liability £7,500 paid on same date	Maximum penalty 30% × potential lost revenue (£2,250). If disclosure is unprompted then may be reduced to nil. Notification should be by 30 November 2013, therefore less than 12 months late
Tax return for accounting period ended 31 July 2012 submitted 30 September 2013	£100 – return due 31 July 2013, ie less than three months late
Destroyed records on 10 August 2016 for accounting period ended 31 December 2012	£3,000 – should have kept records until 31 December 2018
Tax return for accounting period ended 31 October 2012 submitted 30 November 2014, corporation tax due of £10,000 paid 30 September 2014	£2,000 – for return filed late. The return was due 31 October 2013, ie over 12 months late so £100 plus £900 plus £500 (5% of tax due subject to minimum of £300) plus further £500 once 12 months late (unless deemed to be as a result of the deliberate withholding of information in which case penalty could be up to 100% of the unpaid tax)

£1,500 – for tax paid late. 5% penalty at filing date and at three and nine months after filing date

Total minimum penalty for late filing and late payment is £2,000 + £1,500 = £3,500 |

1   A – 13 January 2015

The return was due on 31 January 2014 and was submitted on time. HMRC has until the first anniversary of the actual submission of the return to give notice of a compliance check.

2   B – 15 May 2014

HMRC has nine months from the actual submission date to make corrections to a self assessment.

3   C – 5 October 2013

The business began in 2012/13 (5 May 2012) and James must notify HMRC by 5 October following the end of that tax year.

4   B – £100

The tax return was due on 31 January 2013 and so is less than three months late.

5   C – 31 January 2015

Personal tax records must be retained for one year after 31 January following the end of the tax year (for 2012/13, 31 January 2015).

6   B – by 31 May 2013

7   C – 14 April 2012

The second instalment is due in the 10th month of the accounting period.

8   D – 28 February 2019

Records must be kept for a minimum period of six years after the end of the accounting period.

9   B – £1,000

As the return is filed less than six months late only the fixed £100 late filing penalty plus the 90 days at £10 per day penalty apply, giving a total penalty of £1,000.

10 B – for y/e 30 November 2012 by 1 September 2013, for y/e 30 November 2013 by instalments.

S Ltd is a large company for the first time in the year ended 30 November 2012 and so does not have to pay tax by instalments in that year. It is also a large company in the year ended 30 November 2013 and so does have to pay tax in instalments in that year.

11 C – £1,400

The PLR as a result of John's error is £7,000 × 40%   £2,800

John's error is deliberate and concealed (active steps to conceal the error by the creation of false invoices) but he has made a prompted disclosure so the minimum penalty is 50% of £2,800 which is £1,400.

12 A – 100% of potential lost revenue

E – 30% of potential lost revenue.

13 C – All employers must file P14, P35 and P45 forms electronically

D – Only employers with at least 250 employees are required to make payments electronically.

CHAPTER 13

Ethics

Introduction

Examination context

Topic List

Summary and Self-test

Technical reference

Answers to Interactive questions

Answers to Self-test

Learning outcomes

- Identify the five fundamental principles given in the IFAC Code of Ethics for Professional Accountants and the ICAEW Code of Ethics, and the guidance in relation to a tax practice with regard to:

  - The threats and safeguards framework ☐

  - Ethical conflict resolution ☐

- Identify the following:

  - Conflict of interest ☐

  - Money laundering ☐

  - Tax avoidance and tax evasion ☐

The specific syllabus reference for this chapter is: 1f, g.

Syllabus links

The topics covered in this chapter are essential knowledge for the whole of your Taxation studies. They will ensure that advice and communication is appropriate and in keeping with the requirements of the ICAEW.

Examination context

In the examination candidates may be required to:

- Apply the five fundamental principles to given scenarios

- Determine safeguards to be put in place when threats are made to the fundamental principles

- Advise on the ethical resolution of conflicts

- Give appropriate guidance relating to conflicts of interest, money laundering and the distinction between tax evasion and tax avoidance

For extra question practice on these topics go to the section of the Question Bank covering this chapter.

1 Fundamental principles

1.1 Fundamental principles

Definition

Professional accountant: A member of the ICAEW.

Professional accountants have a responsibility to act in the public interest as well as considering their client or employer. The Codes require professional accountants to comply with the following five fundamental principles:

- Integrity
- Objectivity
- Professional competence and due care
- Confidentiality
- Professional behaviour

1.2 Integrity

Definition

Integrity: Professional accountants shall be straightforward and honest in all professional and business relationships.

A professional accountant shall not knowingly be associated with any information where he believes that the information:

- Contains a materially false or misleading statement

- Contains statements or information furnished recklessly

- Omits or obscures information required to be included where such omission or obscurity would be misleading.

When a professional accountant becomes aware that he has been associated with such information, he shall take steps to be disassociated from that information.

1.3 Objectivity

Definition

Objectivity: Professional accountants shall not allow bias, conflict of interest or the undue influence of others to override professional or business judgements.

Relationships that bias or unduly influence the professional judgement of the professional accountant shall be avoided.

Conflicts of interest are considered in more detail later in this chapter.

1.4 Professional competence and due care

Definition

Professional competence and due care: Professional accountants have a continuing duty to:

- Maintain professional knowledge and skill at the level required to ensure that clients or employers receive competent professional service based on current developments in practice, legislation and techniques; and

- Act diligently in accordance with applicable technical and professional standards when providing professional services.

Competent professional service requires the exercise of sound judgement in applying professional knowledge and skill. Competence entails:

- Attainment of professional competence; and

- Maintenance of professional competence, requiring a continuing awareness and understanding of relevant issues.

The professional accountant shall take steps to ensure that those working for him have appropriate training and supervision.

Any limitations relating to the service being provided must be made clear to avoid misinterpretation.

1.5 Confidentiality

Definition

Confidentiality: Professional accountants shall:

- Respect the confidentiality of information acquired as a result of professional and business relationships;

- Refrain from disclosing such information without proper and specific authority unless there is a legal or professional right or duty to disclose; and

- Refrain from using such information for their personal advantage or the advantage of third parties.

A professional accountant shall maintain confidentiality even in a social environment. The professional accountant shall be alert to the possibility of inadvertent disclosure, particularly in circumstances involving long association with a business associate or a close or immediate family member.

A professional accountant shall consider the need to maintain confidentiality of information within the firm. All reasonable steps shall be taken to ensure that staff under the professional accountant's control and persons from whom advice and assistance is obtained respect the professional accountant's duty of confidentiality.

A professional accountant shall also maintain confidentiality of information disclosed by a prospective client or employer.

The need to comply with the principle of confidentiality continues even after the end of relationships between a professional accountant and a client or employer. When a professional accountant changes employment or acquires a new client, the professional accountant is entitled to use prior experience. The professional accountant shall not, however, use or disclose any confidential information either acquired or received as a result of a professional or business relationship.

Confidentiality is considered later in this chapter.

1.6 Professional behaviour

Definition

Professional behaviour: Professional accountants shall comply with relevant laws and regulations and avoid any action that discredits the profession.

This includes actions which a reasonable and informed third party, having knowledge of all relevant information, would conclude negatively affects the good reputation of the profession.

Professional accountants shall conduct themselves with courtesy and consideration towards all with whom they come into contact and shall not:

- Make exaggerated claims for the services they are able to offer, the qualifications they possess, or experience they have gained

- Make disparaging references or unsubstantiated comparisons to the work of others

2 Threats and safeguards framework

Section overview

- The circumstances in which professional accountants operate may give rise to specific threats to compliance with the five fundamental principles.

- The Codes provide a framework to help identify, evaluate and respond to these threats.

- The professional accountant is then able to apply safeguards to eliminate the threats or reduce them to an acceptable level.

- As a result, compliance with the five fundamental principles is not compromised.

2.1 Threats

Professional accountants are obliged to evaluate any threats as soon as they know, or should be expected to know, of their existence.

Both qualitative and quantitative factors should be taken into account in considering the significance of any threat.

Most threats to compliance with the fundamental principles fall into the following categories:

- **Self-interest threats**, which may occur as a result of the financial or other interests of a professional accountant or of an immediate or close family member

- **Self-review threats**, which may occur when a previous judgment needs to be re-evaluated by the professional accountant responsible for that judgment

- **Advocacy threats**, which may occur when a professional accountant promotes a position or opinion to the point that subsequent objectivity may be compromised

- **Familiarity threats**, which may occur when, because of a close relationship, a professional accountant becomes too sympathetic to the interests of others

- **Intimidation threats**, which may occur when a professional accountant may be deterred from acting objectively by threats, actual or perceived

2.2 Safeguards

Safeguards that may eliminate or reduce such threats to an acceptable level fall into two broad categories:

- Safeguards created by the profession, legislation or regulation.
- Safeguards in the work environment.

Safeguards created by the profession, legislation or regulation include, but are not restricted to:

- Educational, training and experience requirements for entry into the profession

- Continuing professional development requirements

- Corporate governance regulations

- Professional standards

- Professional or regulatory monitoring and disciplinary procedures

- External review by a legally empowered third party of the reports, returns, communications or information produced by a professional accountant

Certain safeguards may increase the likelihood of identifying or deterring unethical behaviour. Such safeguards, which may be created by the accounting profession, legislation, regulation or an employing organisation, include, but are not restricted to:

- Effective, well publicised complaints systems operated by the employing organisation, the profession or a regulator, which enable colleagues, employers and members of the public to draw attention to unprofessional or unethical behaviour

- An explicitly stated duty to report breaches of ethical requirements

The nature of the safeguards to be applied will vary depending on the circumstances.

When applying the conceptual framework, a professional accountant may encounter situations in which threats cannot be eliminated or reduced to an acceptable level, either because the threat is too significant or because appropriate safeguards are not available or cannot be applied. In such situations, the professional accountant shall decline or discontinue the specific professional service involved or, when necessary, resign from the engagement (in the case of a professional accountant in public practice) or the employing organisation (in the case of a professional accountant in business).

3 Ethical conflict resolution

Section overview

- To ensure compliance with the fundamental principles a professional accountant may need to resolve a conflict in applying the principles.

- The conflict resolution process may be formal or informal.

- In both cases the same steps are to be followed.

3.1 Conflict resolution process

When initiating either a formal or informal conflict resolution process, a professional accountant should consider the following five factors:

- Relevant facts
- Relevant parties
- Ethical issues involved
- Fundamental principles related to the matter in question
- Established internal procedures
- Alternative courses of action

Having considered these issues, the appropriate course of action can be determined which resolves the conflict with all or some of the five fundamental principles. If the matter remains unresolved, the professional accountant should consult with other appropriate persons within the firm for help in obtaining resolution.

Where a matter involves a conflict with, or within, an organisation, a professional accountant should also consider consulting with those charged with governance of the organisation such as the board of directors.

It is advisable for the professional accountant to document the issue and details of any discussions held or decisions taken concerning that issue.

If a significant conflict cannot be resolved, a professional accountant may wish to obtain professional advice from the relevant professional body or legal advisors, and thereby obtain guidance on ethical and legal issues without breaching confidentiality. The ICAEW runs a confidential ethics helpline service.

If, after exhausting all relevant possibilities, the ethical conflict remains unresolved, a professional accountant should, where possible, refuse to remain associated with the matter creating the conflict. The professional accountant may determine that, in the circumstances, it is appropriate to withdraw from the engagement team or specific assignment, or to resign altogether from the engagement or the firm.

Interactive question 1: Ethical conflict resolution   [Difficulty level: Exam standard]

James, a member of the ICAEW, is the reporting accountant of a high profile charitable organisation. Over the years he has become firm friends with the financial controller, Gordon.

Recently he has become concerned that funds have been withdrawn from the bank account without the correct approval. James has mentioned this to Gordon, who explained that there was no problem with this.

James does not wish to upset Gordon but is not satisfied with the explanation.

Requirement

Identify the six factors to be considered by James when initiating a formal or informal conflict resolution.

See **Answer** at the end of this chapter.

Interactive question 2: Ethical conflict resolution [Difficulty level: Exam standard]

The same facts as above.

After considering the six factors James decided to consult the Finance Director of the charity, Brenda.

James feels that Brenda has not taken sufficient steps to resolve the issue.

Requirement

Outline the options open to James.

See **Answer** at the end of this chapter.

4 Conflicts of interest

Section overview

- Part B of both the IFAC Code and the ICAEW Code illustrates how the fundamental principles are applied in certain situations for professional accountants in public practice.

- One of the illustrations given in part B contains details relating to conflicts of interest.

4.1 The threat of a conflict of interest

A professional accountant shall take reasonable steps to identify circumstances that could pose a conflict of interest. These may give rise to threats to compliance with the fundamental principles.

A conflict may arise between the firm and the client or between two conflicting clients being managed by the same firm, for example, where a firm acts for both a husband and wife in a divorce settlement or acts for a company and for its directors in their personal capacity.

Worked example: Conflict of interest

A professional accountant in public practice competes directly with a client or has a joint venture or similar arrangement with a major competitor of a client.

Requirement

Which fundamental principle may be threatened by this conflict?

Solution

A threat to objectivity may be created.

Evaluation of threats includes consideration as to whether the professional accountant has any business interests or relationships with the client or a third party that could give rise to threats. If threats are other than clearly insignificant, safeguards should be considered and applied as necessary.

4.2 Safeguards

Depending upon the circumstances giving rise to the conflict, safeguards should ordinarily include the professional accountant in public practice:

- Notifying the client of the firm's business interest or activities that may represent a conflict of interest

- Notifying all known relevant parties that the professional accountant is acting for two or more parties in respect of a matter where their respective interests are in conflict

- Notifying the client that the professional accountant does not act exclusively for any one client in the provision of proposed services (for example, in a particular market sector or with respect to a specific service)

In each case the professional accountant should obtain the consent of the relevant parties to act.

Where a professional accountant has requested consent from a client to act for another party (which may or may not be an existing client) and that consent has been refused, then he must not continue to act for one of the parties in the matter giving rise to the conflict of interest.

The following additional safeguards should also be considered:

- The use of separate engagement teams

- Procedures to prevent access to information (eg strict physical separation of such teams, confidential and secure data filing)

- Clear guidelines for members of the engagement team on issues of security and confidentiality

- The use of agreements signed by employees and partners of the firm to ensure actual and perceived confidentiality

- Regular review of the application of safeguards by a senior individual not involved with relevant client engagements

Where a conflict of interest poses a threat to one or more of the fundamental principles that cannot be eliminated or reduced to an acceptable level through the application of safeguards, the professional accountant should conclude that it is not appropriate to accept a specific engagement or that resignation from one or more conflicting engagements is required.

5 Anti-money laundering

Section overview

- The ICAEW Members' Regulations and guidance includes anti-money laundering guidance.

- This guidance has been prepared to assist professional accountants in complying with their obligations in relation to the prevention, recognition and reporting of money laundering.

- Failure to take account of the guidance could have serious legal, regulatory or professional disciplinary consequences.

5.1 Introduction

Accountants are required to comply with the Proceeds of Crime Act 2002 (POCA) as amended by the Serious Organised Crime and Police Act 2005 (SOCPA) and the Money Laundering Regulations 2007 (the Regulations).

The ICAEW Members' Regulations and guidance includes guidance issued by the Consultative Committee of Accountancy Bodies (CCAB) in December 2007.

5.2 Money laundering

Definition

Money laundering: The term used for a number of offences involving the proceeds of crime or terrorist funds. It now includes possessing, or in any way dealing with, or concealing, the proceeds of any crime.

Someone is engaged in money laundering under POCA where they:

- Conceal, disguise, convert, transfer or remove (from the United Kingdom) criminal property

- Enter into or become concerned in an arrangement which they know or suspect facilitates (by whatever means) the acquisition, retention, use or control of criminal property by or on behalf of another person

- Acquire, use or have possession of criminal property

Criminal property includes (but is by no means limited to)

- The proceeds of tax evasion or any other crime

- A benefit obtained through bribery and corruption (including both the receipt of a bribe and the income received from a contract obtained through bribery or the promise of a bribe)

- Benefits obtained, or income received, through the operation of a criminal cartel

- Benefits (in the form of saved costs) arising from a failure to comply with a regulatory requirement, where that failure is a criminal offence

Where a professional accountant suspects that a client is involved in money laundering he should report this to his Money Laundering Reporting Officer (MLRO) on an internal report or directly to the Serious Organised Crime Agency (SOCA) in the form of a suspicious activity report (SAR).

5.3 Tipping off

Care should be taken not to tip off a money launderer, as this will constitute an offence under POCA. The offence can be committed when there is knowledge or suspicion that a SAR has been made. Similarly, if any disclosure is made which is likely to prejudice any investigation by the authorities, an offence may be committed.

5.4 Tax-related offences

Tax-related offences are not in a special category. The proceeds or monetary advantage arising from tax offences are treated no differently from the proceeds of theft, drug trafficking or other criminal conduct.

Tax evasion consists of seeking to mislead HMRC by either:

- Suppressing information to which HMRC is entitled, for example by:

  – Failing to notify HMRC of a liability to tax
  – Understating income or gains
  – Omitting to disclose a relevant fact (eg duality of a business expense)

  or

- Providing HMRC with deliberately false information, for example by:

  – Deducting expenses that have not been incurred
  – Claiming capital allowances on plant that has not been purchased

Minor cases of tax evasion are generally settled out of court via the payment of penalties. However, there is a statutory offence of evading income tax that can be dealt with in a magistrates court.

Serious cases of tax evasion, particularly those involving fraud, continue to be the subject of criminal prosecutions which may lead to fines and/or imprisonment on conviction.

Furthermore, tax evasion offences will fall within the definition of money laundering and in certain cases individuals may be prosecuted under one of the money laundering offences. This includes both the under declaring of income and the over claiming of expenses.

Thus where an accountant is aware of or suspects that a client has committed tax evasion, he himself may commit an offence under money laundering legislation if he has in any way facilitated the evasion. Even if the accountant was not involved in the tax evasion itself, failure to report such a suspicion is also an offence.

No offences are committed where the client reduces his tax liabilities using tax avoidance methods. Tax avoidance is a legal method of reducing the tax burden, for example by taking advantage of tax shelters such as ISAs.

5.5 Anti-money laundering procedures

Businesses need to maintain the following procedures, in respect of all relevant business:

- Register with an appropriate supervisory authority (see below)

- Appoint a Money Laundering Reporting Officer (MLRO) and implement internal reporting procedures

- Train staff to ensure that they are aware of the relevant legislation, know how to recognise and deal with potential money laundering, how to report suspicions to the MLRO, and how to identify clients

- Establish appropriate internal procedures relating to risk assessment and management to deter and prevent money laundering, and make relevant individuals aware of the procedures

- Carry out customer due diligence on any new client and monitor existing clients to ensure the client is known and establish areas of risk

- Verify the identity of new clients and maintain evidence of identification and records of any transactions undertaken for or with the client

- Report suspicions of money laundering to the Serious Organised Crime Agency (SOCA), using a suspicious activity report (SAR)

Records of client identification need to be maintained for five years after the termination of a client relationship by any part of the firm providing relevant business. Records of transactions also need to be maintained for five years, from the date when all activities in relation to the transaction were completed.

5.6 Client confidentiality in relation to money laundering

The money-laundering legislation requires an accountant to disclose confidential information without client consent in certain circumstances. In order to disclose confidential information, the accountant must have knowledge or suspicion, or reasonable grounds for knowledge or suspicion, that a person has committed a money laundering offence.

Disclosure without reasonable grounds for knowledge or suspicion will increase the risk of a business or an individual being open to an action for breach of confidentiality.

5.7 Penalties

Offences may be tried in a Magistrate's Court or in a Crown Court depending on severity. Cases tried in the Crown Court can attract unlimited fines and the following terms of imprisonment:

- Up to fourteen years, for the main money laundering offences
- Up to five years, for the failure to report offence and the tipping off offences
- Up to two years imprisonment for contravention of the systems requirements of the Regulations

5.8 Supervisory bodies

The 2007 Regulations require all businesses to be supervised by an appropriate anti-money laundering supervisory authority. The ICAEW is one of the approved supervisory authorities for the accountancy sector. Accountants not regulated by one of the approved bodies will be supervised by HMRC.

6 Tax avoidance and tax evasion

Section overview

- Tax evasion is illegal and tax avoidance is legal.

- Tax evasion could lead to prosecution for both the client and his accountant.

- Tax avoidance may not be possible due to the decision in the Ramsay case.

6.1 Tax evasion

Tax evasion consists of seeking to mislead HMRC by either:

- Suppressing information to which HMRC is entitled, for example by:

    - Failing to notify HMRC of a liability to tax
    - Understating income or gains, or
    - Omitting to disclose a relevant fact (eg duality of a business expense).

    or

- Providing HMRC with deliberately false information, for example by:

    - Deducting expenses that have not been incurred, or
    - Claiming capital allowances on plant that has not been purchased.

Minor cases of tax evasion are generally settled out of court via the payment of penalties. However, there is a statutory offence of evading income tax that can be dealt with in a magistrates court.

Serious cases of tax evasion, particularly those involving fraud, continue to be the subject of criminal prosecutions which may lead to fines and/or imprisonment on conviction.

Furthermore, tax evasion offences will fall within the definition of money laundering and in certain cases individuals may be prosecuted under one of the money laundering offences. This includes both the under declaring of income and the over claiming of expenses.

Thus where an accountant is aware of or suspects that a client has committed tax evasion, he himself may commit an offence under money laundering legislation if he has in any way facilitated the evasion. Even if the accountant was not involved in the tax evasion itself, failure to report such a suspicion is also an offence.

6.2 Tax avoidance

Tax avoidance is not defined, but is broadly any legal method of reducing the tax burden, for example taking advantage of tax shelters in legislation, such as ISAs and venture capital trusts.

In the past HMRC has responded to major tax avoidance schemes by changing legislation as the scheme has come to its attention. However there is a general presumption that the effect of the changes cannot be backdated.

In recent years there has been a requirement for promoters of certain tax avoidance schemes to disclose their schemes to HMRC, and for taxpayers to disclose details of which schemes they have used. This may enable HMRC to take action more rapidly to close the loopholes.

The courts have also struck down some planning schemes, by effectively ignoring elements of transactions which have no commercial purpose or effect. They have done so by applying purposive construction to the relevant statutory provisions. The leading case in relation to tax avoidance schemes which has applied this principle is *Ramsay v IRC (1982)*.

In *Ramsay* the taxpayers had a tax avoidance scheme consisting of a circular series of pre-planned transactions, designed to create two debts due to the taxpayer. The scheme ensured that one debt produced a gain for the taxpayer and the other an equivalent loss. This would leave the taxpayer in a neutral financial position. The aim of the scheme was to create the gain as a tax exempt gain, but the loss as tax deductible. If the scheme had been successful the taxpayer could have set off this loss against other 'real' gains. The House of Lords refused to allow the loss.

Later cases have also demonstrated that the *Ramsay* doctrine cannot be applied to counteract all tax avoidance even when it includes transactions or terms which have no commercial effect. In particular, there have been several cases where the courts have concluded that the planning which had been undertaken was consistent with the purpose of the legislation. There have also been cases where the courts have decided that the legislation was formulated in such a way that it was not possible to discern its purpose. This has been primarily in areas where there are complicated statutory rules to determine the amounts which are taxed, which do not relate to commercial ideas of profits or losses.

6.3 Tax evasion versus tax avoidance

The distinction between tax evasion and avoidance is usually obvious as avoidance has no intention of misleading HMRC.

The accountant should take care in situations, for example where a client believes that his tax avoidance has been successful and so does not submit a tax return.

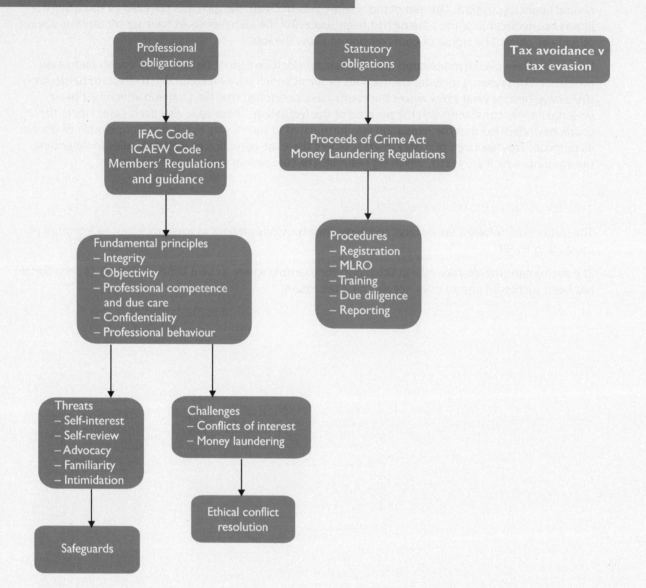

Professional obligations

Statutory obligations

Tax avoidance v tax evasion

IFAC Code
ICAEW Code
Members' Regulations and guidance

Proceeds of Crime Act
Money Laundering Regulations

Fundamental principles
– Integrity
– Objectivity
– Professional competence and due care
– Confidentiality
– Professional behaviour

Procedures
– Registration
– MLRO
– Training
– Due diligence
– Reporting

Threats
– Self-interest
– Self-review
– Advocacy
– Familiarity
– Intimidation

Challenges
– Conflicts of interest
– Money laundering

Ethical conflict resolution

Safeguards

Self-test

Answer the following questions.

1 Which **two** of the following are fundamental principles as stated in the ICAEW Code of Ethics?

   A Integrity
   B Conflict of interest
   C Objectivity
   D Disclosure of information

2 Which **one** of the following situations will **never** be considered to be a breach of the fundamental principle of confidentiality?

   A Discussion of a wife's personal tax return with her husband. They work in partnership together as solicitors

   B Disclosure of an apparent understatement of income on a client's tax return directly to HMRC

   C Providing client files to the courts to protect the accountant's own professional interests in legal proceedings

   D Using information obtained about a client to suggest to a family member that he buys shares in the client company. A substantial profit is made by the family member on a subsequent sale of the shares

3 A professional accountant suspects that the finance director of a client is extracting funds from the bank account for his own purposes. The finance director is a golfing partner of the accountant.

   Select which of the following is **not** an appropriate course of action.

   A Tell the finance director of his suspicions to give him a chance to repay the funds

   B Contact the board of directors to make them aware of the issue

   C Document in his files the suspicions regarding the transactions

   D Obtain advice from the ICAEW ethics advisory group giving full details of the client and the finance director involved

4 A professional accountant is considering performing services for clients who are in dispute with each other in relation to the matter or transaction in question.

   Which **two** of the following fundamental principles are threatened in this situation?

   A Objectivity
   B Professional competence and due care
   C Confidentiality
   D Professional behaviour

5 Which of the following actions by a taxpayer would not constitute tax evasion?

   A Obtaining tax free interest by investing in an ISA
   B Claiming capital allowances on a fictitious item of plant
   C Omitting to declare rental income received
   D Overstating the value of purchases

Now go back to the Learning outcomes in the Introduction. If you are satisfied you have achieved this objective please tick it off.

IFAC Code of Ethics for Professional Accountants

ICAEW Members' My guide to regulations: Code of Ethics

ICAEW Members' My guide to regulations: Professional conduct in relation to taxation

ICAEW Members' My guide to regulations: Anti-money laundering guidance for the accountancy sector

Proceeds of Crime Act 2002

Money Laundering Regulations 2007

The main source of guidance from HMRC on dealing with errors by it is 'Complaints and putting things right'. This is found at http://www.hmrc.gov.uk/factsheets/complaints-factsheet.pdf

Information Commissioner's Office http://www.ico.gov.uk/

ICAEW Ethics helpline service +44 (0)1908 248 250 http://www.icaew.com/members/advisory-helplines-and-services

---

This technical reference section is designed to assist you when you are working in the office. It should help you to know where to look for further information on the topics covered in this chapter. **You will not be examined on the contents of this section in your examination.**

Answer to Interactive question 1

When initiating either a formal or informal conflict resolution process, James should consider the following:

- Relevant facts
- Relevant parties
- Ethical issues involved
- Fundamental principles related to the matter in question
- Established internal procedures
- Alternative courses of action

Answer to Interactive question 2

James may wish to seek professional advice from the ICAEW or legal advisors, and thereby obtain guidance on ethical issues without breaching confidentiality. James should consider seeking legal advice to determine whether there is a requirement to report.

If the ethical conflict remains unresolved, James should refuse to remain associated with the matter creating the conflict. He may determine that, in the circumstances, it is appropriate to resign altogether from the engagement.

1   A and C – Conflict of interest and Disclosure of information are issues which may challenge the fundamental principles.

2   C – This example is directly stated in the Code of a situation where the principle of confidentiality is not considered breached.

3   A – In a situation of conflict resolution within an organisation, it is appropriate to approach those charged with governance, to document action taken and to approach a relevant professional body. If the finance director is engaged in money laundering, option A could constitute tipping off.

4   A and C

5   A – This is an example of legitimate tax avoidance, whereas the others all constitute tax evasion.

PRINCIPLES OF TAXATION

Tax Tables FA 2012

The tax tables reproduced on the following pages are identical to the tax tables you will be given in the exam. Familiarise yourself with the content so that you know what you need to learn and what you can access in the exam from the tax tables.

In the actual exam, for ease of use on screen, your tax tables are divided into sections in accordance with the five key syllabus areas. You will find that for each question in the actual exam you will only be able to access the part of the tax tables relevant to that part of the syllabus. This is to minimise the amount of time you will need to spend scrolling through the tax tables.

Questions on each syllabus area will therefore only be able to access the pages of the tax tables as follows:

SYLLABUS AREA: ADMINISTRATION

SUBMISSION DATES

Submission dates for 2012/13 personal self-assessment tax returns

Return filed online	Later of: • 31 January 2014 • 3 months from the date of issue of return
Paper returns:	Later of: • 31 October 2013 • 3 months from the date of issue of return

Submission dates for corporation tax returns

Must be filed by 12 months from the end of the period of account

Submission dates for PAYE returns

Forms	Filing date
P14, P35	19 May following the tax year end
P60 (to employees)	31 May following the tax year end
P9D and P11D	6 July following the tax year end

PAYMENT DATES

Payment dates for income tax

First interim payment [(1)]	31 January in the tax year
Second interim payment [(1)]	31 July following the tax year end
Balancing payment	31 January following the tax year end

(1)   Interim payments are not required if:

- the tax paid by assessment for the previous year was less than £1,000; or
- more than 80% of the tax liability the previous year was collected at source.

Payment dates for capital gains tax

Capital gains tax is payable by the 31 January following the tax year end

Payment dates for corporation tax

Corporation tax	Nine months and one day after the end of an accounting period
Corporation tax by instalments	The 14th day of months 7, 10, 13 and 16 counted from the start of a 12 month accounting period

Payment dates for VAT

Online return	Due date
Electronic payment	7 calendar days after the last day of the month following the end of the return period
Direct debit payment	Collected automatically 3 working days after electronic payment due date

SYLLABUS AREA: ADMINISTRATION

MAIN PENALTY PROVISIONS

Individuals: penalties

Offence	Maximum Penalty
Failure to notify chargeability by 5 October following tax year end	See below: penalties for failure to notify
Late return	See below: penalties for late filing of returns
Late payment of income tax or capital gains tax: [1] • Unpaid 30 days after payment due date • Unpaid 6 months after payment due date • Unpaid 12 months after payment due date	5% of tax unpaid Further 5% of tax unpaid Further 5% of tax unpaid
Failure to keep and retain tax records	See below: record keeping penalties

(1)   Late payment penalties do not apply to payments on account

Companies: penalties

Offence	Maximum Penalty
Failure to notify that have commenced to trade within 3 months of start of first accounting period	Fixed rate penalty not exceeding £300
Failure to notify chargeability within 12 months of end of accounting period	See below: penalties for failure to notify
Late return	See below: penalties for late filing of returns
Late payment of corporation tax: • Unpaid at filing date • Unpaid 3 months after due filing date • Unpaid 9 months after due filing date	5% of tax unpaid Further 5% of tax unpaid Further 5% of tax unpaid
Failure to keep and retain records	See below: record keeping penalties

PAYE: penalties for late returns

Forms	Initial delay	Continuing delay	Delay exceeds 12 months
P14, P35		£100 monthly per 50 employees	Further penalty not exceeding 100% of the income tax and NICs payable for the year of assessment but not paid by 19 April (22 April for electronic payments) following the end of the tax year
P9D and P11D	£300 per return	£60 per day	

PAYE: penalties for late payment

Penalties for late payment of in-year PAYE depend on the number of defaults in any 12 month period	No of late payments	% of tax unpaid[1]
	1st 2nd, 3rd & 4th 5th, 6th, 7th 8th, 9th, 10th 11th or more	nil 1% 2% 3% 4%
Where a penalty has been imposed and the tax remains unpaid at 6 months		5%[2]
Where a penalty has been imposed and the tax remains unpaid at 12 months		5%[2]

(1)   The percentage penalty is applied to the total amount that is late in the tax year, but ignoring the first late payment in the year.

(2)   The 6 month and the possible further 12 month penalties are in addition to the initial penalty for late payment

SYLLABUS AREA: ADMINISTRATION

VAT: penalties

Offence	Maximum Penalty
Failure to notify liability for registration or change in nature of supplies by person exempted from registration	See below: penalties for failure to notify
Failure to keep and retain tax records	See below: record keeping penalties

VAT: penalty for late filing of VAT returns

	Monthly returns	Quarterly returns
Initial penalty	£100	£100
Further late returns within penalty period (expires 12 months after the most recent late return)	1st to 5th late return: £100 6th and subsequent late return: £200	1st late return: £200 2nd late return: £300 3rd or subsequent late return: £400
Further penalty if return still unfiled after 6 months	5% of the tax due (minimum £300)	
Further penalty if return still unfiled after 12 months	Tax geared penalties apply (minimum £300): • 100% of tax due if deliberate and concealed • 70% of tax due if deliberate but not concealed • 5% of tax due in all other cases	

VAT: penalty for failing to file VAT return online

Annual VAT exclusive turnover	Penalty
£100,000 and under	£100
£100,001 to £5,600,000	£200
£5,600,001 to £22,800,000	£300
Above £22,800,000	£400

VAT: penalty for late payment of VAT

Amounts in respect of	Monthly returns	Quarterly Returns
Penalty for default within penalty period	1st, 2nd or 3rd default: 1% 4th, 5th or 6th default: 2% 7th, 8th or 9th default: 3% 10th or subsequent default: 4%	1st default: 2% 2nd default: 3% 3rd or subsequent default: 4%
After 6 months	5% of tax still unpaid	
After 12 months	5% of tax still unpaid	

VAT errors

An error made on a VAT return can be corrected on the next return provided it was not deliberate and does not exceed the greater of:

* £10,000 (net under-declaration minus over-declaration); or
* 1% x net VAT turnover for return period (maximum £50,000)

Alternatively, a 'small' error which is not deliberate may be corrected via the submission of form VAT652.

Errors which are not 'small' or errors which are deliberate should be notified to HMRC on form VAT652.

SYLLABUS AREA: ADMINISTRATION

PENALTIES FOR INCORRECT RETURNS

The penalties are a percentage of the potential lost revenue

Reason for penalty	Maximum penalty	Minimum penalty with unprompted disclosure	Minimum penalty with prompted disclosure
Deliberate and concealed action	100%	30%	50%
Deliberate but not concealed action	70%	20%	35%
Careless action	30%	Nil	15%

PENALTIES FOR FAILURE TO NOTIFY

Failures to notify chargeability to tax, or liability to register for tax that leads to a loss of tax will result in a penalty. The penalties are a percentage of the potential lost revenue.

Reason for penalty	Maximum penalty	Minimum penalty with unprompted disclosure		Minimum penalty with prompted disclosure	
Deliberate and concealed action	100%	30%		50%	
Deliberate but not concealed action	70%	20%		35%	
Any other case	30%	>12mths 10%	<12mths Nil	>12mths 20%	<12mths 10%

PENALTIES FOR LATE FILING OF RETURNS

The penalties for late filing of a return are as follows:

Offence	Maximum Penalty
Late return	Immediate £100 fixed penalty
Return more than 3 months late	Daily fixed penalties of up to £10 per day for maximum 90 days
Return more than 6 months but less than 12 months late	Tax geared penalty of 5% of tax due (minimum £300)
Return 12 months late	Tax geared penalties apply (minimum £300) : • 100% if deliberate and concealed[1] • 70% if deliberate but not concealed[1] • 5% in all other cases

(1)   These tax geared penalties are reduced for disclosure as per penalties for incorrect returns.

RECORD KEEPING PENALTY

Offence	Maximum Penalty
Failure to keep and retain tax records	£3,000 per tax year/ accounting period

SYLLABUS AREA: ADMINISTRATION

INCOME TAX RATES

	2012/13
Starting rate for savings income only	10%
Basic rate for non-savings and savings income only	20%
Basic rate for dividend income	10%
Higher rate for non-savings and savings income only	40%
Higher rate for dividends	32.5%
Additional rate for non-savings and savings income only	50%
Additional rate for dividends	42.5%
Basic rate band	£1 – £34,370
Higher rate band	£34,371 – £150,000
Starting rate band for savings income only	£1 - £2,710

INCOME TAX RELIEFS

	2012/13
Personal allowance	£8,105
– age 65–74	£10,500
– age 75 or over	£10,660

CGT RATES

	2012/13
Gains falling within the remaining basic rate band	18%
Gains exceeding the basic rate band	28%

CORPORATION TAX RATES

	FY 2012	FY 2011
Main rate	24%	26%
Small profits rate	20%	20%
Profit limit for small profits rate (lower limit)	£300,000	£300,000
Profit limit for marginal relief (upper limit)	£1,500,000	£1,500,000
Standard fraction	1/100	3/200

NIC CLASS 1 CONTRIBUTIONS

	2012/13		
	Annual	Monthly	Weekly
Lower earnings limit (LEL)	£5,564	£464	£107
Primary earnings threshold (PET)	£7,605	£634	£146
Secondary earnings threshold (SET)	£7,488	£624	£144
Upper earnings limit (UEL)	£42,475	£3,540	£817
Class 1 Primary contributions on earnings between PET & UEL	12%		
Class 1 Primary contributions on earnings above UEL	2%		
Class 1 Secondary contributions on earnings above SET	13.8%		
Class 1A contributions	13.8%		

NIC CLASS 2 CONTRIBUTIONS

	2012/13
Normal rate	£2.65 pw
Small earnings exception	£5,595 pa

NIC CLASS 4 CONTRIBUTIONS

Annual lower earnings limit	£7,605
Annual upper earnings limit	£42,475
Percentage rate between limits	9%
Percentage rate above upper limit	2%

VAT

Standard rate of VAT	20%
Reduced rate of VAT	5%

SYLLABUS AREA: INCOME TAX & NIC

INCOME TAX RATES

	2012/13
Starting rate for savings income only	10%
Basic rate for non-savings and savings income only	20%
Basic rate for dividend income	10%
Higher rate for non-savings and savings income only	40%
Higher rate for dividends	32.5%
Additional rate for non-savings and savings income only	50%
Additional rate for dividends	42.5%

Basic rate band	£1 – £34,370
Higher rate band	£34,371 – £150,000
Starting rate band for savings income only	£1 - £2,710

INCOME TAX RELIEFS

	2012/13
	£
Personal allowance	£8,105
– age 65–74	£10,500
– age 75 or over	£10,660
Married couple's allowance (relief is given at 10%)	
– At least one spouse/partner born before 6 April 1935	7,705
– Maximum income before abatement of relief	25,400
– Minimum allowance	2,960

COMPANY CARS, VANS AND FUEL

Company cars

Cash equivalent   11% of list price for cars emitting 100-104g/km
Increased by 1% per 5g/km over the 100g/km limit
Capped at 35% of list price
3% supplement on diesel cars (subject to 35% cap)

Qualifying low emission cars

Cash equivalent   0% of list price for cars with no CO_2 emissions
5% of list price for cars emitting 1-75g/km
10% of list price for cars emitting 76-99g/km
3% supplement applies to diesel cars

Private fuel provided for company car

£20,200 x company car %

Van scale charge

£3,000 if van has CO_2 emissions

Additional £550 if private fuel provided for the van

Neither charge applies if either:
CO_2 emissions are nil; or
There is insignificant private usage

CAPITAL ALLOWANCES

First year allowances available

100% on new energy saving plant or machinery
100% on low emission cars (not more than 110g/km CO_2 emissions)
100% on new and unused zero emissions goods vehicles

Annual investment allowance

£25,000 (£100,000 before 6 April 2012) of expenditure incurred by any business on certain plant and machinery

SYLLABUS AREA: INCOME TAX & NIC

NATIONAL INSURANCE CONTRIBUTIONS

NIC CLASS 1 CONTRIBUTIONS		2012/13		
		Annual	Monthly	Weekly
Lower earnings limit (LEL)		£5,564	£464	£107
Primary earnings threshold (PET)		£7,605	£634	£146
Secondary earnings threshold (SET)		£7,488	£624	£144
Upper earnings limit (UEL)		£42,475	£3,540	£817
Class 1 Primary contributions on earnings between PET & UEL	12%			
Class 1 Primary contributions on earnings above UEL	2%			
Class 1 Secondary contributions on earnings above SET	13.8%			
Class 1A contributions	13.8%			

NIC CLASS 2 CONTRIBUTIONS	2012/13
Normal rate	£2.65 pw
Small earnings exception	£5,595 pa

NIC CLASS 4 CONTRIBUTIONS	
Annual lower earnings limit	£7,605
Annual upper earnings limit	£42,475
Percentage rate between limits	9%
Percentage rate above upper limit	2%

PAYE CODES

L   tax code with basic personal allowance

P   tax code with full personal allowance for person aged 65-74

Y   tax code with full personal allowance for those aged 75 or over

K   total allowances are less than total deductions

SYLLABUS AREA: CAPITAL GAINS

	2012/13
Annual exempt amount	£10,600
Gains falling within the remaining basic rate band	18%
Gains exceeding the basic rate band	28%
Basic rate band	£1 – £34,370

SYLLABUS AREA: CORPORATION TAX

Financial year	FY 2012	FY 2011
Main rate	24%	26%
Small profits rate	20%	20%
Profit limit for small profits rate (lower limit)	£300,000	£300,000
Profit limit for marginal relief (upper limit)	£1,500,000	£1,500,000
Standard fraction	1/100	3/200

Marginal relief

$$(\text{Upper Limit} - \text{Augmented Profits}) \times \frac{\text{TTP}}{\text{Augmented Profits}} \times \text{Standard Fraction}$$

CAPITAL ALLOWANCES

First year allowances available

100% on new energy saving plant or machinery
100% on low emission cars (not more than 110g/km CO_2 emissions)
100% on new and unused zero emissions goods vehicles

Annual investment allowance

£25,000 (£100,000 before 1 April 2012) of expenditure incurred by any business on certain plant and machinery

SYLLABUS AREA: VALUE ADDED TAX

Standard rate		20%
Reduced rate		5%
Annual registration limit	From 1 April 2012	£77,000
De-registration limit	From 1 April 2012	£75,000
VAT fraction (standard rated)		1/6

	From 01.04.07
Cash accounting	£
Turnover threshold to join scheme	1,350,000
Turnover threshold to leave scheme	1,600,000

	From 01.04.06
Annual accounting	
Turnover threshold to join scheme	1,350,000
Turnover threshold to leave scheme	1,600,000

	From 04.01.11
Flat rate scheme	
Annual taxable turnover limit (excluding VAT) to join scheme	150,000
Annual total income (including VAT) to leave scheme	230,000

Index

Notes

ICAEW

ICAEW